DAILY LIFE IN COLONIAL PERU

1. Torre Tagle Palace, Lima

DAILY LIFE IN
COLONIAL PERU

1710-1820

Jean Descola

Translated by Michael Heron

THE MACMILLAN COMPANY
New York

Library of Congress Catalog Card Number: 68-29129

FIRST AMERICAN EDITION 1968

Translated from the French *La Vie Quotidienne au Peru au Temps des Espagnols,* © Hachette, Paris, 1962

The Macmillan Company, New York

PRINTED IN THE UNITED STATES OF AMERICA

CONTENTS

ILLUSTRATIONS

ACKNOWLEDGEMENTS

'The laziness of the governors when it came to keeping archives and our own carelessness in the past about chronicling events were unparalleled and make it extremely difficult to write an accurate history of the age of the viceroys today. I must have inhaled great clouds of dust while consulting old chronicles and deciphering manuscripts in countries where the scarcity of archives made research difficult for those who wanted to consult them . . .'

I am tempted to appropriate this disillusioned remark by the celebrated Peruvian chronicler, Ricardo Palma.[1] Not that I have lacked documentation. On the contrary. In fact it was the profusion and variety of documents that complicated my task. My problem was not to find archives, which exist in great numbers, but to choose those most revelant to my subject from among the great mass of documents that have passed through my hands.

I have had to cover a period of about a century, for 'daily life in Peru' cannot be allocated to a specific decade of its history, even though it scarcely changed throughout the last century of the Spanish viceregal period.

It can also be claimed of a large part of the population of Peru

[1] The name of Ricardo Palma will recur frequently in this book. So it seems advisable to give his biographical details now.

Ricardo Palma was born at Lima in 1833. At first a paymaster in the Navy, he entered politics while still young and then embarked on a consular career. After travelling all over the world, Palma returned to his own country where he was given the task of reconstituting and directing the National Library of Peru, sacked by the Chileans during the conflict between Peru and Chile.

Palma is mainly known for his *Tradiciones peruanas*. The first series appeared in 1872, the eighth and last series in 1891. It was thanks to his post as librarian—he held it for twenty-seven years—that Palma was able to carry out this enormous labour, drawn from the most reliable sources. The *Tradiciones peruanas* not only represent Peruvian letters, but they also mark two important victories of Hispano-American consciousness. Firstly, Palma had realized that to be really faithful to the national spirit, it was necessary to recall the colonial period, which was equivalent to the European Middle Ages for Spanish America. Secondly, in the place of the historical novel he put tradition, which, based on authentic texts, revived the real past of Peru.

The *Tradiciones peruanas* achieve the best synthesis in existence of national life in Peru from the Conquest to the Emancipation.

—the mountain Indians and the Negroes—that their almost exclusively vegetative daily life had no history. Sleeping on the ground, grinding toil, not much to eat—there was little historical material there. In his *Memoirs* Viceroy Amat refers to them by the old Latin word *plebs*. Undoubtedly, this soldier, who was also something of a jurist, used the term deliberately. In fact, they were the plebs, i.e. a civic group, with certain rights, theoretically protected by laws, but actually vegetating miserably while waiting for better days.

That explains why in certain parts of this book, for lack of 'daily events', I have had to limit myself to sketching the general background, to suggesting what daily life was by evoking everyday preoccupations.

If this book has any value, in spite of its inevitable imperfections, I owe it largely to all those people in France and Peru who gave me the benefit of their advice and knowledge. In France, I mainly consulted Sr. Alberto Jochamowitz, cultural attaché to the Peruvian Ambassador in France, Sr. Hector Boza. In Peru, my contacts with Peruvian specialists were greatly facilitated by M. Léon Brasseur, the French Ambassador, his cultural attaché M. Olivier Dollfus and M. Vellard, Director of The French Institute of Andean Studies.

Among the Peruvians who have been of great assistance, I should like to mention Sr. Raoul Porras Barranchea and his collaborators, Sres. de la Puente Caudamo, Dean of the Catholic University, Enrique Carrion and André Rutkowski, of the Riva Aguero Institute, Sr. Hector Velarde, a great architect and President of the Alliance Française at Lima, Sr. Hector Garcia Ribeyro, Mayor of Lima, Sr. César Miro, Sr. Cristobal de Losada y Puga, Director of the National Library, and his assistants, Sres. Alberto Tauro and Raoul Rivero Serna. I am indebted to all of them for helping me to compile an extensive bibliography, only part of which appears as an appendix.

Lastly, I must mention the friendly reception given me by Doctor Manuel Prado, President of the Republic of Peru. He took an interest in my work that could not fail to stimulate it.

J. D.

INTRODUCTION

What is the age of the Spaniards in Peru? To many Peruvians and Spaniards it is still the 'time of la Perricholi'. Consequently, three questions arise: Who was la Perricholi? Where did she live? And in what period?

We shall get to know la Perricholi later on in the chapter which comments on the theatre—for she was an actress, a *comica*. All we need to say here is that la Perricholi—her real name was Micaela Villegas—was a Creole born at Lima in 1748, that she appeared on the stage very young and won the heart of the Spanish Viceroy, Don Manuel Amat, whose admitted and official favourite she became. He indulged all her fancies, even allowing her to flaunt herself in a carriage, an honour reserved for the highest aristocracy. She died at Lima.

What is left at Lima of la Perricholi, its extravagant heroine, and her loves? Very little. Almost nothing. The house in the Calle del Huevo where la Perricholi spent her youth disappeared when the Avenue Tacna was built. The casa del Rincón grows a little more dilapidated every day and a baker's shop window now occupies its façade. The cement premises of the Backus and Johnston Brewery now occupy the site of the house in the Almeda de los Descalzos where Micaela lived for much of her last years. Beer flows and barrels roll where la Perricholi dreamt away her life. It is nobody's fault that the demolishers' pickaxe has once again broken the poets' lyre. But one wishes so ardently that things had not changed. Retrospective lovers of la Perricholi are reduced to the somewhat melancholy flights of their imagination. I should add that their task is facilitated by the Peruvians themselves who, belatedly realizing the wrong done to la Perricholi's memory by the progressive obliteration of evidence about her life, automatically take the visitor to the Quinta de la Presa, situated behind the present day Presidential Palace in the neighbourhood of the Malambo quarter, beyond the three-hundred-year-old bridge which crosses the Rimac.

The Quinta de la Presa achieves a perfect synthesis of the colonial style of the end of the eighteenth century and French

Rococo. It belonged to the lords of Presa y Salazar, Carrillo de Albornoz, Counts of Montemar y Monteblanco. Viceroy Amat, a great friend of the Presas and passionately interested in architecture, had offered to draw up the plans for it. This made people think for a long time that he intended the future house for la Perricholi. To tell the truth, neither the Viceroy nor Michaela ever set foot in the Quinta de la Presa. However, popular tradition has got into the habit of situating the loves of la Perricholi and Don Manuel in this delightful little house which is at the same time Moorish and in the style of Versailles. This statue of Bacchus, standing in the middle of the garden, is the bust of la Perricholi. This pool beneath the arbour is the one in which Micaela used to bathe stark naked, spied on by her lover. This bathtub of Italian marble, carved from a single block, was used for her toilet and their erotic games. Even the carriage which seems to await the favourite's pleasure is there. The Quinta de la Presa is a possibly unique example of the adaptation of completely different styles. Its façade has three sections, in the classical French style. The architecture is Louis XV, but it is redolent of the Spanish style handled in the Creole manner. Adobe and plaited reed frameworks replace brick and marble. Inside, one would imagine oneself in the Trianon: Rococo consoles, copings, mirrors and doors. Staircases decorated with *azulejos* lead to a series of salons with doors in line which give onto a large gallery facing the garden. This gallery embraces the whole width of the rear façade and separates each of the three sections of the building by loggias with light, delicate, pale blue arcades which make the perspective look longer than it is. The same is true of the outside staircase with two arms, imitating those at Chantilly and Fontainebleau—in the materials at least— and which gives this eighteenth-century boudoir the appearance of a small château. But one final disappointment awaits the lover of la Perricholi. The Quinta de la Presa has become an infantry barracks.

Nevertheless, this is the place where one can still best evoke the memory of the celebrated favourite. What could be more natural? What traveller has not trembled with emotion when walking through the alleys of Argamasilla de Alba, where the skinny ghost of Don Quixote floats, or the streets of Toboso still echoing with Dulcinea's laughter? It must be admitted that on the whole the Peruvians have respected the early decoration of the colonial palace. Even if the ground floor of la Quinta has been taken over for military offices, the first floor and the galleries have been turned into a museum and the garden has not changed. As for the troops, they occupy an adjoining building. So la Perricholi is present at the Quinta de la Presa, on the first floor and in the garden at least. We meet her at every step—leaning on the balcony, running down the paths of the garden '*à la française*' or playing hide-and-seek with her lover behind the white-trunked palm trees. She bathes in the round swimming pool, while the Viceroy spies on her from the top of an open-work wooden loggia erected high up in a tree, where he loved to enjoy the cool breeze after his bath in the square pool used by the men. We lose sight of her behind a mountain of blood-red geraniums, she bobs up through the blue tufts of plumbago. She darts onto the staircase with its landings at right angles. With a light step she walks through the salons whose glassless windows have wrought-iron grilles and are closed by heavy solid carved shutters. She seems to glide over the waxed parquet floors. The furniture—it came from Spain, France and Portugal—has been caressed by her hand. Here is a large portrait of Viceroy Amat, forming a pendant to portraits of King Ferdinand VII, Alvarado and some Presidents of the Audience. How disarming, beside these stiff, formal effigies, is this miniature of la Perricholi, with her great laughing eyes, her round face, her full smiling mouth, her coquettish nose and her black hair with an enormous gardenia in it! The great reception hall is separated from the bedroom by two doors which conceal mirrors set in a frame of carved wood, in the manner of a Louis XV medallion. La Perricholi slept in this bed of cedarwood carved with rural motifs and formerly surmounted by a canopy. And perhaps these Manilla embroideries, this Chinese kimono, these doll's slippers and this enormous tortoise-shell comb belonged to her. And there she is, fleeing, after having thrown one last look at the Viceroy's private altar—*el oratorio compendiado*—embedded in the wall of the gallery and closed by a door with two leaves. She goes down the stairs again, runs past the austere building in which the slaves lived, then disappears into the misty blue distance down the Alameda.

Even though she never lived there, la Perricholi appears as she really was in this genuine setting. A historical personage, she symbolizes the zenith, the decline and death of the Spanish Empire. The banquets over which la Perricholi presided were among the last given in the great western viceroyalty—the last in Spanish America too. Born a few years after the arms of Philip V had gained a spectacular triumph over an Indian Revolt, la Perricholi died two years before the proclamation of the Independence of Peru. Thus she was at the junction of two worlds, because she only just missed knowing in turn the height and the collapse of Spanish power. But, above all, la Perricholi is the incarnation of *la Limeña* (the woman of Lima). Coquettish, but not really vicious, fond of luxury, without being frankly mercenary, playing on her charms with a sort of amused candour. In short, a nice girl.

And above all she was gay. She laughed. In this country where love was still savage, where intrigues entwined and disentwined in a shadow that was still feudal, it was audacious to mingle sexual pleasure and laughter. An even greater audacity to love in broad daylight, for la Perricholi was not afraid to broadcast her love affairs—not out of cynicism, but out of naïve pride. Lastly, the episode of the carriage, so variously interpreted, acquires an almost political significance with the passage of time. Our little minor actress was not so much intent on scandalizing the aristocracy of Lima as on asserting publicly that she and they had equal rights. Although we must not exaggerate nor attribute revolutionary afterthoughts to a woman who after all was nothing more than a charming little Pompadour of the Spanish Indies.

'The time of la Perricholi' covers quite a long period, since it begins in the middle of the eighteenth century and ends during the first quarter of the nineteenth century. It happens that this period—which actually begins with the first years of the eighteenth century and goes on into the middle of the nineteenth century—is at one and the same time one of the most brilliant in Spanish colonial history and the harbinger of its end. Never had the overseas empire of the Spanish Bourbons shone so brightly, and yet it was flaring up for the last time. Soon it would be extinguished.

Between the hour of Micaela's birth and the hour of her death, Peru was to see ten Viceroys succeed each other: the Conde de Superunda, Manuel de Amat, Manuel Guirior, Agustin de Jauregi, Teodoro de Croix, Francisco de Taboada y Lemos, Ambrosio de O'Higgins, Gabriel de Avilés, Fernando de Abascal and Joaquin de la Pezuela. Four kings were to succeed each other on the throne of Spain: Ferdinand VI, Charles III, Charles IV and Ferdinand VII. Events of capital importance took place in Europe, deciding the future of Spain: the signature of the Family Pact, the naval battle of Trafalgar, the war of Independence against Napoleon. And if Micaela had lived a few months longer, she would have been able to witness the last Viceroy's farewells and the triumphal entry into Lima of San Martin, Protector of Peru. The 'time of la Perricholi' can certainly be included among the 'historic' periods, for it comes exactly between the apogee of Spanish viceroyalty and the proclamation of Peru's independence. So that, during her long life, the witty actress—if she had taken an interest in politics—would have been admirably placed to witness to them. But her affairs of the heart and self-interest kept her away from affairs of the world. She simply lived her own life.

Lima, Spring 1958
Paris, Summer 1960

PART ONE

THE SETTING, THE COUNTRY AND THE INHABITANTS

CHAPTER ONE

BEFORE LA PERRICHOLI

Where is Peru?

Let us take a look at the map of America.

Composed of two triangles whose apexes are turned southwards and which are connected by a narrow strip of land, the American continent extends from latitude 71° N to latitude 56° S, i.e. 127°. What is commonly known as South America begins, politically speaking, with Panama, the point where the Atlantic joins the Pacific, and geographically north of the Equator. It extends southwards and measures about 5,000 miles from one extremity to the other—from Punta Gallinas, in Colombia on the Caribbean, to Cape Horn. At its widest part—from Brazil to Peru—it covers some 3,000 miles.

THE THREE FACES OF PERU

Peru begins below the Equator. After Brazil and Argentina, it has the third largest area in South America. It is twice as big as France, four times as big as Italy, six times as big as Great Britain. But in the days of the Inca Empire and during the period of the Spanish viceroyalty, Peru was much larger: it embraced Ecuador, Bolivia and zones that today belong to Colombia, Argentina and Chile. Situated in the most westerly part of South America, on the Pacific Ocean, Peru is dominated by a giant defence wall—the Cordillera of the Andes. A formidable barrier, extending from north to south, the Cordillera is Peru's spinal column, so to speak. In the north, it opens into three branches, which unite in the centre to separate again and finally rejoin in the south. The grandiose lay-out of the Andean chain gives Peru its three faces.

The first face is the coast. Desert-like, sandy and sometimes crossed by the rivers which rush down from the Andes, the Peruvian coast contracts as it descends from north to south. Whereas the lofty escarped granitic buttresses of the Andes plunge directly into the sea in the centre and south, they can only be seen in the far distance in the north. Thus ends the ascent to the sun of vertiginous submarine depths—depths of over 18,000 feet.

The second face is the mountains. An ever-present face which shows the traveller its stone profile whether he arrives by land, sea or air. Soon after leaving the coast one finds oneself suddenly in the midst of the eternal snows. It takes three hours to go by car from Lima, at sea level, to peaks 12,000 feet high. A strange journey! From scorching desert, the traveller comes to vast expanses of sand intersected by luxuriant valleys. The ascent is imperceptible, but there are no better altimeters than the cactus, cotton plants and sugar cane. At the very top, he reaches the peaks and the fine powdering of the eternal snow. Gay and peaceful in the north, hollowed out in the centre by the harsh valley of the river Mantaro, harsh and melancholy in the south, on the high plateaux of Lake Titicaca, the Peruvian mountain chain disgorges snow and rains into the inland plains which are crossed by rivers whose tumultuous courses bear the offering of water to the bronze-coloured Amazonian forest.

The third face is the forest. It appears as early as the eastern buttresses of the Cordillera and extends westward for thousands of miles. Sometimes cool and Virgilian, sometimes stifling, sometimes reflected in the mirror-like waters of the Amazon, the 'father of rivers', but most often hidden in the heart of inaccessible valleys, the Peruvian forest imposes its sinister law on man.

Such is the triple face of Peru. A triple world, too. The coast, inhabited by innumerable birds, lined with the *guano* islands, is the world of fire. The mountains—and the Andean highlands, surmounted with ridges with fantastic contours, carved out with majestic valleys lit up by the sapphire reflection of Lake Titicaca —are of the world of the sky. The forest is the world of water. The alchemy of these three worlds is Peru.

IN THE TIME OF THE INCAS

If we draw a line from Quito, capital of present-day Ecuador, on the Pacific coast of Peru, and extend it to Lake Titicaca, we obtain a wide-open obtuse angle that embraces what was formerly called Tahuantinsuyu, the Inca empire. The word makes us dream.

But the Inca empire existed and its reality exceeds anything we can imagine in our dreams. In the dawn of time, a demi-god, Viracocha, laid the foundations of this empire, then vanished mysteriously into legend. Much later—about the year 1000—Manco Capac and his wife Mama Ocllo came from Lake Titicaca and reached the Andean plateau. Manco Capac founded the first Inca dynasty. Gifted with political genius, he assembled under his sceptre the hitherto intractable tribes scattered between Bogota and Tiahuanaco, in present-day Bolivia. At his death he left a state of comparatively modest dimensions, but endowed with a political and administrative framework which ensured that it would last. But it was after 1420, under the reign of the Inca Pachacutec, that the empire reached its apogee, embracing Ecuador, Bolivia, Peru and the greater part of Argentina and Chile. Indeed, a fabulous empire.

What was the secret of Inca power? Meticulous organization, inexorable authority, a rigid hierarchy. All the land in the empire belonged to the Inca by right, but in practice, it was divided into three parts, those of the Inca, the State and the community respectively. In fact, the land belonged to the State, the farmers keeping part of the harvest for their personal use, but not being allowed to sell, transfer or bequeath land. Ownership of the soil did not exist. In any case there was absolutely no need for the Peruvian of the Inca period to be a land-owner, since the State looked after him from birth to death. His extremely close dependence on the State and the fact that he drew his subsistence from it alone prevented the Peruvian from showing even a token of personal initiative. He knew nothing of the majority of the usual preoccupations of individuals living in a community, because the State looked after the future of his children, in the same way that it satisfied all his needs and supplied him with necessities—and even with superfluities. Save up for his old age? Save for his daughters' dowries? Develop his inheritance? Even if it had been legally possible, what was the point? The State knew better than anybody what suited the people and the people did not complain. Besides, even if they had wanted to, they could not have done so. In short, the Inca society worked like a transparent and perfectly adjusted clock whose wheels were well oiled. There were no beggars, no anarchists and no adventurers. At the top an individualized élite. At the bottom, a socialized mass. And everybody was obliged to work.

Were the Inca citizens happy? They were resigned, at any rate, since the word happiness had no meaning in the Inca city. How could *joie de vivre* flourish 'in this dreary geometrical Empire where everything was done with the inexorability of a fatality'?[1]

Towards the end of his reign, in 1525, the Inca Huayna Capac was informed by his coast guards at Tumbez that 'large floating houses' full of 'bearded monsters'—a great surprise to these beardless men—were cruising off the Gulf of Guayaquil. The Inca died suddenly at the moment when he was preparing to send a reconnaissance mission. In his will, he had divided his enormous heritage into two parts. One, to the south, with Cuzco as capital, went to his legitimate son, Huascar. The other, in the North, around Quito, was intended for Atahualpa, his natural son. The monarch believed that he had acted wisely. In fact, although he did not suspect it, his attempt to be fair had unfortunate consequences. The rivalry, and soon the discord, between Huascar and Atahualpa facilitated the fall of the Empire of the Sun.

Who were these bearded men? 168 Spaniards, who, under the leadership of Pizarro, had disembarked in the Bay of San Mateo, coming from Panama. It was by no mere chance that these intrepid men had advanced so far into the unknown world. For long months the sole topic of conversation at Panama had been a mysterious country, situated to the north-east of the Gulf of Darien and governed by a king of divine origin, with untold wealth. No Spaniard had yet penetrated this kingdom where, it seemed, the streets were paved with gold and which the Indians, pointing to the coast, gave the name of *Pirú*. However, for a quarter of a century already the conquistadores had enormously enlarged the colonial domain of the Spanish kings. Cortés had taken Mexico, Balboa had discovered the Pacific and Charles V could already evaluate the dimensions of his empire 'on which the sun never set'. But the other side of the American continent, glimpsed from far away by Andagoya in the course of a recent expedition and guessed at by Balboa, was still to be discovered and conquered. This was the work of Francisco Pizarro.

As a child Pizarro had been found on the steps of a church in Trujillo, Estramadura. He became successively a swineherd, sailor and private soldier. Although unscrupulous, he had indomit-

[1] BAUDIN (Louis): *Les Incas du Pérou*, Librairie des Médicis, Paris, 1947.

22

able courage. He got the idea into his head of reaching the kingdom of gold. Nothing was going to stop him, neither the enormous difficulties of the enterprise, nor tenderness of conscience. After bogging down in the mud of the tropics and crossing the vertiginous passes of the Cordillera of the Andes, Pizarro's men reached the camp of Atahualpa, in the month of November, 1532. The conquistador seized the Inca, easily overcame the weak resistance that was offered him and, to complete his conquest, he had Atahualpa garrotted, after seizing his treasure: a mass of gold and silver worth more than 700,000 pounds sterling. Meanwhile, Huascar had died in prison, strangled on his half-brother's orders. In a few weeks, Pizarro and his comrades had made themselves masters of a territory which extended, between the Pacific Ocean and the Cordillera of the Andes, from the second parallel of latitude north to the thirty-second parallel of latitude south. An empire as vast as Spain, France, Germany and former Austro-Hungary put together.

IN THE TIME OF THE VICEROYS

On August 29, 1533, the wind of the Andes dispersed the ashes of the last Inca. Two years later, almost to the day, Pizarro founded *Ciudad de los Reyes,* Lima. The era of colonization succeeded to the brutal era of conquest. The Empire of the Sun became the viceroyalty of Peru. Towns arose, industries were established. It took only a few decades for Peru to assert herself as the most brilliant jewel of the Spanish overseas empire. For a long time, incidentally, all the provinces which today form the South American Republics—with the exception, of course, of Brazil— were a dependency of the viceroyalty of Peru. This explains the magnificence with which the viceroys surrounded themselves, as well as the aversion they sometimes showed to carrying out instructions from Madrid. The *cabildo*[2] of Lima spent so much money on the ceremonial receptions of new viceroys that in 1718 a royal *cedula* fixed the maximum expenditure on such occasions at 12,000 pesos. But nothing prevented the rich citizens of Lima from

---

2 I shall deal further on (Part I, Chapter 3) with the *cabildo*, in connection with the political organization of the viceroyalty of Peru. The *cabildo* was a local assembly somewhat like our town councils, whose members carried out administrative and judicial functions. The *cabildo* enjoyed considerable independence with regard to the viceroy and the monarchy.

arranging for credits to be overstepped. It was at this period that an English traveller, W. Burk, wrote:

'There are at Lima fifty-four churches, twenty monasteries, among which there are two, one with 500 monks and lay brothers, the other with 700; twelve convents, one of which has no less than 300 nuns; twelve hospitals, not to mention numerous foundations for providing poor girls wth dowries. However, it is claimed that the number of inhabitants does not exceed 30,000 souls.'[3]

To W. Burk's list should be added the palace of the *cabildo* and of the Audience, the viceroy's palace, the Royal University—the first in the New World—and the University of San Marcos.

I should say here that among the viceroys who exercised the power in Peru, nearly all were effective and some were excellent, whether it was Francisco de Toledo—the man who made audacious innovations—or Pedro de Toledo y Leiva, who was both a humane administrator and a far-seeing strategist, since he interested himself as much in the social condition of the Indians as in the protection of the Peruvian coasts from the attacks of the Dutch and English pirates. For piracy and social disturbances never ceased during the three centuries of Spanish administration in Peru. However, they were lesser calamities than the earthquakes.

In any case, and in spite of the Indian revolts, the inroads of corsairs and the earthquakes, Peru was still one of the most beautiful jewels in the Spanish empire, when Conde Manso de Velasco, Conde de Superrunda and thirtieth Viceroy, disembarked there in 1745, three years before the birth of la Perricholi.

[3] Quoted by Hugo D. Barbagelata in his *Histoire de l'Amérique espagnole,* Armand Colin, Paris, 1949, p. 151.

CHAPTER TWO

THE MEN

The people who populated Peru in the time of la Perricholi were even more diversified than the landscape. Three races had supplied the three fundamental colours of this human palette. The Indian race, rooted in the soil, the African race, transplanted from overseas, and the Spanish race which came as a conqueror. But the amalgamation of these three races had enlarged the scale of human colouring in a remarkable way. In fact, the Peruvian type included seven colours—like the solar spectrum. The *white* of the European, the brown of the *Creole*—two centuries of existence below the Equator had tanned his skin—the *red* of the Indian, the *olive* hue of the half-breed or *Cholo,* the *black* of the Negro, the *grey* of the mulatto and the *chocolate* colour of the *Zambo.* These colours were distributed unevenly over the fabric of the Peruvian people, a veritable multi-coloured *poncho* in which the *olive* hue of the half-breed predominated.

In fact, the racial question could be reduced to two fundamental distinctions. First of all there were the *original bloods*: the *White Man,* the man with 'blue blood', *sangre azul* (a curious expression which confused the ideas of race and aristocracy), the *Red Man* —the autochthonous Indian—and the *Negro,* imported from Africa.

And then there were the *people of mixed blood* or *gente de medio pelo,* i.e. the half-breeds with all their derivatives, although the word *mestizo* applied more precisely to the *Cholo,* a mixture of White and Indian.

THE WHITE MAN: EUROPEAN AND CREOLE

The White Man, a native of Europe, who came to Peru to fill an administrative post, or to run a business or industry, was also called *Chapetón.* He was the 'Spaniard from Spain', as opposed to the Creole, a descendant of the first Spaniards of the Conquest and the early days of colonization, who, living in Peru for several generations, proudly called himself an 'American Spaniard'. Although both of them were scions of the conquering race, the European and the Creole disliked each other cordially. The European believed that he was superior to the Creole by the very fact of having come from Europe. The Creole loudly proclaimed his consanguinity with the conquistadores—hence his superiority over the European, the last arrival in the country that his ancestors had conquered. Opinions varied about this point. 'The Creoles of these provinces', wrote an official of the Inquisition at Lima in 1757, 'are not fitted to administer the Law.' To which Solorzano retorted: 'The Creoles are surely more fitted to administer Justice than those who are born in Europe, since they surely have more affection for the soil and the country where they were born.'[1]

It should be noted that, sometimes and to some extent, the Creoles had good reason to claim that they were superior to the white Europeans, for there were Creoles and Creoles. Those who from their youth had been brought up in the cult of tradition and pride in their ancestors, and who were required to produce, in order to be admitted to the College of Nobles, *'las pruebas de limpieza de sangre y nobleza que deben dar los individuos que solicitan entrar en el Colegio de Nobles americanos,* the proofs of purity of blood and nobility which individuals who request entry into the American College of Nobles must produce', considered themselves more Spanish than the Spaniards. In fact, these proofs of 'pure blood', minutely examined, without any possibility of trickery, did testify to an aristocratic origin. The majority of Creoles in this category went into the Administration or the Church, thus becoming brilliant servants of the viceroyalty, in more or less open competition with the Whites of the Metropolis. In the same way and inversely, the White European of quality did not want to have anything to do with the 'little white' or 'poor white' who was stranded in Peru as the result of a shipwreck or some other misfortune. Living by his wits, refusing all kinds of manual work which he judged unworthy of his 'colour', 'the poor white' led a wretched existence, his usual company being the Indians and negroes on whom he sometimes depended for his subsistence. A remark here

[1] Quoted by Salvador de Madariaga in *Le Déclin de l'Empire espagnol d'Amérique,* French translation, Albin Michel, Paris, 1958, p. 51.

26

that is not without its importance: when a white European is mentioned here, he is of course the Spaniard born in Spain and not another European. There were certainly Europeans other than Spaniards in Peru—French and German for the most part—but their number was infinitesimal, not more than a few dozen in all. They were generally travellers passing through who prolonged their stay or 'engineers' on a job. Very few of them had settled in Peru and if they did, they kept their status as foreigners.

The antagonism between Spaniards from Spain and Spaniards from America greatly amused Frézier, a French engineer at the beginning of the eighteenth century, a native of Saint-Malo, whom King Louis XV had sent on a mission 'in the south seas and to the coasts of Chile and Peru'. He wrote at the time:

'As regards intelligence in general, the Creoles of Lima have no lack of it, they are quick-witted and have an aptitude for the sciences; the mountain Creoles have it to a slightly lesser degree; but both of them believe in themselves much more than the European Spaniards, whom they call *caballos,* i.e. beasts, among themselves; perhaps this is a result of the antipathy that reigns between them, although they are subjects of the same king. I believe that one of the main reasons for this aversion is perpetually seeing these foreigners occupying the highest offices in the State and doing the best business, which is the only occupation of the Whites, who disdain to apply themselves to the Arts, for which they have no liking.

Moreover, they are quite averse to war, the languid tranquillity in which they live makes them fear the loss of their repose; nevertheless they stand the fatigue of long land journeys very easily.'[2]

The permanent rivalry between European and Creole became acute when it was a question of obtaining an important post in the colonial Administration. It must be admitted that, in this field, the Spaniards from Europe were constantly favoured at the expense of the American Whites. In the whole of the Spanish Overseas Empire, out of 166 Viceroys and 588 Captains General, only eighteen were Creoles.[3] This preference of the Spanish kings for metropolitan administrators is explicable not so much on

[2] FRÉZIER (François Amédée): *Relations du Voyage de la mer du Sud aux côtes du Chili et du Pérou,* Paris, 1716, vol. 2, p. 439.
[3] Salvador de Madariaga, *op. cit.,* p. 48.

grounds of efficiency as because they distrusted the tendency of the Creoles to consider the New World, not as an annexe of the Spanish kingdom, but as their own empire.

THE INDIAN

So called by Christopher Columbus at the time of the discovery of what he believed to be an advanced point of India, the Indian of Peru had obvious similarities with his racial brothers in the other Spanish colonies. Long exploited by the white man, whether he came from Spain or America, and even by the half-breed, the Indian tried to recapture the place he had held in Peruvian society before the arrival of the Spaniards. This might seem perfectly normal, for, among the extraordinary variety of men living in Peru, it could not be denied that the Indian represented the genuinely autochthonous element. To be sure, the Indian type was infinitely varied. The Indian of the Pacific coast, who was found at Lima, had a round face, a flattened nose, thick lips and narrow eyes with yellow sclerotics, slanting and slit at the corners like those of the Chinese and Mongolian races. The mountain Indian—or Quechua—had an oval face, prominent cheek-bones, a nose like an eagle's beak, slanting wide-open eyes and abundant smooth black hair. To tell the truth, the Incas had subjugated and collected under the same law many tribes of uncertain origin, but who shared the undeniable fact in common of belonging to the so-called 'red' race. But this race, once powerful and proud, had long since ceased to rule in Peru. It no longer furnished the cadres. It supplied the manpower. It supplied the land with *mitayos*.[4]

In fact, it was the Indian who bore the crushing weight of Peru's natural setting: he who faced geographical conditions that were among the harshest in the world. Whether on the barren coast, at great heights or on the edge of the forests, one found Indians fighting desperately against hardship.

[4] Among the native peoples, the *mita* was a levy by lottery of contingents of Indians for compulsory service on public works. The Indians subjected to this tribute were called *mitayos*. Many concessionaries of public works had carried this abuse so far as to erect gallows at work places and to threaten disobedient or unsatisfactory Indian *mitayos* with hanging. The viceroy of Peru, Nicolás Caracciolo (1716–1720), had asked the king of Spain to abolish the *mita*. But the monarch did not even consider his request.

The orographic structure of Peru—the alternation of lofty peaks and deep valleys and those islands of vegetation which suddenly appeared in the arid plains—gave its human geography the appearance of an archipelago of populations separated by enormous distances. The most important human island was in the hot valleys where all the plants necessary for feeding the country and for its industries were concentrated. The work was comparatively easy there and the Indian could be considered relatively happy. But he was also found on the coast, where water was scarce, in the forest, where there was too much water, and on the peaks, where the melting of the ice wiped out the work of a whole season at one blow. The constant pressure of the environment on the Indian had left a deep mark on him. He had had to learn to walk slowly to conserve his forces, to practise patience and resignation, to adapt himself to the circumstances that nature imposed on him, at the same time preserving his apparent good humour—the mask of his indifference—without ceasing to earn his living by the sweat of his brow, in the literal sense of the word.

Thus the Indian of Peru was the only person who could legitimately claim his title of Peruvian, since he was descended from the inhabitants of pre-Columbian Peru. However, he found himself paradoxically deracinated in his own country, because the pattern of his life, both spiritual and material, had been radically upset. Under Spanish constraint, the Indian had had to transform his modes of existence, become a miner, pay tribute to the *encomendero*[5] and worship one God, when his ancestral vocation was agriculture, he detested servitude and he worshipped the stars. But the Indian's submission to the new demands—to progress—was only apparent. His inner mentality remained intact. The hard work in the mines did not stop him from cultivating his own piece of land. And his exemplary attendance at divine service, his demonstrable piety, perhaps had their explanation in the fact that in his heart of hearts he naïvely attributed the eternal virtues of his abolished gods to the saints of Catholic martyrology.

[5] The system of exploiting the Spanish colonies was based on the *ecomienda*, which assigned districts to the colonists. The natives living in these districts became *encomendados*, that is to say they were 'handed over' to the colonists, or *encomenderos*, who levied taxes on them and employed them, on condition that they instructed them in the Christian faith and protected them. This system was finally abolished by Charles IV on June 10, 1791.

THE HALF-BREED OR CHOLO

The half-breed or *cholo* was the offspring of a white man and an Indian woman. The fusion of the two races began very early in Peru, because the first conquistadores had not brought any women with them. As the Incas represented a far more clearly defined aristocracy than in Mexico, there were numerous marriages between the Spanish captains and women of royal blood—the *goyas*. So that many Indian princesses helped to found the great families of Peru. It was thus that Dona Inés, Pizarro's ex-concubine, gave birth to the Ampuero family—the first in Peru—and that the granddaughter of Manco Capac, by marrying Ones de Loyola, nephew of St Ignatius, was the founder of the noble family of Oropesa, universally respected throughout South America.

Of course, with the passage of time, the half-breed degenerated, although without losing his essential characteristics, which Salvador de Madariaga summed up as follows:

'Nothing is more complicated than the soul of a half-breed. Compared to it, the most subtly varied soul of a man of pure blood—white, negro or Indian—is as transparent as water. The typical feature of the soul of the half-breed is its hue, which changes rapidly and recalls those iridescent colours or shot silks which pass from green to blue and react to the slightest variation in the angle of the light . . . The half-breed is always at least two people: a white man and an Indian . . . The half-breed has in him the energy of the conquistador, the calm pride of the colonist, the effective charity of the first monks, the vicious and lewd epicureanism of the brutal priest, the cupidity of the corregidor . . . But he does not possess them in their natural spontaneous state. All these traits that exist in him are constantly in intimate opposition with his other self, the Indian self which is their object and often their victim.'[6]

In the time of la Perricholi, the half-breed played an important role in the city. It was he who made up the majority of the urban populations. He was soldier, craftsman and priest. Although excluded from high administrative office and kept in check by authority, the half-breed gradually showed that he was indispensable to Peruvian society. Even though he had the same rights as

[6] Salvador de Madariaga, *op. cit.*, pp. 130 and 131.

the Spaniards, the half-breed was the victim of a constant ostracism, when he was not actually persecuted. He was neither Indian nor Spaniard, secretly despised by the one, openly persecuted by the other. It was undoubtedly because of this unjust treatment that the half-breed, kept in a state of permanent revolt, drew from this very revolt the secret of his inexhaustible vitality. In any case, the half-breed of Peru, disdaining the Indian who remained shut up in his primitive circle and dreamt nostalgically of the past, measuring himself fearlessly against the white man he often outclassed, was the perfect incarnation of this eighteenth-century colonial society of which he represented the driving turbulent element.

THE NEGRO

'The Indian was the original inhabitant of the New World; he was there. The Spaniard forced his way in and settled there. The negro was not there and did not want to go there. He was brought there by force to work as a slave. A good intention was at the basis of the idea. There were already negro slaves in Spain and some of them went to the New World with their masters. But, as a general measure, the idea was advanced by the intransigent defender of the Indians, Las Casas. In his ardent desire to reduce to a minimum the violence done to the Indians, he proposed another possibly worse violence: he had the negro slave brought over.'[7]

That is Madariaga's harsh summing up of the negro problem in the New World. But his point of view, although strictly historical, calls for a correction or, at least, must be considered in the atmosphere of the period.

Slavery in Spanish America was an institution that appeared normal to everybody. The Spanish colonists made extensive use of negro manpower, which offered the double advantage of economy and docility. But what went on in English America?

Humboldt, who travelled in America shortly after the time of la Perricholi, noted that

'all the Spanish colonies, including the islands of Cuba and Puerto Rico, have, over an area which exceeds that of the whole of Europe by at least a fifth, a smaller number of negroes than the State of Virginia alone. In the country formed by New Spain

[7] *Ibidem*, p. 99.

and Guatemala, the American Spaniards provide the unique example of a nation of eight million inhabitants, governed according to European laws and institutions, cultivating sugar and cocoa, wheat and vines, and possessing hardly any slaves snatched from African soil'.[8]

Humboldt concluded that by far the best country as far as slavery was concerned was New Spain—the Spanish name for Mexico in the time of viceroyalty—where it was practically non-existent, pointing out that Spanish legislation on this point was humane, even though it proved inadequate to protect the slaves. In this connection, Humboldt recalled that Spanish legislation acknowledged that the slaves had four rights that the other countries refused him, namely: the right to seek a better master, to whom his former proprietor was required to relinquish him; the right to marry as he wished; the right to purchase his freedom at the lowest market price or to earn it as a reward for his good services; lastly the right to own property and to be able to buy the emancipation of his wife and children. Humboldt compared this system 'of wisdom and gentleness' with the legislation inflicted on the slaves in the French and English possessions.

The situation of the negro slaves was less idyllic in Peru, where their condition proved to be wretched.

Ricardo Palma recalled how slaves of the female sex were punished:

'Should one of them chance to throw propriety to the winds or fail to keep her mouth shut about some gallant of her mistress, the bakery of Don Jaime the Catalan or some other pitiless *señor* was not far off. The unfortunate woman spent weeks or months there, whipped every day, fasting as in Lent, working harder than she was physically able to and enduring all the rigours of the most barbarous treatment.'

At the time the kneading of bread was carried out in particularly miserable conditions. Consequently it was reserved for slaves.

But the worst punishment was being sent to the Island of St Lawrence, off Callao, a place of exile for negroes and mulattos who had been condemned for some crime to work there quarrying stone for public buildings. This punishment was compared to

[8] Quoted by Salvador de Madariaga in *L'Essor de l'Empire espagnol d'Amérique*, French translation, Albin Michel, Paris, 1953, p. 301.

that of the galleys in Europe. In fact the western point of the island bore the name of 'galley'.

However, the negroes' situation improved during the eighteenth century. While a royal edict, during the viceroyalty of Carracciolo, forbade the branding of slaves with red-hot irons, people saw 'developed' negroes gradually entering Peruvian society, to the great indignation of the whites—Europeans and Creoles—who, in agreement for once, made common cause against the negroes.

When the king of Spain granted coloured people—and consequently negroes—the right to hold public offices in 1795, the Creoles protested vehemently:

'How is it possible for the Crown to entrust the safety of the nation and the defence of its whites to men, who, far from seeing the home of their happiness in Spain, will naturally look to the inhabitants of that Africa from whence they came, so that they may protect them and incite them to revolt against the Spaniards, against whom they say they have grievances?'

How could they help having grievances!

THE MULATTO AND THE ZAMBO

Contrary to what one might think, sexual relations took place more easily between whites and negroes than between whites and Indians, because the negroes lived in proximity to the whites more than the Indians. Whether slaves or servants, they formed part of the household. Moreover, the negroes exercised a mysterious influence over the whites, apart from their undeniable sensual attraction. It was none the less true that marriages between whites and negroes were rare and, naturally, looked much askance on in Peruvian society. For a long time mulattos had been considered as 'the fruits of sin'. But gradually their situation had improved, firstly because of the ease with which established families absorbed coloured people, and secondly because of their aptitude for carrying on mechanical trades. They excelled as blacksmiths. At Lima, the mulattos formed a class above the Indians and even the half-breeds. And so the streets of Lima were traversed by wealthy, well-fed mulatto workpeople, dressed in cloth of gold and silver like personages of high rank. If it had not been for their dark hue, they could have passed for noble lords.

We must believe that the negro male possessed very special aptitudes, since it was he, rather than the white man or even the Indian, his racial brother, whom the Indian woman preferred without shadow of doubt, when she had a choice in her loves. A poor but voluptuous compensation for so many social disgraces! The union of an Indian woman and a negro—or of a negro woman and an Indian—produced the *Zambo* or *Zambavigo*. The number of *Zambos* had grown so rapidly that the public authorities were disturbed by it, so much so that a predecessor of Viceroy Amat had received from Spain a royal document enjoining him 'to keep an eye on the matter, so that men resulting from such mixtures who are mostly vicious do not cause troubles and do damage in the kingdom'. As a result, the *Zambos* were not allowed to carry arms nor live other than under the guardianship of a master.

But the situation was complicated by the fact that the half-breeds, the mulattos and the *Zambos*, who after all only represented the mixture of two out of three colours—red and white, black and white, black and red—mingled in their turn, either with one of their two original colours, or with the third. Hence an infinity of hues. Mulatto and white produced the *Tercerón*, who, mating with a white, engendered the *Cuarterón*, who still with a white, produced the *Quinterón*. When a *Tercerón* married a mulatto woman or a *Cuarterón* married a *Tercerona*, the children's colour was not changed. They were called *Tente en el aire*—hold yourself in the air. Conversely they called the children of a *Cuarterón* and a negro woman *Salto atras*—a jump backwards. Basically everyone's ideal was to resemble the white man as much as possible. All the coloured men who were lucky enough to be neither as copper-coloured as an Indian or as black as an African, did not hesitate to assert that they were Spaniards endowed with reason, *Gente de razón*. A drop of white blood, however minute, authorized them to look down on the pure Indians and Africans who were only fit to till the soil and carry burdens, and only fit for that, provided that they were whipped by them, the men of mixed blood—the near whites.

THE WOMAN OF LIMA, THE PARISIENNE OF PERU

How was the Peruvian population distributed throughout the country? Most unevenly as regards number and 'colour'. While

34

most of the rural and mountain population in fact remained Indian, that of the towns was a picturesque blend.

Walking through Callao, a few years after la Perricholi, Max Radiguet noted:

'The population of Callao as a whole consists of whites, and more particularly of *Cholos* (Indians) and *Zambos* (the result of crossing the Indian race with the white race). The crossing of these three primitive races has endlessly multiplied the shades of skins, and only the practised eye of the inhabitants of the country can infallibly detect the original type of various individuals. The *Cholos* and *Zambos* are distinguished less by the colour of their skin than by the shape of their face: they have narrow foreheads, heavy prominent jaws, lively black eyes slanting Chinese fashion and hair smooth and brilliant as jet; their physiognomy, full of gentleness, bears the impress of melancholy and resignation.'[9]

The most populous town in Peru was naturally Lima, the capital, and the number of whose inhabitants grew from year to year. From 37,259 in 1689, the population of Lima had increased to 54,000 in 1755, excluding 'slaves and Indians',[10] but taking into account the monks and nuns who 'occupied at least a quarter of the town'.[11] Altogether, there were no more than some 12,000 whites, the rest being made up of half-breeds, Indians, negroes, mulattos and *Zambos* of every category.

Cutting across these diverse human types, the woman of Lima asserted herself by her original and piquant charm. Although of different origins and sometimes from different social backgrounds, the woman of Lima, like her Parisienne contemporary, had engendered a unique model: the *Limeña*.

All the travellers agree in celebrating the charms of the woman of Lima, the least gallant being—who would have thought it?—the Frenchman Frézier, when he observes that the beauty of the ladies of Lima is largely formed by the contrast with the mulattos, negresses and Indian women 'and other hideous faces which form the greatest number in the whole country', in which he showed himself doubly unjust—both to the women of Lima, whose charm owed nothing to the effects of contrast, and to the coloured women,

[9] Max RADIGUET, *La Revue des Deux-Mondes*, April–May–June, 1852.

[10] *Mercurio peruano de historia, literatura y noticias públicas*, May–June–July, 1792.

[11] FRÉZIER, *op. cit.*, p. 379.

some of whom, mainly the negresses, were stunningly beautiful. Unlike Frézier, his countryman Max Radiguet lavished praises on the woman of Lima:

'The woman of Lima has at one and the same time something of the wasp and the humming-bird. She has, like the former, a fine corsage and a sting, which is the epigram; she has the dazzling colour and the capricious uneven flight of the latter, and from both an immoderate love of flowers and perfumes. One sees her beneath the *portales* flitting covetously from one stall of *mistureras* to another and sometimes she practises on the passer-by of a certain kind all sorts of wheedling ways and fine words to win some copper-coloured bouquet from his generosity. At the period when the manœuvre we are talking about flourished with a brilliance which is disappearing daily, the site occupied by the flower-girls was called *Calle del Peligro* (the Street of Danger). The sirens there practised such irresistible wiles that the *cicateros* (misers) made vast detours to avoid this perilous passage, or, if they ventured into it by chance, it was not until they had previously stopped up their ears like Ulysses' seamen in the Tyrrhenian Sea.'[12]

Two chroniclers contemporary with la Perricholi, Jorge Juan and Antonio de Ulloa, complete this rather frivolous picture with indications of a moral and intellectual order:

'Of medium size, beautiful and charming, their skin very white without artifice, to the perfection of their lively fascinating eyes, to all their physical perfections, they add those of the mind, for they have a clear and perspicacious intelligence. The power of pleasing comes naturally to them with a certain distant air which, while making them more friendly, places them within the limits of respect; a kind of hauteur which forbids them to submit to the will of anyone else, even that of their husband; but decent as they may be, they know how to conquer men by their charm; they respect their matrimonial obligations with a discretion and a solid friendship in which it is impossible to compare them to anyone in any other country. Witty, never at a loss for a phrase, gay and smiling, they love music passionately and with so much taste that even in the very humble classes one hears nothing but skilful and

[12] Max RADIGUET: *Souvenirs de l'Amérique espagnole*, Michel Levy Frères, Paris, 1859.

harmonious songs. They are helped in this by the fact that they have very beautiful voices. They are also addicted to dancing.'[13]

A fascinating look, the will to please, coquettish manners, gaiety on all occasions, a love of perfumes and flowers, plenty of wit, a little malice, an absolutely natural aptitude for singing and dancing . . . And there we have the finished portrait of la Perricholi— wasp and humming-bird.

[13] *Relación histórica del Viaje a la América meridional hecho de orden S.M. para medir algunos grados de Meridiano terrestre* by Jorge Juan and Antonio de Ulloa, Madrid, 1748, 4 vols., pp. 79–82. Quoted by Madariaga.

CHAPTER THREE

THE ADMINISTRATION

This mass of men, unevenly distributed, of different origins and tendencies, sometimes separated by everything—race, social background, conditions of existence—was nevertheless contained within the bounds of an apparently homogeneous administrative community from which only certain isolated tribes in the Andes, practically inaccessible to the officials of the viceroyalty, were exempt. This awkward amalgam was made possible thanks to a political structure that, while not without its faults, was solid.

The Spanish colonial system formed a whole. So before tackling the politics and administration of Peru, it is necessary to give a brief picture of the general framework of the organization of the Spanish empire.

THE GENERAL FRAMEWORK

Vast and powerful, the Spanish empire in America extended from California to Cape Horn over an area of about 3,250,000 square miles and comprised a population of some 18,000,000 inhabitants, including 4,000,000 whites, 8,000,000 Indians, 5,000,000 half-breeds and mulattos, and 1,000,000 negroes and *Zambos*.

The longevity of the Spanish empire—it was to last for three centuries—was due not so much to the virtues of its founders and maintainers as to the joint effectiveness of a colonial system founded on a strange mixture of implacable authority and tolerance, of scrupulous order and local improvisations.

The first administrative act relating to colonization dates from the very beginning of the conquest. It consists of the Capitulations of Santa Fé, in April 1492. This charter granted to Christopher Columbus by the Catholic Kings even before his flotilla had set sail conceded exorbitant privileges to the future discoverer, without any serious guarantee for the Monarchy. To tell the truth, the Catholic Kings were so unconvinced by the success of the under-

CALIFORNIA

ATLANTIC

LOUISIANA

• San Francisco
• Los Angeles
• Santa Fé

CAROLINA

Christopher Columbus 12·Oct.1492

OCEAN

WEST
INDIES

• Durango

Vera
Cruz

NEW

• Mexico
Oaxaca •

SPAIN   Guatemala •

• Trujillo

TERRA   FIRMA

HONDURAS

Cartagena •

• La Guaira

Panama •

Caracas •

• Bogota
• Popayán

Guayaquil •
• Quito

GUYANA

• Tabatinga

• Trujillo

PERU

Callao •

• Lima

• Manoa

• Cuzco

BRAZIL

• Potosi

• Túcuman

• Asunción

CHILE

Valparaiso •
Santiago •

THE
PLATE

Concepcion •

• Buenos Aires

PACIFIC

OCEAN

Magellan's Straits

C. Horn

SPANISH EMPIRE
IN AMERICA

Before 1550

1550 — 1650

1650 — 1850

taking that they did not think they risked much by promising Christopher Columbus and his heirs the admiralty and viceroyalty of the lands to be discovered, as well as the tenth part of the profits made from them. But when they were faced with the *fait accompli* —the triumph of Columbus—the Spanish sovereigns bitterly regretted their generosity. From the moment that it was no longer a question of imaginary kingdoms, but of 'solid, profit-earning', lands, they had to become a 'royal affair' and the Treasury had to be the sole usufructuary. So the Monarchy decided to establish as quickly as possible a supervisory and controlling organization—a sort of net—which would catch the riches of the New World when they entered the Spanish ports. This was the *Casa de Contratación*. It is worth pointing out that, ten years before its foundation—the same year in which Christopher Columbus returned from his first voyage—the Catholic Kings had created a Superintendence of Indian Affairs, the delegation of which at Santo Domingo bore the name of 'audience'—the first one. The two sovereigns, conscious of their carelessness at the time of the negotiations of Santa Fé, had acted quickly. Hardly was America discovered before they made certain of their ownership of it, by legal means.

The role of the *Casa de Contratación* was to supervise the application of the laws concerning trade with America. It registered the ships which sailed from or returned to Spain, and settled in both civil and criminal law all disputes relating to the traffic with the New World. The *Casa* also had powers which were strictly speaking maritime. It combined the functions of a Chamber of Commerce, a Consular Office, a Naval School and a Chamber of Cartography. Eight years after the foundation of the *Casa de Contratación*, Ferdinand the Catholic created the Royal Council of the Indies— a veritable Colonial Ministry—composed of personalities 'specializing' in American questions, which exercised its jurisdiction over all the affairs of the 'Indies', civil, military, commercial and religious. All the officials in the New World, from the highest to the lowest, were subordinate to it. The headquarters of the Council of the Indies was in Madrid. It was more of a directory than an assembly; there were only seven councillors including the President. The deliberations were held in camera. Only the king could be present at the sessions. The work of the Council of the Indies was considerable: the study of reports drawn up by overseas officials, exchange of correspondence, administrative decisions, appointments, punishments, reprimands and congratulations—in short, everything that normally falls within the province of a ministry.

So the metropolitan administration had two instruments at its disposal: the *Casa de Contratación* and the Council of the Indies, which were soon completed by a third body. This was the *Consulado de Indias*, more specifically concerned with the control and supervision of ship-owners. This three-headed metropolitan administration was duplicated by a multiple local administration. First of all, the viceroy, an omnipotent personage, Grand Master of War, Justice and Finance, supreme judge between individuals and the law courts, incarnation of the common weal. He enjoyed royal prerogatives over the extent of his territory. However, at the expiration of his mandate, he was obliged to render an exact and faithful account of it. This was the 'judgment of residence'. Far from being a mere formality, this explanation sometimes turned out very badly for the viceroy, if he had consciously omitted some troublesome detail of his government. Thus, the Monarchy asserted its intention, by considering the viceroys as simple servants subject to the common law, of reigning *de facto* and *de jure* over the most far-flung jungles of its empire.

In the time of Charles V, Spanish America was divided into two viceroyalties, Mexico and Peru. New Granada—Colombia—and the Rio de la Plata, long subordinate to Peru, were not elevated to viceroyalties until much later. Guatemala, Venezuela, Chile and Cuba were captaincies general. The provinces of minor importance were called *gobernaciones*. They were administered by governors. Lastly, each province included districts placed under the command of a *corregidor*. There was an *alcalde* at the head of every commune. The communal administration was in the hands of a municipal council—the *cabildo*—whose members, chosen from the most representative local elements, enjoyed comparative independence as regards power. By extending to the New World under the name of *cabildos* the system of *fueros* functioning in the north of Spain, the kings of the golden century had unwittingly prepared the way for the future South American democracies. Apart from the viceroys and captains general, the sovereign appointed the governors and the *corregidores*. The last named were required to pay a deposit before taking up office and solid moral guarantees were required of them. They acted as colonial administrators rather than prefects, since they were empowered to judge the civil and criminal disputes

41

that arose in their territory. In case of appeal the affair was brought at the second or third instance before the royal audiences which sat in the capitals.

The audience was a more ancient institution than the viceroyalty, for it came directly from Spain. It had the same authority and the same competence as that of Spain, but, because of the distance from the metropolis, it had been invested with supplementary powers which came within the province of the Royal Council of Justice in Spain. Consequently, it had the right to inspect the local judiciary and political authorities, for example, the governors and *corregidores*. It had a mandate from the Council of the Indies to watch over the 'education and good treatment of Indians in spiritual and temporal matters', and even 'to protect them from the avidity of the clergy'.

So exclusive was the competence of the audience in legal matters that it was empowered to hear appeals against the execution of a judgment pronounced by the viceroy. When the viceroy died while in office, the audience of the principal city took over his functions in the interim. Moreover, in every royal territory, an auditor specially nominated for the purpose was given the mission of constantly travelling round the country, observing in some cases, listening in others, studying living conditions and, if necessary, settling difficult cases.

The auditors (*oidores*, literally 'hearers'), who were also appointed by the king, were subject to very strict rules. They were forbidden to contract marriage in their place of residence, to become friendly with the Indians and to deal with personal affairs. Responsible directly to the Council of the Indies, they were not subject to the viceroy's authority and sometimes even kept him in check. They wore a black robe called a guranacha and every well-brought-up citizen who met an auditor dismounted from his horse and offered to escort him.

So the audience was more than a mere law court. A semi-political, semi-judicial body, it supplemented the viceroy, sometimes even took precedence over him and, in any case, was responsible for keeping a check on him. Moreover, in certain territories situated outside the limits of the viceroyalty, it was the audience that was invested with the supreme authority under the name of presidency: the presidency of Quito, for example.

If I add, to conclude this outline of the colonial organization,

that the king frequently sent out 'visitors' to make enquiries and seek information, the reader will have an idea of the vast network that linked the court of Madrid with Spanish America.

THE VICEROYALTY OF PERU: THE MISAPPLICATION OF WHAT WERE FREQUENTLY GOOD PRINCIPLES

It was Viceroy Amat himself who specified in his *Memoirs* the dimensions of the territory which he administered. 'The viceroyalty of Peru is composed of seventy-two provinces and *gobernaciones*, excluding the provinces of Tucuman, Paraguay and Buenos Aires.' Which meant that the Viceroy of Peru had under his sway—in addition to Peru—Chile and the countries known as Rio de la Plata, comprising the present-day territories of Argentina, Paraguay, Uruguay and Bolivia. It was an immense territory, since it included nearly all the countries of South America, with the exception of Portuguese Brazil, the viceroyalty of New Granada and the captaincy of Venezuela. The area of the viceroyalty of Peru covered about 2,300,000 square miles, more than ten times that of Spain.

Broadly speaking, the organization of the viceroyalty of Peru was much the same as the organization applicable to Spanish America as a whole.

The viceroy, who was the echo and representative of the king of Spain, had the most powerful influence of all. His title of 'royal person' made it his duty to hear and receive all his subjects, whoever they might be. He had three reception rooms in his palace for this purpose.

'In the first, hung with portraits of all the viceroys, he received the Indians and half-breeds, in the next one the Spaniards and in the innermost hall, where could be seen beneath a sumptuous canopy the portraits of the reigning king and queen, he received the ladies who wished to hold private conversation with him, without risk of being recognized.'

In addition to his audiences, the viceroy presided over the deliberations of the courts of justice, and also over those of the councils of finance and war, for he was also grand treasurer and captain general of the armies on land and sea. In fact, generally speaking, the viceroy dominated problems from a remote height. So-called 'government' affairs were actually dealt with by a Secretary of State, advised by a 'specialized' assessor.

As we have already seen, the tribunal of the audience was competent in legal matters. The audience of Lima consisted of eight auditors and one *fiscal*, assuming the functions of Public Prosecutor. The peculiarity of the audience of Lima was that the viceroy assumed its presidency, which reinforced his personal power.

It held sessions in the viceregal palace in four halls, each with its own special function. In the first deliberations went on, in the second public pleading took place and the third was reserved for debates in camera. In the fourth hall, criminal cases were judged before a special court which included four *alcaldes de corte* and two *fiscales*, one for the prosecution and the other for the defence.

Financial matters came under the Chamber of Accounts, presided over by a regent and composed of five masters of general accounts. This body had the task of examining and controlling the accounts of the *corregidores* responsible for collecting taxes. Parallel to the Chamber of Accounts, the tribunal of the Royal Treasury was responsible for inspecting the taxation lists by 'sampling'. These two important bodies of the viceroyalty functioned at Lima, for it was there in the capital that the revenues from all the taxes levied in Peru were centralized, including the tributes levied on the Indian mountain communities, and the *alcabalas*—the *quint* or fifth of the produce of the mines.

The municipal administration—at least in the large urban centres of Lima, Cuzco and Arequipa—was carried out by the *municipal officers*. Its main officials, recruited among the flower of the local nobility, were the *regidores* or municipal magistrates, the *alferez real*—lieutenant-general of police—and two *alcaldes* performing the function of justices of the peace.

Lastly, the merchants came under the *consulados*, a kind of chamber of commerce, possessing considerable powers in matters of justice, administration and taxation.

Thus no activity or person escaped the viceregal administration, not even the dead, for there was at Lima a *tribunal of the fund of the dead* responsible for judging cases of heirs *ab intestat*.

One question immediately springs to mind: how could the viceroyalty keep such a vast complex in check?

First of all, it should be noted that the population of Peru bore no relation to its area: not more than 6,000,000 inhabitants altogether—4,000,000 Indians and half-breeds, and 2,000,000 whites—which was very little in view of the country's vast size. Moreover, this population was very unevenly distributed. Whereas the active population—composed mainly of whites and half-breeds—was concentrated in the principal towns or their environs, the *cercados*, the Indian population remained fixed in its villages or *pueblos*, in the mountains or on the coast. Both of them, separated by endless desert expanses, were mutually ignorant of each other and made no effort to get to know each other. The majority of Indians of the sierra had never left their house and their fields, their travels hardly ever went beyond the market of a neighbouring *pueblo*. They lived and died where they were born and spoke to each other of Cuzco and Lima as inaccessible paradises.

The political, administrative and judicial organization described above was valid, of course, for the whole of the viceroyalty, but in fact it applied mainly to the large urban collectivities. The inhabitants of the pueblos only resorted to it on rare occasions. For a matter to be brought before the viceregal jurisdiction through the intermediary of the local *corregidor*, it had to be extremely important or else the *corregidor* had to have a personal interest in it.

In effect, in the districts remote from the big centres, it was the *corregidor* who combined all the various offices: tax collector, justice of the peace, chief of police—hence the name of *corregimientos* given to these multiple posts. The task of the *corregidores* was facilitated by the fact that it was supported by a local organization that was rudimentary, to be sure, but perfectly suitable for its purpose. The first Spanish administrators had been careful not to disturb the framework of local institutions, being content to 'supervise' them. In the same way, at the time of the 'carving up' of the viceroyalty, they had taken into account the territorial divisions instituted by the Incas. Thus, so long as they did not infringe in any way on the precepts of the Catholic Church, the Indians could, though still under the supervision of the *corregidores*, preserve their own administration and customs, devote themselves to working the land for their own benefit or put themselves in the service of the *corregidores*, provided that their work was duly remunerated. They only had direct dealings with their cacique or *alcalde*—an

Indian like them—who negotiated with the *corregidor* in their name.

Does this mean that everything was for the best in the best of all possible worlds? Better in any case since the Bourbon dynasty had succeeded the Hapsburgs on the throne of Spain. The French of Philip V, by arriving at Madrid, had brought new ways of life with them and a premonitory breath of 'enlightened ideas'.

This light breeze crossed the sea and stimulated the New World. Thanks to the reorganization of the system of fleets and galleons, the ships were travelling quicker, which tightened up and improved contacts between the metropolis and the colonies. The press crossed the Atlantic in a few weeks. The news in the *Gaceta de Madrid* was still topical when it arrived in Peru. Certain colonists preferred to consult their local paper, the *Mercurio Peruano*, of Lima, which gave interesting information about the major world events. Thus no one was left unaware of what happened in Europe.

Spanish America was no longer that stifling, closed, impenetrable universe of the first years following the Conquest. It had opened up, enlarged its horizons, let in fresh air. One could breathe more easily there.

The modernization of the merchant marine, the increased number of ships and the fact that traffic by sea was faster and safer gave the colonial trade a new physiognomy. It was no longer possible, in these conditions, to keep the monopoly of commercial exchanges for the benefit of the merchants of Seville alone. Other ports *habilitados* for the trade were opened, reaching the figure of fifteen in Spain and twenty-five in America. The royal regulations henceforward permitting all Spaniards to trade with the colonies had had the dual result of developing exports and imports, and increasing the State's revenues. The traders, in fact, made a fortune, but paid heavy taxes, which helped to swell the public resources, such as the *almojarifazgo*, a customs duty paid when merchandise entered and left, the duty of 'the consulate' earmarked for the maintenance of the *consulados* and the duty 'of the fleet', the income from which was set aside for coastal defence.

The fact that manpower was used more considerately was also a sign of the times. Work in the mines became optional. The conditions of the *mita* were less harsh and slavery gradually disappeared. Lastly, a more flexible legislation, better adapted to regional contingencies, while enabling affairs to be settled rapidly offered—in principle, at least—a means of defence to the most humble social categories.

However, if the general situation in Peru had improved considerably since the Conquest, it was still far from perfect. The Spanish administrative system was ingenious. It functioned quite well on the whole, as a good juridical machine, more fitted to manufacture texts than to weigh souls. But if the principles were good, their application too often left much to be desired. One thinks of the famous remark made by Belalcazar, the conquistador of Ecuador, two centuries before: '*Lo que el Rey manda se obedece, no se cumple*. What the King orders is obeyed, but not carried out.' Without going so far, it can be said that in Peru the law was always respected, but often slackly carried out, especially when powerful private interests were concerned. In short, the law was dispensed with when it was troublesome.

It was the whites—or certain well-placed half-breeds—who profited by this new political climate in the viceroyalty. There had always been exploiters and exploited. The highly placed official was often venal, the big land-owner tried to obtain the best return from his workers at the lowest cost, the clergyman made profitable use of his moral prestige. The rich man had not become impoverished. The poor man had not become rich, or rather the poor man remained poor. The wind of liberalism that blew from Madrid swelled the sails of the merchants. It had barely touched the Indian workers.

The condition of the Indians—whether they were employed in the mines, in the fields or in workshops—was still precarious, if not wretched. It had aroused the pity of Jorge Juan and Antonio de Ulloa during their scientific mission to Peru on behalf of Philip V in 1735. So much so that they put their observations in writing in a secret report which they presented to the king on their return. These two gentlemen wrote at the time about the exploitation of the Indians by their landed proprietors: 'Corn was very scarce and the land-owners treated the Indians with terrible harshness and went so far as to stock-pile the corn—which is the Indians' sole food —to sell it at a higher price, thus causing a high native mortality rate throughout the provinces.'[1]

But it seems that the lot of the Indians working in the mills for weaving cloth—the *obrajes*—was even more distressing. Shut up

[1] Jorge JUAN and ULLOA: *Noticias secretas de América*, p. 270.

4. a. Lima: The River Rimac and the Piedra Bridge

b. Lima: the Calle de las Nazarenas

5. a. Lima: a house in the Descalzos
 b. Lima: the Calle de Valladolid

from dawn to dusk in unhealthy premises, they 'often died of priva-
tion, their tools in their hands', for lack of the care of which they
were deemed unworthy.

'The employers cannot imagine that a sick Indian deserves to be
sent to a hospital, unless he is so weak that he dies before reaching
that charitable institution, and happy are those who retain enough
strength to manage to die inside the hospital.'[2]

And this is how Juan and Antonio de Ulloa concluded the
gloomy picture of the existence of the weavers in the *obrajes*:

'The custom that condemns the Indians to work in these abominable places has become so widespread that they are sent to this
civil death for several other reasons: a short-term debt, even if it is
contracted with a private person, suffices, if it is unpaid, for anyone,
on his own authority, to impose this kind of punishment on them.
On the roads one frequently meets Indians tied by their hair to the
tail of a horse ridden by a half-breed who is taking them to the
factory . . . Vehemently as we insisted on the despotic domination
practised by the *encomenderos* over these Indians during the first
years of the Conquest, it is hard for us to believe that it was as cruel
as that which we have seen inflicted on these same Indians by the
Spaniards and *mestizos*; and although, in that period, the *encomenderos* treated their Indians as slaves, the Indian had only one
master, his *encomendero*, whereas now their masters are the *corregidor*, the owners of the textile workshops, the cattle-owners . . .'[3]

The *corregidor* often crops up in the chronicles of the period as
a greedy and shameless character, which he was in reality, with
few exceptions.

Established at the time of the Conquest to help and defend the
Indians against the excesses of the colonists—which was very laudable—the office of *corregidor* had gradually become in effect one
of the most profitable appointments in Spanish America. 'The
sword of justice is confused with the sword of trade,' was Viceroy
Amat's amusing remark about them. The truth is that the *corregidores* made money out of their influence and their powers. For
example, instead of transmitting to the audience the legitimate
recriminations of Indians oppressed by their masters, they sup-
pressed them, at the same time accepting from the latter a few

[2] *Idem*, p. 275.
[3] *Idem*, p. 279.

supplementary tributes which the Viceregal Treasury never saw the colour of. In addition, they were responsible for collecting taxes from the Indians, of which they naturally retained a large part for their own benefit.

So that there was scandalous collusion, of which no one, not even the viceroy, was ignorant, between the *corregidores,* on the one hand, and *obrajeros* (owners of obrajes), *cañavereros* (sugar cane merchants), *dueños de coca* (coca owners), *mineros* (mine owners) and other *hacendados,* on the other.

Moreover, the *corregidores* were in the habit of 'trading' with the Indians, a euphemism meaning that they sold to them at very high prices objects which were completely useless to them. In effect, what use was *ropa de Castilla* (linen of Spain) to them, when they wore cloth woven and made up by themselves? What would they have done with the 'mirrors, silk stockings, razors, pens, ink, paper, playing cards, combs, rings, buttons and books' which the *corregidores* compulsorily supplied them with? Only the 'wax of Castille' was of some use to them, to burn in the churches on holidays. Most of the time, the Indians resold what they had bought so dear at ludicrous prices.

The *corregidores'* tyranny over the Indians had struck the French merchant Gauver. He tells the following anecdote on this subject, when he took leave of the people of a little Indian village of the *sierra*:

'As I was about to mount a mule, the Indians of the town assembled to watch me and wish me a good journey. The oldest of the band took the floor and said: "So you're going, sir! Oh when you see that great King, our Lord and master, tell him that we are poor people and that we suffer greatly from the tyranny of the *corregidores.*" These peoples cannot distinguish between ranks. The King being white, they concluded that being white too, I must be his comrade. The truth is that the tyranny of the *corregidores* or governors over these poor people is excessive.'

And what if a *corregidor* wanted to fulfil the duties of his office honestly and to the letter? There was nothing to stop him of course, but then he had to reckon with the ill will of employers and landowners. Juan and Antonio de Ulloa tell the story of a gentleman, Don José de Eslaba, who had tried to take his task as controller of *obrajes* seriously. Seeing this, the owners of *obrajes* quite naturally offered Eslaba whole sacks full of silver. What could be more normal than to buy the conscience of a conscientious *corregidor*? To their great surprise, Eslaba refused their offers. Then, 'convinced that men were forced to burden their consciences, in all the offices in this country, if they acted according to the corrupt customs of Peru or risked losing their lives if they tried to reform those customs', he joined the Jesuits and was ordained priest.

At the same period—and according to the same chroniclers—Don Baltazar de Abarca, appointed 'inspecting magistrate' by the viceroy, 'shortly after leaving the town of Quito to begin his circuit, was forced to flee the province of Lima even before he had begun it, because, when the *obraje* owners realized that he meant to inspect them properly, they plotted to kill him, so determinedly that he had not even time to inform the viceroy about it'.

However I must be careful not to conclude this summary of the administrative organization of the viceroyalty of Peru on too pessimistic a note, which might give a wrong impression of its essential features. It was not the political system that was at fault, but the culpable use that its bad servants made of it for personal ends—even though not all the *corregidores* were corrupt and it sometimes happened (in spite of everything) that the Indians on the *haciendas* found good masters.

In the same way it was not inevitable that royal officials despairing of fulfilling their functions correctly had to choose between flight or entering a monastery. Some of them, less fearful, stayed at their posts and filled them worthily. There were even cases of *corregidores* who did not make their fortune.

But even if the exploitation of the Indians by the whites was not universal, it was considered as common and almost permissible—sometimes by the very people who suffered from it. As if everyone, exploiter and exploited, felt obscurely that it was almost impossible, at least within the existing political framework, to provide any drastic cure. One simple reason, among so many others, made this exploitation inevitable: the distance separating one administrative body from another. A separation at two degrees, in a sense, since it included the distances separating the king of Spain from the viceroy and the latter from his provincial officials. How could the master's eye, however piercing it might have been, have seen from Madrid to Lima and from Lima to the huts of the Andean *sierra*?

It is a fact that, once it had reached the stage of the audience at Lima, a request, even one emanating from the humblest of Indians, had every chance of being granted. The difficulty was in getting the file transmitted.

In the same way, when an affair reached the highest instances— the Council of the Indies, and sometimes the Royal Cabinet—it was assured of a reception that was at least well-disposed. The attitude of the Spanish sovereigns with regard to their Indian vassals had not changed since Isabel the Catholic, who died in 1504, instructed her heirs in her will: 'That they do not allow or cause the Indians . . . to suffer any damage to their persons or their property . . . On the contrary they shall see to it that these peoples are treated with justice and kindness.'

The Crown's solicitude for its 'subjects in the Spanish Indies' has never been in doubt since then. One has only to refer to some of the countless royal *cédulas*, including this one, issued by Philip V's predecessor:

'I desire you to give me satisfaction and to give satisfaction to the world, as to the way in which our vassals are treated; if they were not well treated and the guilty persons were not punished in an exemplary fashion, I should consider that I was very ill served.'

The interest taken in the Indians by the kings and their direct representatives was not confined to Platonic declarations. One of the most celebrated viceroys of Peru, Francisco de Toledo, had drawn up regulations covering work in the mines that not only witnessed to a remarkable knowledge of the technique of extracting metals, but also formed a genuine code of labour legislation and industrial medicine. In that, the Spaniards were ahead of their time, for hardly anything had been done in the English colonies, or even in Europe, to regulate the work of miners and protect them against accident and sickness.

Perhaps this will lead the reader to ask whether the political system in Peru was fundamentally bad. It was both good and bad, or rather it contained the seeds of the best and the worst, administratively speaking.

The viceroyalty of Peru shared with the other dominions of the Spanish crown the inconveniences of a system which suffered alternately from an excess of centralization and an excess of decentralization, as if it were permanently traversed by two forces moving in opposite directions, one centrifugal, the other centripetal. Conceived by its theoreticians to function over a territory with the normal dimensions of a European country, such as Spain, it lost its effectiveness as soon as it was applied to areas over which there was no direct control. A chain of intermediaries and weeks of travel separated king from viceroy, and viceroy from cacique.

Those are some of the reasons that made the viceroyalty of Peru into a composite whole that was both prosperous and wretchedly poor, anarchical and disciplined. It is not surprising that it disconcerted the foreign observer with such a profusion of contradictory features. In point of fact, there was not a single assertion that could not be immediately contradicted by another, both of them being equally verifiable by the facts. One can go on *ad infinitum* opposing the cruelty of the soldiers to the missionaries' charity, the missionaries' apostolic spirit to the bureaucratic attitude of the secular clergy, the contempt of the whites for coloured people to the royal policy of assimilation, the paternalism of the Creoles to the pro-slavery policy of the European whites, the despotism of the king to the free and easy ways of his officials, the opulence of certain classes to the destitution of others. These contradictions were those that characterized every Spanish enterprise, which was dominated, whatever its goal, by the eternal conflict between the original purity of its plans and the varying temperaments of the men responsible for putting it into practice.

The Spanish 'phenomenon' does not lend itself to a summary or simplified view. It is made up of many fine gradations, as Salvador de Madariaga remarked when he wrote:

'Spanish life is particularly subtle and eludes definition. When dealing with Spanish problems, all opinions that are limited to forms and institutions are necessarily superficial. The truth can only be perceived by the fleeting observation of the individuals who come to life behind these forms and institutions.'[4]

Lastly, to finish with this survey of the Spanish organization in Peru, it is only fair to state that the viceroys had no reason to be ashamed of their stewardship when they handed over this fragment of an Empire turned Republic to the *libertadores*. Indeed, if we

[4] Salvador de MADARIAGA: *L'Essor de l'Empire espagnol d'Amérique*, p. 403.

take up a position midway between the *leyenda negra*[5] and the official Spanish thesis, if we stick to the practical achievements, we cannot deny that they were very real. The kingdom of Atahualpa, in the form that Francisco Pizarro had captured it, was still very rudimentary and very static, in spite of the ingenuity of Inca socialism. It was organized and disciplined, but also feeble and apathetic. By imposing on Peru an entirely new style that it was to keep until the contemporary period, two centuries of Spanish rule had transformed it into a powerful and prosperous colony. This material success was due to the strict application of three principles: the integration of the natives into political and economic life, the development of communications between the various regions of the country and the rational exploitation of Peru's vast natural resources.

Moreover, far from diminishing, the native population of the viceroyalty of Peru, including Bolivia and Ecuador, had increased from 2,600,000 Indians in 1570 to 3,000,000 at the beginning of the nineteenth century, in addition to whom there were a million half-breeds of all shades.

The main thing is whether the Spanish administration in Peru must be judged by its achievements or the means it employed.

OUTBURSTS OF INDIAN NATIONALISM

The achievements, of course, would not have been possible without the means, among them the intensive use of Indian manpower. In fact, it was hundreds of thousands of Indians who, in the absence of machines, had carried out the enormous public works which the viceroys decided on: mountain roads, dams, mine shafts, military works. Well trained, commanded by men of his own race, accustomed to servitude for centuries, the Indian obeyed the Spaniards as a matter of course, as his ancestors had obeyed the Incas. However, the Indian sometimes rebelled, in spite of his atavistic indolence. But he needed a leader and he actually found leaders who were descended from his great ancestors—or claimed to be.

The Inca dynasty was not extinguished with the arrival of the Spaniards and the execution of Atahualpa. In the sacristy of the

[5] The *leyenda negra* or 'black legend' is applied to the defamatory and in any case harsh campaign conducted against Spanish colonialism by its opponents, particularly the Protestants and the English.

cathedral at Cuzco people could still see the Imperial family tree of the thirteen Incas who had reigned over Peru from the foundation of the city to its capitulation. Painted on Chinese taffeta at the end of the sixteenth century, it listed, side by side, the names of Juan Atahualpa, son of the last Inca sovereign, and Francisco Atahualpa, bastard son of Pizarro and a daughter of Atahualpa. The lot of these Incas was very pleasant. Some of them lived at the expense of the viceroyalty; Cristobal Paulo, for example, who had retired with his favourites to the valley Yuncay and whose descendants bore the honorary title of *adelantado*. Others accepted posts as caciques or *alcaldes*. Most of them were painlessly integrated into the Spanish regime. Some of them, on the other hand, conspired against it in secret and preached revolt to their coloured brethren. They had no lack of arguments. Indeed it was only too obvious to everyone that the aims and interests of the Spanish State and those of its American vassals were increasingly divergent, that the exercise of political power and tenure of government offices were reserved for officials from Spain, that the administration of the Colony was a source of wealth for them and lastly that it was Spain alone that decided the principal problems and not the Peruvians themselves—i.e. the Indians. But this excessively political language was beyond the comprehension of the Indian masses, whose self-respect, deadened by centuries of servitude, was hard to arouse. Nor were many of them very responsive to hearing the memory of their great ancestors recalled; they listened more readily to promises to improve their lot. This shows how premature it was to speak of 'Indian nationalism' as an organized movement pursuing definite objectives. The explosions of this nationalism, which were often terribly violent, reflected the brutal expression of legitimate discontent much more than the desire to see specific claims met.

Nevertheless, Inca rebelliousness gave the viceroyalty some nasty knocks. Indeed, it had to take up arms twice in fifty years in order to repress risings that endangered its authority.

The first of these revolts was called the 'conspiracy of the Amencaes'.

In the mountains of Chanchamayo, in 1743, the Inca Juan Santos had proclaimed himself the last Inca under the name of Atahualpa II, King of the Andes, and, at the head of savage tribes, had seized possession of the *cerro* of la Sal, threatening to invade Tarma,

Huancayo, Huanuco and other villages. The Spanish authorities defended themselves and bombarded the fort of Quimiri, which had fallen into the hands of the rebels, who had pitilessly cut the throats of the soldiers taken prisoner. In 1749 the rumour went the rounds that Juan Santos had been assassinated by his partisans. The Indians of the civilized villages, who sympathized and even kept in touch secretly with this rebel chief, began to conspire openly at Lima. Their meetings were held, beginning in January of that year, on the hill of the Amancaes, in the environs of Lima, and there were more than 2,000 conspirators in the capital of the viceroyalty alone. Their plan was as follows: taking advantage of the fact that it was customary on September 29th, the day of the archangel St Michael, for the Indians and negroes to assemble in masked bands, armed by their masters with blunderbusses and sabres, they proposed to set fire to the four corners of the city, taking advantage of the confusion and uproar to surprise and assassinate the viceroy and all the Spaniards. The town of Callao was also supposed to rise and only priests were to be spared in the general slaughter.

The conspirators were betrayed by a half-breed called Jorge Gobea who revealed the conspiracy to the viceroy, the Conde de Superunda. Long before the date fixed, the whole city was put in a state of alarm. The government arrested and imprisoned not only the leading Indians in the plot, but also some negroes.

The auditor, Don Pedro José Bravo de Castilla, did not let the grass grow under his feet. Thanks to the torture inflicted on the accused (the speediest way 'of making the dumb sing'), everything was over in forty-eight hours; six of the leaders were hung, drawn and quartered, and their heads exposed on the triumphal arch of the bridge and at the gates of Lima. Many of the men who had been implicated in this affair were condemned to forced labour for life. Such was the epilogue to the conspiracy of the Amancaes.

The viceroy thought that this example had terrorized the Indians and averted the rebellion. However, the revolution broke out suddenly on the day fixed, September 29th, at Huarochiri, almost at the gates of Lima, where more than 20,000 Indians were assembled, determined to fight without giving quarter. The royal troops, commanded by the Marquis de Monterrico and the Count de Castillejo, were ordered to pursue the rebels to their most remote strongholds. But months passed, the rebels received continual reinforcements, and the soldiers of the viceroy did not succeed in reducing the Indians, who had taken refuge in the precipitous, thorny *maquis*. Had it not been for the anarchy and treason that infiltrated the rebels' camp, the viceroy would have been forced to treat with the rebels of Huarochiri on equal terms and grant them privileges and favours. But from May, 1750, onwards the royalists got the upper hand and on July 6th the two main leaders were hanged in the square at Lima.[6]

The second revolt was led by Tupac Amaru. Owing to its size and the quality of its leader, it can be considered as a veritable popular and racial insurrection directed by the Indians against the Spaniards, the only serious attempt to achieve Indian unity in opposition to the white man. Tupac Amaru claimed to be the great-grandson of the sixteenth Inca, who, under the same name, had been executed in 1571 in the main square of Cuzco. 'Mounting the scaffold, he had raised his hand to impose silence on his subjects, whose muttering was disturbing the arquebusiers. When his head fell beneath the scimitar of an Indian, the crowd had uttered a prolonged groan.' Self-styled heir of the despoiled Inca emperors and claiming the crown of Peru, he espoused the complaints of the natives oppressed by the *corregidores* and the *mita*, and aimed at driving out the Spaniards. Tupac Amaru, whose real name was José Gabriel Condorcanqui, was cacique of the province of Tuita. He had been an outstanding student at the College of Nobles at Cuzco. To earn his living, he had become a transport agent. His *arrieros* (Andean muleteers) carried gold, silver, maté and salt from valley to valley, at the same time as they spread the news abroad. Indian troubadors, they accompanied their long marches with melancholy and martial songs in which they recalled the lofty deeds of the Inca kings.

On November 4, 1780, Tupac Amaru seized the *corregidor* Don Antonio Arriaga and had him executed on the 10th in the main square of the village. How? By forcing him to drink molten gold. Thus began a revolution that soon spread throughout the whole country. Condorcanqui was an able but impulsive leader. He shared his 'power' with another Indian, Thomas Catari, and with a strange character who was both miner and gravedigger. The last-named masqueraded under a mixed name, Tupac-Catari, and gave himself the titles of Inca and viceroy. After many campaigns,

6 Ricardo PALMA: *Tradiciones peruanas*, p. 571.

in which the Indians fought courageously, whereas the leaders of the royal forces were often outshone owing to the indiscipline and cupidity of their troops, the Indian leaders were taken and condemned to the severest tortures. After having had his tongue cut out, Tupac was drawn and quartered by four horses, and then decapitated. His dislocated limbs were transported on mule-back in leather bags to be exposed in all the towns he had incited to rebellion.

Three years later, the revolt broke out again, when Felipe Velasco involved the Indians of Huarochiri in another rebellion. He took the name of Tupac Inca Yupanqui and spread the rumour that Tupac Amaru was not dead. He, too, was captured and drawn and quartered.[7]

LA PERRICHOLI'S VICEROY: DON MANUEL DE AMAT

The viceroyalty had succeeded in strangling at birth or mastering by force of arms the Indians' attempts at rebellion. But although authority ultimately triumphed over disorder, its triumph was by no means solely due to institutions. The personality of the man who incarnated them—the viceroy—had a great deal to do with the maintenance of the Peruvian colony's at least apparent submission to the sceptre of the Kings of Spain.

In fact, the first quality of a viceroy, if he wanted to make himself respected, was to show his strength constantly and, when necessary, to use it.

We shall see further on that the viceroy's worries did not stop at the frontiers of the viceroyalty. They also had to watch over the security and integrity of the territory, prevent or suppress enemy inroads, and never lose sight of the maritime horizon against which the black sails of pirate ships were sometimes silhouetted.

Were all the viceroys equal to their task? Obviously not, and it would be irrelevant to examine in detail the administration of the ten odd viceroys who succeeded each other at Lima between the birth and death of la Perricholi. But the official who must be mentioned here is Don Manuel de Amat y Juniet Planella Aymerich y Santa Pau, Viceroy of Peru from 1761 to 1776. Fifteen years which represented the best of the time of la Perricholi.

[7] Salvador de MADARIAGA: *Le Déclin de l'Empire espagnol d'Amérique*, p. 252.

Amat was the second son of the Marquis de Castellbell, a title which the latter had won 'at sword-point' during the Austrian War of Succession. He was descended from one of the most ancient and noble families of Barcelona. The young Amat spent his early years in a warlike atmosphere. There was fighting in Spain. There was fighting in Europe. So Amat burned with desire to fight. He was given the chance when he was barely seventeen. Admitted to the Order of St John of Jerusalem, he embarked for Malta where he distinguished himself during the battle of Bitonto. After fighting hard for five years in the African theatre of operations, where he was considered one of the bravest officers in the famous regiment of Dragoons of Sagunto, Amat received his warrant as Governor and President of the Audience at Chile at the age of fifty-one. Four years later, he was confirmed in his office and added to his titles that of Lieutenant-General in the army. Finally, six years later, he was appointed Viceroy Governor, Captain General of Peru and President of the Audience of Lima.

So, when Amat disembarked in Peru at the end of 1761, he could pride himself on following a 'fine career'. But his rise came to an end at Lima—perhaps because of la Perricholi! In July, 1761, he gave up his viceregal mandate, left Peru for ever and, after a brief stay in Majorca, settled at Barcelona in the ancestral palace. He married at the age of seventy-two!—and died six years later.

However, Amat's personality cannot be properly defined in this brief biographical sketch. We must welcome him on his arrival at Lima, when he was still full of fire and surprised his entourage by his unusual vigour. The fame he had acquired in Chile by killing recalcitrant Indians had preceded him to Peru. People already knew that he had an agile enterprising mind, a quick, sometimes irascible character and a firm hand. Esteemed by his leaders, feared by his subordinates, Amat, however, had many friends whom he knew how to use admirably.

At the time when Amat took the destinies of Peru in his hands, he was approaching sixty. There are still two portraits of him in existence, one in the Quinta de Presa at Lima and the other in the Hotel of the Vicereine on the Rambla de los Flores at Barcelona. His face is wide and florid, his chin thick, his shoulders heavy, but his look is piercing. We see a sensualist, but also a man with a brain.

His qualities? Unusual energy, extraordinary zeal in serving the cause of Spain and the king. Extreme vigilance over everything concerning 'royal affairs'. One of his historiographers, although not given to treating his subject kindly, noted: 'Without any doubt, Amat had been an active and pertinacious mandate-holder.' We shall see proof of this later. As for his military talents, the viceroy supplied plenty of evidence of them, including the mobilization he organized when Spain entered the Seven Years' War and the reorganization of the Peruvian army. A man of war and administration, Amat was also very enthusiastic about architecture and town-planning. He had the fortifications of Lima rebuilt and took part in the beautification of the city. His name is linked with the Plaza de Toros, the pit for cock-fights, the Coliseo de Comedias and most of all with the Alameda de los Descalzos, Lima's elegant promenade, and the Paseo de Aguas, the Promenade of the Waters, intended for la Perricholi's baths, but which remained unfinished after the viceroy's departure. The construction of hospitals and the repairing of many palaces and churches should also be put down to his credit.

His faults? Excessive authoritarianism. 'Haughty, arrogant, wilful, he would not listen to anyone's advice,' noted Barras Araña.[8] And Carlos Pereyra criticized 'his rigid and often grotesque way of materializing the empire by order, which turned those under his administration from citizens into subjects'.[9]

It must be admitted that Amat's contemporaries put the emphasis on his faults rather than his good qualities. This is how a malicious chronicler expresses himself on the subject of Amat's administration:

'His civil list, in his capacity of viceroy, was 60,000 pesos and more than 12,000 for the gratification of fees for bulls, state tobacco monopolies and other things, which in fourteen years nine months of governorship make 1,080,000 pesos—more than 700,000 pounds sterling. To that must be added the 300,000 pesos he made year in, year out, from the sale of the seventy-six *corregimientos* (posts of *corregidores*), twenty-one royal offices and countless other appointments for which he received 3,000 duros in thanks . . .'

    [8] Diego BARRAS ARAÑA: *Historia general de Chile*, Santiago, 1886–1894, vol. VI, p. 217.
    [9] Carlos PEREYRA: *Historia de la América española*, Madrid, Aguilar, vol. VII, p. 310.

The viceroy also made himself unpopular by trying to expro-priate the nuns' convents, sell their lands and open up new roads, thus splitting up convents that occupied more than two and a half acres. But the protests were so great that he had to abandon his project.

The malicious chronicler omits to say that, although Amat was by no means devout, he spent 100,000 pesos on rebuilding the tower of Santo Domingo, that he designed the niche of the Virgin de las Mercedes, paying for the work out of his own pocket and that he traced the plans of the Church of the Nazarenas himself, directing the work of the masons and carpenters in person.

As happened later to Abascal,[10] people even spread the calumny that he had failed in the loyalty sworn to his king, and that he had formed a plan to proclaim Peru independent and have himself crowned king. This was a calumny pure and simple!

One thing that was not in doubt was the viceroy's excessive love of money. But his venality, although often invoked by his enemies —and heaven knows he had enough of them—has never been proved by specific facts. In reality, Amat's haughty character and his inexorable severity had made him many more enemies than friends, which enabled the *fiscal* of the Council of the Indies to speak of 'a malicious conspiracy' against him. Incidentally, this conspiracy of jealousy and resentment did not prevent the ecclesias-tical authorities from proclaiming, on the expiration of his man-date, that Amat had set 'the highest example' of religion, by fighting against the immorality of certain circles in Lima.

However, many anecdotes about him went the rounds of the salons of Lima. It was said that he had secretly had three millions in gold for his personal use transferred from Chile to Spain in boxes ostensibly containing tobacco. At the same time, some boxes of chocolate addressed to a provincial father of the Company of Jesus, each ball of which contained one ounce of gold, were opened on his orders in the port of Callao. Must we then believe Ricardo Palma when he declared: 'Amat, like Louis XV and la Pompadour discovered that morals and a strict life were good for the governed, but not for those who governed, that they were compulsory for the masses, but flexible in the case of the authorities?'[11]

Perhaps there is an element of truth in Palma's assertion. But it

---

[10] Thirty-eighth viceroy (1806–1816).
[11] Related by Ricardo Palma, *op. cit.*

is probable that such a campaign of libels would never have been launched against Amat if he had not been ordered by Charles III in 1767 to see that the Jesuits were expelled from Peru. He made deadly enemies at the time and they soon showed their power to harm him.

At the end of the eighteenth century, a poem by Simon de Ayanqué, alluding to the tombs of Amat and one of his predecessors, the Marquis of Villagarcia, uses these words:

> *Verás en la catedral*
> *en las gradas, otros de estos*
> *que las noches de verano*
> *hablan juntos de gobierno,*
>
> *Del Señor Villagarcia*
> *hacen mención varios de ellos*
> *Y otros del Señor Amat,*
> *teniéndole por muy recto.*

'You will see in the cathedral—on the steps, people—who, on summer nights—talk together about the government—Some of them mention—Señor Villagarcia—And others Señor Amat—considering him to be a very upright man.'

This homage to Amat's rectitude—unless it expresses the posthumous flattery of a grateful courtier—confirms, that whenever affairs of state, and not his loves or personal fortune were concerned, Amat passed for a just and perspicacious man.

PART TWO

THE BACKGROUND TO PUBLIC AND PRIVATE LIFE

THE CITY AND THE STREET

Until Philip V ascended the throne of Spain on April 14, 1700, Peru had remained virtually closed to the rest of the world, or had only opened its doors to a handful of duly authorized travellers. The ban prohibiting foreign ships from trading with Spanish America was not calculated to encourage 'business voyages', a clandestine monopoly that the smugglers reserved for themselves. The only foreigners regularly admitted to Peru were sailors who put in at a Peruvian port, missionaries sent for by their monastery and diplomats *en poste*. Their attitudes to the country and its people were completely at variance. The seaman, especially when he professed the Protestant religion, as the English and Dutch sailors did, made fun of them or waxed indignant. The monk, on the contrary, seeing everything from the angle of the apostolate, was inclined to optimism. As for the diplomat, cossetted by Lima high society, he found the country pleasant, the Peruvians easy to get on with and the women of Lima charming. Rather vague opinions. None of these foreigners penetrated deeply enough into the country or stayed there long enough to form an accurate idea of men and affairs.

THE EVIDENCE OF FRENCH TRAVELLERS IN PERU

In the early years of the eighteenth century everything changed or was in the process of changing. The restrictions covering trade between foreign ports and South American ports were not lifted, but it was easier to infringe them or to be made exempt from them, owing to the increasingly liberal granting of special privileges or *licencias*. Ships flying foreign flags could, exceptionally and by virtue of private agreements concluded between the viceroy and certain merchants approved by Madrid, load and unload merchandise in Peru—and even trade on behalf of the King of Spain. The main beneficiaries of these privileges were, of course,

65

the French, who had recently become the great friends and allies of Spain. Consequently, the first foreigners able to travel 'on business' and move about freely in Peru were the French, whom the Spaniards mockingly called the *Gabachos*.[1]

The adventurous spirit of these Frenchmen was only rivalled by their temerity. They needed plenty of both to undertake the voyage to Peru. For, although wealth might lie at the end of it, there was no guarantee that they would acquire it, even if they avoided shipwreck and eluded the pirates. So many risks threatened them, including the risk of losing their health—or their life! So it was that in November, 1706, a merchant called Vincent Bauver, acting on behalf of a commercial company, left Brest on the *Comte-de-Toulouse* in order to dispose of his merchandise in the ports on the Chilean and Peruvian coasts. Bauver's troubles began with his departure from Brest. He was counting on the protection of M. de Chavagnac's squadron, composed of three ships of the line. It did not deign to wait for the unfortunate merchant, who then decided to put to sea without an escort. A Dutch privateer, armed with thirty cannon, forced him to delay his departure. At last, the *Comte-de-Toulouse*, evading the pirate's traps, weighed anchor. It doubled Cape Finistère and arrived at the Canary Islands, after holding an English ship to ransom in the approaches to Madeira. The harvest was twenty casks of wine and a few boxes of candied lemons. This practice was common and considered quite fair. The weather was so bad that Bauver could not pass through the Straits of Magellan. He retraced his steps, went round the coast of Tierra del Fuego and called at Valparaiso. He visited the Chilean ports of Coquimbo and Cobija, but in order to get permission to sell his wares he had to go in search of the governor of Atacama and cross a large part of the Cordillera of the Andes in the process. He got his *licencias*, visited Indian villages, went down to the coast again, rejoined his ship, then, leaving Chile, reached Pisco. From there he went to Lima, where he stayed for several weeks. Finally he returned to Coquimbo, whence he set sail for Brest, in which port he tied up after an absence of sixteen months.

Next year, Bachelier, surgeon on board the *Ville-de-Bourg*, disembarked at Lima and made a lengthy stay there. Three years

---

[1] The word *gavacho* or *gabacho* which the Spaniards applied to the French is pejorative. It probably comes from the Arabic *cabach* meaning 'dirty, detestable, of dissolute morals and character'.

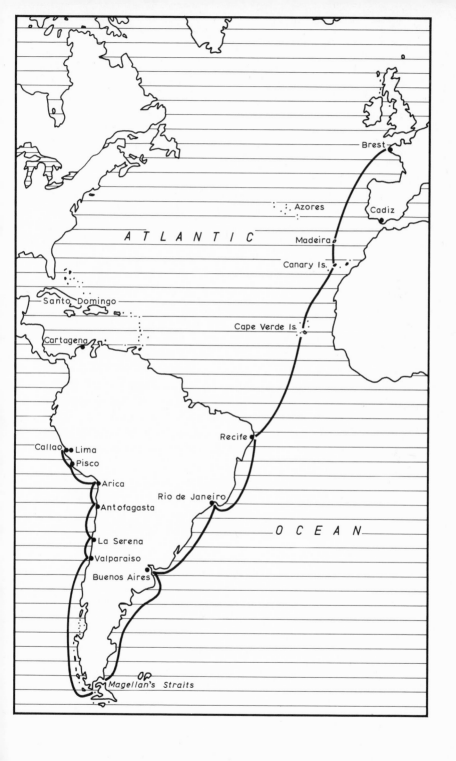

Brest

Azores

Cadiz

ATLANTIC

Madeira

Canary Is.

Santo Domingo

Cartagena

Cape Verde Is.

Callao Lima
Pisco

Arica

Antofagasta

Recife

Rio de Janeiro

La Serena

OCEAN

Valparaiso

Buenos Aires

Magellan's Straits

later it was the turn of Amédée-François Frézier, fortifications engineer in the service of the King of France and native of Saint-Malo, to make a voyage of investigation to Chile and Peru, where he stayed three years.

After the merchants and the engineers on special missions came the scientists. It was the time when scientific and intellectual collaboration between France and Spain was the order of the day. It was in this climate that the two crowns of France and Spain organized, from 1735 to 1740, a combined expedition in order to 'determine the shape and size of the earth' by measuring degrees of latitude. Two groups of scientists were sent out simultaneously, one towards the polar circle, the other below the Equator. Both groups were to take the exact measurements of a terrestrial degree. With this information, it was believed that it would be possible to decide whether the earth was a perfect sphere or slightly flattened at the poles. The three French scientists were chosen by Louis XV himself. The party consisted of Jussieu, a botanist, Seniergues, a surgeon, Moranville, a draughtsman, and Hugot, a clock-maker, completed by three eminent members of the Academy of Sciences: Bouguer, La Condamine and Gaudin. The first, celebrated for his work on hydrography and his invention of the heliometer, disputed the leadership of the expedition with La Condamine. Less scholarly, perhaps, than Bouguer, but more brilliant, La Condamine surpassed him in the difficult art of negotiation. His curiosity about men and material things was well known and had earned him his full share of unusual experiences. One day, during a journey in Italy, he stopped in a village which legend had it would be swallowed up by the floods if a certain candle venerated by the population was extinguished. La Condamine blew it out to see what would happen. He was nearly torn to pieces. He was present at the execution of Damiens and when one of the executioner's assistants tried to push him away, the executioner made this remark: 'Leave him alone, he's an enthusiast.' This lust for universal knowledge caused his death. He insisted on a risky new operation being performed on him, begging the surgeon to go more slowly so that he could see better. But he never saw the end of the operation, for he died before it was finished.

Gaudin, the astronomer, more specifically in charge of the scientific equipment, was one of the few Frenchmen to be present during the earthquake that destroyed most of the town of Lima and the port of Callao in 1746. Dazzled by his scientific knowledge, the viceroy offered Gaudin a chair of mathematics at the University of Lima and he accepted it. A similar experience befell Jussieu. The Peruvians appreciated his medical knowledge and begged him not to leave the country until an epidemic that was raging had come to an end. Once the epidemic was over, Jussieu in his turn decided not to return to France until thirty-six years later, after he had visited the whole of Spanish America. He returned home so worn out and with his memory so impaired that he was unable to publish the results of his discoveries and his travels.

The French expedition, leaving from San Domingo, rejoined the Spanish mission at Cartagena de las Indias, the port of New Granada, present-day Colombia. The two Spanish scientists, appointed by the court of Madrid, were also men of ability. They were Don Jorge Juan, 'Commander of Aliaga in the Order of Malta and Commander of the Marine Guard of Gentlemen,' and Don Antonio de Ulloa, Lieutenant in the same company, both 'rated captains in the naval army of the King of Spain'. Juan was a specialist in the natural sciences, Ulloa shone in mathematics. Although both were young—Ulloa was not yet twenty—they belonged to various scientific societies, including the Royal Society of London and the Academy of Sciences at Paris. But as we have seen in the last chapter, their mission was not confined to scientific investigation alone. They were perhaps even more interested in the study of men and institutions. It is only necessary to refer to their *Noticias secretas,* in which there is more about the politics of the viceroyalty of Peru than about the terrestrial meridian.

Setting out from Cadiz in the *Conqueror,* of sixty-four guns, Juan and Ulloa reached Cartagena de las Indias four months before their French colleagues. They killed time by studying the geographical and botanical peculiarities of the Colombian coast. Then they welcomed the French academic mission with great demonstrations of politeness and respect. And the band of scholars, after having fraternized under the sign of the Bourbons, hastened off in the direction of the Cordillera.[2]

Thus, as from the middle of the eighteenth century, Peru, which

[2] Most of the facts about the travels of Bauver and the 'Academicians' have been taken from *L'Amérique du Sud au XVIIIe siècle, Mélanges anecdotiques et bibliographiques* by Régine Pernoud (a work quoted in the bibliography).

had long remained *terra incognita* to all Europeans except Spaniards, began to unveil its face. Businessmen, seamen, 'technicians'—most of them French—had as it were rediscovered it, clearing the way for the travellers of the future, for those whom one still does not dare call 'tourists'. Many years were to elapse before Europeans had the means, the time and the intrepidity to go to Peru for pleasure. For a long time they went to Peru on business or as diplomats, or on scientific and naval expeditions, of which the most famous were that of the German naturalist Alexander von Humboldt and Bonpland in 1799 and, much later, that of Max Radiguet, secretary to Admiral Dupetit-Thouars, in the frigate *La Reine Blanche*.

The French travellers mentioned above, whether mariners or men of science, were serious and truthful people by profession and temperament, trained in the strict school of mathematical observation. So their evidence—log-books, reports, memoirs—can be taken into consideration, even though it is sometimes rather on the dry side. On the whole, it confirms the narratives of the Spanish travellers fairly exactly, as regards the mathematical details at least. Spanish accounts were of necessity very numerous, since thousands of Spaniards from the most varied social classes and fortunes, from the starving emigrant to the president of the audience, came and went between the metropolis and the viceroyalty.

In any case, all these travellers, whether French or Spanish, whether they came from Brest or Cadiz, burning to get rich or simply wanting to see the country, followed the same itinerary. Let us follow in their footsteps and disembark at Callao en route for Lima. The time of our 'retrospective' arrival in Peru is a cold day in the spring of 1771, i.e. twenty-five years after the partial destruction of Lima and Callao, and ten years after the arrival in Peru of Viceroy Don Manuel de Amat. The earthquake of 1746 is no more than a memory, Callao and Lima have been rebuilt and Amat's administration is at the height of its powers.

ARRIVAL AT CALLAO

As a rule night is falling when ships from Europe come in sight of Callao. It is the end of a long voyage, begun in a French or Spanish port, with these principal stages: Madeira, the Canary

Islands, the Cape Verde Islands, Pernambuco (Récife), Rio de Janeiro, Montevideo, Buenos Aires, the Straits of Magellan and Valparaiso. The ship has had to sail round almost the whole of the South American continent, put in scores of times both on the Atlantic coast (Brazil, Uruguay and Argentina) and on the Pacific coast (Chile). There has been no lack of incidents and sometimes accidents on the voyage. The reefs off the coast of Tierra del Fuego have made holes in the bilges. A sailor was killed by a Patagonian during a trip ashore. Fortunately, the voyage from Valparaiso to Callao was calm. The sea was motionless, like a great blue lake, and at night the golden arms of the Southern Cross twinkled in the southern sky between Carina and Centaurus. An uneventful but lengthy voyage, for the ship had to drop anchor in each of the eighteen *intermedios* (intermediate ports) between Valparaiso and Callao: Coquimbo, Antofagasta, Cobija, Arica, Pisco, etc.

The harsh light of the tropical sun accentuated the bareness of this arid coast, which looked like an endless sand-dune with only the green shadow of an occasional oasis to break its monotony.

The ship has entered the roads by a fairway situated between the coast and the island of Callao which gave its name to the port and the town. Callao means 'calm', for the sea is calm at this point and vessels can moor there in perfect safety. In order to prevent smuggling the customs regulations forbid the disembarkation of passengers and merchandise by night. So the ship will stay in the roads until the next morning. By moonlight we can see the white houses of Callao, dotted with luminous points, the broken line of roofs against the greyish horizon, in the distance the domes and bell-towers of Lima, and blocking the horizon a dark mass—the Cordillera of the Andes.

The night passes quickly, enlivened by the sailors' tales. They recall the gigantic tidal wave of 1746 that had hurled ships onto the mole and the quays, submerged Callao and then flowed back into the sea, leaving nothing but ruins in the place of the hundreds of houses lining the coast. The old sailors say that if you lean over the rails at midnight you can see the old city that was swallowed up by the sea and the shades of dead fishermen, sitting outside their doors. The sailors also assert that if you listen hard you can even hear cockcrow rising from the depths of the sea at dawn. Fabulous tales that put some travellers to sleep and keep others awake.

Daybreak is announced by a deafening hubbub: the awakening of the birds. Heavy, clumsy pelicans, chequered with silver and ebony plumage, petrels with hooked beaks and white seagulls describe wide concentric circles above the ship and utter piercing cries, punctuated by the beating of their wings. A line of white houses, dominated by the squat bell-tower of the cathedral, appears in the foreground. To the left, the two forts of the Castillo aim their threatening batteries seawards. To the right, the sinister island of San Lorenzo, to which criminals are sent, forms a grey patch on the ocean. In the distance, beyond the muddy plain, the roofs and spires of Lima flash in the rising sun in a violet haze that gradually turns to purple. Still farther away, drowned in a milky transparency, is the mountain range of the Andes. Such, seen from the sea, is the first vision of Peru that strikes the traveller.

Permission to disembark is given by the port authorities. Boats come to meet the passengers and take them to the quay, past the mole built by Viceroy Amat and which is the apple of his eye. How delightful it is to set foot on land after such a long voyage! Not for long, for transport to Lima is infrequent and must be taken advantage of whenever possible. There is a *calesa*, a sort of calash harnessed to a mule and generally constructed to hold four passengers besides the driver. (But some were bigger; they could hold a dozen travellers and were drawn by two mules.) The passengers pack into one of the large *calesas*, happy to know that they will not have to walk the six miles that separate the port from the capital. Jolting and wobbling, the old rattletrap threads its way through the main street of Callao, paved with cobble-stones and lined with houses painted in soft colours. The town is waking up. The gaudy roller-blinds of the balconies are pulled up, creaking on their rollers. Women are enjoying the cool of the morning outside their doors. Children run afer the *calesa,* but they soon stop, out of breath, for the driver has set his mules off at full speed with a loud crack of the whip and soon the carriage, with groaning axles, is nothing but a black dot on the dusty track that leads to the City of Kings.

Once they have settled on the wooden seats as best they can, the travellers take a look at their fellow-passengers, three Peruvians of widely differing appearance: an officer, a monk and a half-breed girl from the country.

The officer wears a pink cap braided with silver, at a rakish angle, a blue poncho with long fringes protects his blue uniform from the dust and he mechanically smooths the gold bands on his purple trousers. The monk belongs to a confraternity, the *Hermandad de la Buena Muerte*, which is responsible for burying corpses. A vast black felt hat with a wide brim, from which hang black silk tassels, balances on his rosy pate, like an enormous mushroom. A large red cross stands out against his black cloak. The cholita, intimidated by such neighbours, lowers her eyes beneath her Guyaquil straw hat, tied under her chin with a black ribbon.

The wheels of the *calesa* grate on the grey sand that is dotted with pebbles. About half a mile from Callao, a cross stands by the side of the road. The driver crosses himself. It is the site of an astonishing miracle that took place on October 28, 1746. When the famous earthquake was at its height, an enormous wave deposited a ship of heavy tonnage on the sand. Then it ebbed at breath-taking speed, leaving the ship stuck in the ground like a spear and its crew safe and sound. A few hundred yards farther on, clumps of grass announce the presence of water. Here it is, springing in small jets from the channels fed by the Rimac. The driver crosses himself a second time before the statue of Our Lady of Carmel, erected exactly half-way between Callao and Lima on the spot called the *Legua* (the league), one league from Callao and one league from Lima. The appearance of the countryside changes. It is less arid. We begin to see fields of corn and clover, or *alfalfa*. Trees are more and more numerous. The greenery expands and grows denser. Lima is not far now. We enter it by a handsome avenue of willows planted by Viceroy Abascal, who dreamt of extending it as far as Callao. The *calesa* crosses the *puente* of Callao, over the Rimac, at a gallop, traverses a vast portico decorated with stucco mouldings, goes along the Calle de los Mercaderes, Lima's shopping street, then, with a great tinkling of bells, it stops suddenly at the entrance to the Plaza Mayor. The travellers have arrived.

LIMA'S GENERAL APPEARANCE

'Lima, paradise for women, purgatory for men and hell for *borricos*.'

It is indeed likely that donkeys in Lima were so ill-treated that they believed they were in the abode of the damned, and that

women, on the contrary, were as contented there as in the kingdom
of the blessed. But the really malicious part of the old saying is
the reference to Lima as a place of penitence for men. 'Penitence
is sweet . . .' would certainly have been the sinners' refrain. How
many *hacenderos,* bored to death in the depths of some valley in
Upper Peru, would have liked to purge themselves of their sins
at Lima!

Of course, there were also Cuzco, Arequipa, Callao and Pisco,
not to mention other charming cities hidden away in delightful
sites. It was pleasant to go to them for a short period of rest, to
make a retreat there. But one only really lived at Lima. And the
sole ambition of Peruvian towns other than Lima was to resemble
the capital, to borrow its way of life, in short, to imitate it in
every way.

The 'Town of Kings', as its founder, Francisco Pizarro, had
christened it on Epiphany Day, was, towards the middle of the
sixteenth century, a bucolic country town, surrounded by pomegranate trees, citron trees and grapefruit trees, 'looking more like
a wood than a city'.[3] Indeed, once the period of conquest was over,
the Spaniards had undertaken to turn the conquered country and
especially the district of Lima into agricultural colonies. The
soldiers became farmers, leaving the sword for the plough and
spending their time acclimatizing to Peru the vines and lemon
trees, wheat and rose bushes, cows and doves brought from Spain.

'Outside the town, on both sides, there are many farms and rural
estates where Spaniards keep their cattle and their dove-cotes, as
well as many vines and cool, pleasant orchards, full of fruits native
to the country and fig trees, banana trees, pomegranate trees, sugar
cane, melons, oranges, lemons, citrons, grapefruit and vegetables
brought from Spain.'[4]

But a city full of vitality was growing behind this green belt.
From the seventeenth century onwards, Lima, the seat of a powerful
viceroyalty, had the whole of South America under his sway, except
Brazil. In the days of la Perricholi, it had reached its apogee and
incarnated the glory and opulence of the Spanish Empire in
America. Thousands of masons and architects from Spain, especially Andalusia, had given the city that Hispano-Moorish look that

---

[3] J. Regina de LIZARRAGA: *Description et Population des Indiens.*
[4] *Chroniques* of Cieza de León.

surprised the visitor. Dominated by the steeples and domes of its churches, Lima seemed to extend endlessly, with its wide streets laid out absolutely straight. Under a clement sky, the humid warmth of the town made flowers bloom and softened the will-power of the great-grandsons of the conquistadores. In fact, over a long period, cross-breeding had watered down the vigorous blood of the *extremeño* captains.

Some people said of Lima that it was the second town of Spain; others whispered that it was the first. People spoke about the court of Lima as naturally as if it was the court of Madrid, and some-times more respectfully. In fact, it really was the second town of Spain after Madrid, and the capital of Spanish America, after the separation of the viceroyalties of New Granada and Buenos Aires in 1718.

Descriptions of colonial Lima abound, but they are generally poetically vague. Thus the Chilean historian Vicuna Mackenna paints Lima as a

'nymph of idleness, asleep on the banks of the flowering Rimac, softly resting on the very spot that its masters first designated for it, surrounded by green fields, crowned with rustic diadems, lifting its voluptuous forehead to the caresses of a cloudless sky, she whose climate consists of light breezes without rainfall and a light that wears the impress of an eternal calm.'

I prefer the Frenchman Bauver's clearer description to this exaggerated ode:

'Lima is a big town, like Lyons or Rouen, on a gentle slope, along the top of which runs a torrent coming from the mountains which has been "bled" in order to channel into the majority of the streets, which are all dead straight, several streams of excellent water, which supply the town. It would be very clean as a result, if all the streets were paved; most of them are not paved at all and consequently are full of mud and soil, since it never rains there.'

That is the briefly sketched face of Lima as it appeared to foreign travellers. A town of medium size, situated on a hill where the Rimac flows. The streets, some of them paved, are straight and wide and intersect each other on the 'chess-board plan' dear to the first builders of the Spanish Empire. Irrigation channels lead down from the top of the hill that dominates the city and, carried by aqueducts in the form of vaults, transport the water intended for watering the streets and gardens. A stone bridge crosses the Rimac in the middle of the town, which is surrounded by a green belt that adds splashes of shimmering colours.

Thus the landscape gradually takes on more definite lines. But to get a more general impression of Lima, it is necessary to climb to the top of one of the many *miradores* (a sort of belvedere in the form of a tower) that many of the inhabitants have built on the terraces of their houses. In fact, as it never rains in this part of the littoral, the rooftops are not sloped to let the water run away, but form flat surfaces, sometimes laid out as terraces full of flowers (*azoteas*) surmounted by a mirador. From the top of such an observatory and looking towards the coast, it is possible to take in the whole of Lima. Then the observer has a better idea of the geographical situation of Lima, which is imbedded between two natural barriers: in front, the Pacific Ocean, behind, the Cordillera of the Andes. The dark-blue ocean extends from the hills of Anion in the north to the mountain of Chorrillos in the south. From the top of the mirador he can make out the forts of Callao and the sails of the ships, swollen by the coastal wind, that are entering and leaving the port. If he turns round, the spectacle is quite different. Abrupt, rocky, covered with black dust, the granite rampart of the first line of mountains forming the Cordillera separates Lima from the interior of the country, cutting the horizon off short. Just as the maritime frontiers seem boundless—from the high cliffs of the Peruvian coast to the first islands of Polynesia there is nothing but sea for thousands of miles—so the mountain frontiers seem brutally to mark the end of a world and stand for an inexorable 'Thou shalt not pass'. In fact, this back-cloth comprises successive lines of mountains, one behind the other and getting higher the further away they are. There, to the right, quite near, is the cone-shaped mountain of San Cristobal. Starting from its summit and reaching out to the left, a depression formed by the collapse of the terrain ends in a vast plain, the *pampa de amancaes,* so called because in summer it is covered with yellow narcissi (*amancaes*) which the people of Lima flock out of the town to pick.

Behind, another mountain rises, not as high as San Cristobal, but broader at the base. Lastly, behind this first line of mountains a second can be seen and sometimes, when the weather is fine, it is even possible to count seven successive ranges. The most distant peaks are covered with snow. They are over 18,000 feet high.

The observer's gaze moves down to the town again whose general architecture, intelligently laid out, contrasts with the infinite expanse of the Pacific and the formidable rampart of the Andes. However, such neighbours do not crush it; quite the contrary, as if the ocean receding into infinity and the gigantic mountains emphasized, by contrast, the charm of this city that the hand of man has built and rebuilt several times. A somewhat monotonous charm, be it said, with its neatly intersecting streets and its frequently uniform houses.

Here, we recognize the octagonal tower of Santa Domingo, the highest in the town, the square tower of San Agustin and the tower of la Merced. In the distance, the old stone bridge. To the left, even further away, the massive building of San Francisco de Paula and the little painted tower of San Lazaro. To the side of the town clumps of pines line the promenade of los Descalzos. Here, a little closer, the two red brick towers of San Pedro, then the two blackish-brown spires of the cathedral, behind which the twin bell-towers of San Francisco are barely visible. Towers, belfries, domes, and dividing up the town at regular intervals, like the bars of a grille, animated, bustling streets, thoroughfares in which a good part of everyday life seethes and flows by.

IN THE HEART OF THE TOWN AND IN THE STREET

Now that we have seen Lima from a distance and from above, let us penetrate to the heart of the city, and walk through its streets.

The plan of Lima was simple. It did not differ from the plan of other Spanish cities, nor from that of other Spanish American cities. These were the main features of its lay-out.

All the streets intersected each other at right angles, about every hundred yards, thus forming blocks of houses (*manzanas*) of roughly equal dimensions; they were square and surrounded by four streets. Each face of these squares, corresponding to a section of street, was called a *cuadra*. So the city consisted of a series of *manzanas* arranged like the squares of a chess-board. Several *manzanas* formed a quarter (*barrio*), which formed part of a district (*cuarta*).

77

In the time of la Perricholi, Lima consisted of four *cuartas,* thirty-five *barrios,* 209 *manzanas,* 350 streets and 8,222 'house doors',[5] that is to say habitations. Thus the basic feature of the urban plan was the *manzana,* or in other words the block, which we find again as the basis of the architecture of big American cities.

Of the 350 streets (*calles*), only seven deserve to be mentioned because of their size, the others being frequently nothing more than alleys or simple passages in front of a group of houses. They are the streets de los Mercaderes, de las Mantas, del Correo, del Palacio, del Arzobispo, del Melchormelo and de Bodegones. They all started from the parade-ground or Plaza Mayor, the centre of the town. The Calle del Palacio led to the stone bridge crossing the Rimac and continued on the far side of the river, where it assumed the name of Calle de San Lazaro. The Calle de los Mercaderes, too, was continued by the Calles de Espaderos, de la Merced, de Baquijano and de Boza. Apart from the Plaza Mayor, Lima possessed thirty-two squares, the majority of which were situated in front of churches whose names they bore.

It was in these streets and under the *portales* (wooden galleries) surrounding the Plaza Mayor that the popular life of Lima was concentrated. As soon as one moved away from the parade-ground in the direction of the river or the country, one no longer met many people. Only the presence of the *pulperias* (grocers' shops) at the street corners in the outlying quarters aroused a little animation; the maids from the neighbouring houses went there to do their shopping and took the opportunity to chat with each other. In the same way, the banks of the Rimac were not much frequented. I should say that only a very relative cool was to be found there, for the Rimac was only a small river. Nevertheless, the viceroys had three bridges built, the Stone Bridge, the Wooden Bridge and the Balta Bridge, to cross this undersized watercourse that cleared a passage for itself among the big rocks roasted by the sun and only just bathed the foundations of the monumental arches. It is true that at the height of the main bridge the bed of the Rimac underwent a change of level and broadened out into a shallow sheet of water, purling as it fell into the lower part. But it quickly contracted again to pass beneath the wooden bridge.

We have seen that the problem of irrigation had been solved

[5] Information taken from the *Mercurio peruano* (May, June, July and August numbers, 1792). Statistics for the year 1786.

by using, not the section of the Rimac flowing in Lima, but the natural pressure of the waters of the Rimac itself, collected at the top of the town, then led away and distributed in the streets and surrounding countryside by open channels running down a gentle slope.

As for the problem of drinking water—for the water of the Rimac was unfit for consumption—it had been solved as from the end of the fifteenth century, thanks to the discovery and use of an excellent spring, as Father Lizarraga noted in the course of his stay at Lima:

'The water of the river, the Rimac, is not as good as that of the other valleys round about. But the Lord has granted this city a spring situated three quarters of a mile away and whose water is so excellent that perhaps the doctors would wish that it was not so good. I heard one of them—and he was the doyen of all those living at this moment—declare that this water had diminished his income by about 3,000 pesos (2,170 pounds) a year. This water was led to the town, in the centre of which is a big fountain. In each quarter there is a secondary fountain, as well as in all the monasteries, the large surrounding houses and the prisons. There are two in the palace, for the streets being arranged at right angles and the water flowing in conduits which follow the street, it is easy to install it in the houses.'[6]

There were therefore two different sources and two distribution systems, one for irrigation purposes and one for drinking water, the latter being brought by conduits to the fountains where the people came to draw it. The rich citizens had it laid on to their houses.

In spite of their beautiful alignment, the streets of Lima had some disadvantages, the main ones being dust, traffic jams and beggars.

'The incessant trampling of processions of mules loaded with merchandise maintained a litter of dung which, dried by the wind and sun, disintegrated into a powdery and very unpleasant dust. Half the town travelled by coach, either in the sumptuous coaches of the wealthy or in the scarcely less sumptuous *calesas*, two-wheeled carriages drawn by mules and made to carry four persons

[6] Quoted by Salvador de MADARIAGA in *L'Essor de l'Amérique espagnole*, pp. 247–248.

79

in addition to the driver who mounted the mule. The *calesas* were completely gilded and covered with rich ornaments. Although their cost was high (from 800 to 1,000 pesos; from 580 to 720 pounds), there were between 5,000 and 6,000 of them in Lima, and almost as many coaches that were even more magnificent, of course, and much more costly.'[7]

There were also the flocks of vicunas with their long brown silky hair, the lines of mules loaded with lucerne, jumping under the whips of the muleteers, water-bearers perched on their little donkeys, star-gazing, iron-shod pole on shoulder, ringing their bell and keeping their balance on their saddle which supported two barrels of fresh water counterbalancing each other. Here, a herd of lowing cows returns from its pastures to the dairy. There a baker struggles to guide his horse through the crowd; the animal carries two leather bags full of bread on its back, their wooden framework covered with leather as tight as a drum. When he reaches his customer, the breadseller announces himself by striking a series of blows on the bags with a leather thong. A piercing cry echoes him, that of the milkmaid who comes from the country to bring milk to the town. She is mounted on a horse, sitting with legs crossed between two tin cans and sometimes her child, whom she carries on her back wrapped in her *manta,* imitates her call.

At a turn in the road, a herd of white llamas spotted with brown swaying their long necks surrounded with little bells, clashes with a dozen mules loaded with sacks of lime. The terrified llamas escape, the sacks burst, the lime flies in all directions and covers the passers-by, who flee, cursing the clumsy muleteer.

And everywhere one meets itinerant salesmen who announce their passage in different ways. One recognizes the monotonous, drawn-out cry of the cake-seller (*bizcochero*), trotting along with short steps, a basket of biscuits on his head, the raucous cry of the woman selling tisanes, carrying like an amphora her earthenware crock full of an infusion of barley, in which pineapple skins are soaking. The sharp call of the seller of lottery tickets (*suertero*) promising fortune to anyone willing to listen; the wheedling call of the seller of roots to whiten the teeth. As for the seller of jasmin blossom, he shouts himself hoarse: '*¡Jazmin! ¡Jazmin!* young ladies,

[7] Quoted by Jorge Juan and Ulloa.

6. a. Map of the city of Lima

b. Lima Cathedral, 1836

7. a. La Perricholi's house

b. La Perricholi's carriage

don't you want to smell it?' Lima was not made for lovers of silence.

The dust, the noise and the traffic jams seemed less trying than the cynical insistence of the beggars. They were found in every street. They were very well dressed, both men and women. From their earliest years, they were accustomed to this idle way of life and were content to have enough to live on comfortably without having to work for it. Those who ventured to offer them four or five maravédis (a coin worth about fivepence) met with a very hostile reception. They refused with disdain—the least one could give to this sort of beggar was twenty odd maravédis, under penalty of passing for a heartless person or a skinflint.[8]

One last disadvantage was the almost total obscurity of a large part of the town, once night had fallen.[9] Public lighting, in fact, had only just been installed—in 1776—and, with a view to economy, the municipality had restricted it to the centre of the town and the main thoroughfares. As soon as one moved away from this zone, one's progress was haphazard. However, it should be pointed out that for several months of the year, especially in summer, the moonlight was so bright that it supplemented the illumination of the oil lamps. Then visibility was as good as in broad daylight.

Such were the disadvantages of the streets of Lima, to which should be added in conclusion another very unpleasant one that affected people with sensitive feet or a delicate sense of smell. Although the streets of Lima were laid out and intersected each other regularly, like a geometrical design, their paving left much to be desired. The road surfaces bristled with small sharp stones that cut like bits of broken glass and the pavements, though spacious enough, one and a half *vare* wide, about three feet, ten inches), were made of unjoined slabs that gave beneath one's feet. Moreover, in some quarters far from the centre, the middle of the street was occupied by open gutters which were crossed on wooden planks, but their filthy waters often overflowed, resulting in minor floods and a terrible stench.

And yet, in spite of the dust, the traffic problems, the noise, the

[8] After the observations of Bachelier, a French traveller at the beginning of the eighteenth century, quoted by Raoul Porras Barranechea in *Pequeña Antología de Lima*.

[9] Since Lima is situated in the tropics, it is night there all the year round from six in the evening to six in the morning.

beggars, the bad nocturnal lighting and the hazardous pavements, it is amusing to walk through the streets of Lima. Whereas a punctilious hierarchy governs people's relationships within the social structure—whether at home, in the workshop or in the office—the crowd in the street is one big happy family.

Here is an important canon, draped in his *capa* lined with satin, in friendly conversation with a second-hand dealer crouching in front of his stall, which is sheltered from the sun by a parasol mounted on a pole. Here an officer, spurs clicking and white poncho thrown over his shoulder, enters the barber's to have his moustache curled—perhaps also to be bled, for the *peluquero,* as in Spain, was also a surgeon, as is shown by his sign, a hand holding a scalpel from which a gout of blood escapes. Squatting face to face on a rush mat, a *Zambo* with his hair plaited plays dice with a mountain Indian, the black handkerchief over his ear surmounted by a straw hat like a sugarloaf.

Everybody fraternizes in a friendly uproar.

When night comes, the spectacle in the street changes its appearance according as one remains in the centre of the town or moves away from it. In the Plaza Mayor and in the well-lit main streets where the shops stay open till late at night, the crowd is as dense as at midday. Groups of young girls, arm in arm, walk endlessly up and down under the *portales.* They meet similar groups of young men. They look at each other, smile, shout to each other. It is the hour when people in high society are paying calls or on their way to dine in town. So there are many idlers to watch the passage of *calesas* full of elegant women and escorted by fashionable gallants. From ten o'clock in the evening onwards it is impossible for traffic to move in the Calle de los Mercaderes. It is a time-honoured custom for the people of Lima to gather there to watch the elegant women of the town pass by. Leaning against the walls, standing at street corners or sometimes simply installed in chairs at the edge of the pavement, these connoisseurs of beautiful women obstruct the traffic and no one dares to say anything to them. It is the tradition. Then there is a mixture of cries of admiration and flattering remarks: '¡Hombre, ve qué buena moza! Just look at that beautiful girl!' '¡Que ojos tan preciosos! What lovely eyes!' '¡Qué modo de andar tan hermoso! What a superb walk!'

As one moves further away from the Plaza Mayor, the spectacle changes; it is less brilliant, but perhaps more poetical. Incidentally, there is no danger in venturing into the remoter streets as they are well guarded, and the town's topography lends itself to efficient policing. At each corner of the *manzanas* there is a policeman, responsible for keeping order in the *cuadra*—i.e. there were four of them per *cuadra*—and in constant touch with his colleagues. This policeman is called *encapotado,* because of his cape; he wears a round hat and carries a coil of rope for tying up thieves. What he does lack is a weapon. So the *encapotado* will soon be replaced by the *sereno,* a combination of night-watchman and policeman, wearing a short coat and a broad-brimmed hat, and armed with a gun. His job is to walk up and down the *cuadra* that he is responsible for, announce all the hours to the inhabitants, who are sound asleep when he does so, and, of course, keep a check on the comings and goings of passers-by. And, above all, he has to stay awake, otherwise he would be in danger of finding himself minus gun and coat when he woke up.

But nocturnal aggression is rare in Lima. The foreigner can walk through the town in perfect safety, without fear of being robbed or assassinated. If he goes into a *pulperia* where everything is sold from haberdashery to tobacco and liqueurs, he will be welcomed and the owner will probably offer him a glass of *pisco,* the national spirit, even if he does not buy anything. Perhaps a *cholo* musician will even play a tune on the guitar for him. He will run into him again further on in a tavern (*bodega*) that is still open. The calm that reigns in these suburban districts contrasts strangely with the deafening hubbub of the Plaza Mayor. However, total silence does not come until midnight. There will still be a few nightbirds in the streets and even a few humble street vendors (those who have been driven out of the better quarters), such as the icecream man (*heladero*) and the man selling wafers. The *heladero* is usually an Indian from the *sierra,* clad in shirt and trousers held up by a woollen belt of dazzling colours; on his head he carries a wooden pail inside which swirl, surrounded by crushed ice, ices (*helados*) of much lower quality than the ices sold in the elegant confectioners' installed beneath the *portales,* but very cheap. From time to time, he utters a long guttural cry, 'Helado de leche, helado de piña, Milk ices! Pineapple ices!', brandishing the long metal spatula he uses to extract the ices from the bottom of his pail. As for the wafer merchant, he announces his presence by banging his tin.

83

But the noises get fewer and fewer. Sometimes we hear the mournful ringing of the little handbell that precedes the passage of the viaticum, or the bell of the parish sacristan who is dressed in a coloured cape and carries a small lantern, and is collecting money for the souls in Purgatory and for holy candles. At last silence comes broken every hour until dawn by the *sereno* who chants: '*¡Ave Maria purisma!* It is midnight! Long live Peru! The weather is fine!', for his orders are to announce fine weather even if the sky is cloudy.

The City of Kings has gone to sleep.

HOUSES AND FURNITURE

We have seen that all the towns in Peru were laid out on the 'chessboard plan' imposed by the Spanish monarchy ever since the conquest. But this type of town plan went back even further. Indeed, it is striking to note the similarity between the instructions of Philip II in 1573 regarding the rules for the construction of towns and the principles of town-planning set forth in the works of the great Roman architect Vitruvius, who, incidentally, was only picking up the threads of the Greek tradition again. Miletus and the Piraeus were chessboard towns. The architects of the Middle Ages, and later of the Renaissance, were certainly inspired by Greek and Latin documents when they applied this plan to numerous fortified villages and towns in the South of France. And it was the kings of Spain, in their turn, who handed on the heritage of Mediterranean town-planning to the New World. I should add that the Graeco-Roman tradition was very well suited to the thinking of the founders of South America, with their passion for order.

The 'laws of the Indies' had once and for all prescribed *uniformidad en todo* (uniformity in everything), which was equally applicable to persons and things, to administration and architecture. They decreed that everywhere, from Mexico to the farthest boundaries of Chile, there should be the same criss-cross pattern of streets and the same vast, square, Plaza Mayor, in which the cathedral and the viceregal palace stood opposite each other, or, in smaller towns, the church and the *cabildo* (the house of god and the house of the king), incarnating the permanence of the spiritual power and the temporal power, the two pillars of the imperial Spanish pediment.

A DEVELOPING ARCHITECTURE: FROM PLATERESQUE TO ROCOCO

This unity in urban lay-out is found again in the style of buildings in the sense that they all obeyed the same principles or

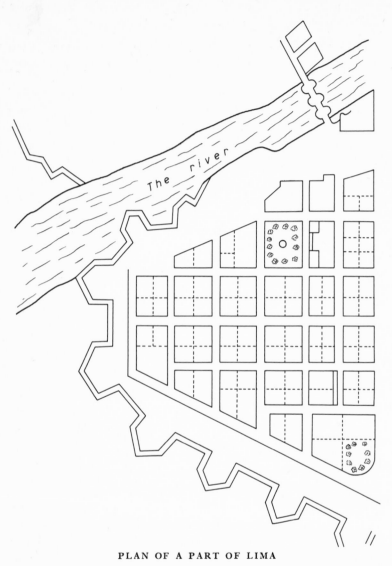

PLAN OF A PART OF LIMA

A *barrio,* surrounded by fortifications. The houses, or *casas,*
grouped in sixes or fours, form *manzanas,* separated by streets, or
calles. Each face of each *manzana* is called a *cuadra.* Several *barrios*
form a *distrito* or *cuarta.*

rather they reproduced, with a certain time lag and some variations in practice, the edifices of Spain. That explains why Peruvian architecture, from Pizarro to Amat, underwent the same development as Spanish architecture.

The development of Peruvian architecture of the 'colonial' type, i.e. the one which was practised in Peru for three centuries, from the end of the Inca empire to the advent of the Republic, can be summed up in a few words.

Even if there were certain rather special aspects of this architecture in a few towns in Peru because of purely local influences (climate, traditions, materials), its main features show that it developed as follows: *Plateresque,* reminiscent of Gothic and Moorish styles, during the period of conquest strictly speaking (from 1532–1534) and the first years of the viceroyalty, *Classical,* from the middle of the sixteenth to the middle of the seventeenth century, *Baroque* from the middle of the seventeenth to the end of the eighteenth century, a period when the influence of *Rococo* began to make itself felt, followed by the *Neo-classical* period which covers the first quarter of the nineteenth century.

However, if this definition is to be absolutely explicit, it calls for a brief commentary and in particular a reminder of what the words Plateresque, Baroque and Rococo mean.

Plateresque (*plateresco,* from *plata,* silver) is a style of Spanish architecture whose ornaments of flowers and foliage are in imitation of those generally seen on fine examples of the silversmith's art. The Plateresque style is characteristic of the first period of the Renaissance. It was imported into Spain by the Catalan silversmith or *platero* Pedro Diez who, on his return from Rome, built at Valladolid the College of Santa Cruz which the critics have recognized as the first building of the Italian Renaissance in Spain.

The word 'baroque' was originally a word used by jewellers to describe bizarre, irregular objects, especially figures that took no account of proportions. Applied by the Italians to architecture, the Baroque became Baroque art and was imported into Spain from Italy towards the end of the eighteenth century. It seems that Baroque had an essentially negative meaning, designating that which was not classical, even though the classical itself is not easily definable when it comes to architecture, unless, going back to antique sources, we restrict ourselves to the three orders recognized by Vitruvius, the Doric, Ionian and Corinthian, the special

87

proportions of which determined the proportions of the whole building. The Baroque, then, was that which was opposed to the classical canons, a sort of reaction or protest against the three Greek orders and the 'academicism' of forms.

This reaction was most extreme in the case of the Catalan architect and sculptor Churriguera, who gave his name to the Spanish baroque style of the eighteenth century (Churrigueresque), recognizable by its polychromy and the use of irregular columns or 'estípites' as opposed to the beautiful geometrical regularity of the Greek columns. An extravagant style in which colour succeeded in confusing forms by covering a tortured sculpture with its violent, often strident tones.

In short the terms Baroque and Churrigueresque should be understood more as a conception of art than as the definition of a specific style.

In art, as in many other fields, reaction inevitably entails an opposite reaction. Baroque and its exaggerated form, the Churrigueresque, were succeeded by Rococo, whose origin must almost be sought in etymology. 'Rococo' is an Italian word meaning 'rockery'. It defines a style of architecture of ornamentation and furnishing in fashion in France at the end of the reign of Louis XV and at the beginning that of Louis XVI, characterized by the use and abuse of spiral scrolls and shell-like forms. Austrian architecture of the end of the eighteenth century was also Rococo. As mannered as Baroque, but less exuberant, the Rococo style can be recognized by bristly façades, by curves and curved and broken pediments, by the profusion of ornaments, bosses and garlands of enlaced flowers.

Such had been the development of Peruvian architecture, in turn Graeco-Roman (a renewal of the antique), Italian, Spanish and French. In fact, it consisted not of a succession, but a superposition and sometimes a confusion of styles, which gave certain buildings a lopsided look, elaborate here, stripped to the bones there, alternating or mingling Moorish reminiscences and Italian motifs, in short, the 'colonial style'.

At Lima, however, in the time of la Perricholi, the Rococo influence clearly predominated for two reasons, one political, the other natural. At the time of the earthquake of 1746, the throne of the viceroyalty was occupied by José Manso de Velasco. He had gone about the reconstruction of Lima with such enthusiasm that he was called its 'second founder'. Velasco arrived from a Spain where architects were already building '*à la française*'. So it was quite natural that the viceroy, imitated by the clergy, the nobility and the wealthy middle class, should hasten to build in the same style. To advise him, he had by his side the Frenchman Louis Gaudin (one of the three academicians on the 1735 mission to Ecuador), who devoted his main efforts to the perfecting of 'antiseismic' processes, i.e. the more rational use of plastic materials in building.

Can it be said that, if the first Lima was Spanish, the second Lima was French? Of course, one must not exaggerate. The master builders, trained for so long in the Spanish manner, could not have broken with their techniques in a few years. They continued to adapt the old Baroque themes to the Lima manner. On the other hand, during the eighteenth century, an Austrian Jesuit architect, Jean Rher, had imported Viennese Rococo motifs, which, mixed with oriental fantasies, produced a confused style which, in spite of that, was given the name of *borbónico*.

At the moment when Louis XV ascended the throne, Philip V, grandson of Louis XIV and French prince, had long been reigning in Spain. He wanted everything to be French, including, of course, the buildings. He surrounded himself with French architects, and built the Royal Palace of Madrid on the model of Versailles. Aranjuez, the gardens of the Prado and the Granja were small-scale Saint-Clouds or Fontainebleaus. Thus French architecture, including the charms of the Regency and the purity of the Louis XV style, had passed into Spain and from there, with a certain time-lag, to Lima.

So with Philip V and until the middle of the eighteenth century French influence made itself felt at Lima, in the form of Rococo, less perhaps in architecture than in furnishing and cabinet-making, with an excess of Louis XV panelling. Need I add that smuggling greatly facilitated the 'Frenchifying' of architecture and furniture in Peru? In the salons of Lima people spoke cryptically of certain arrangements made by viceroys with the captains of French galleys loaded with furniture, paintings and *objets d'art* in the purest Versailles style.

So it was indeed the earthquake of 1746 and the accession of Philip V that marked the last stage in the architectural development of Lima and the flowering of the French style. The builders and engineers of this period, priding themselves on being

89

afrancesados, felt bound to imprint the French trade-mark on stone. It stayed there for a long time to come. In the second half of the eighteenth century, while Ferdinand VI reigned in Spain, the France of Louis XV had already seen the beginning of the Neo-classical style that bore the name of his successor Louis XVI, but continued in Peru long after Louis XVI, until the coming of Independence.

Thus the contemporaries of la Perricholi lived in a setting in which a Versailles rose-window suddenly blossomed, unexpectedly, like a rose rising from the sand, amid the surviving examples of Plateresque, Baroque and Classical.

Such were the main features of Peruvian architecture.

MATERIALS AND TECHNIQUE

An art critic, holding forth on colonial architecture in Spanish America, has wittily evoked 'earthquake baroque', in an attempt to express the idea that builders had been forced to make their techniques conform to the natural conditions of the country and never to lose sight of the eventuality of an earthquake, in short, to build provisionally—even though, against all expectations, a fairly large part of this provisional construction in Peru has miraculously continued to exist, in spite of two earthquakes in the sixteenth, eleven in the seventeenth and seven in the eighteenth centuries.

It is a fact that the almost total exclusion of hard materials and the use of easily modelled plastic materials encouraged the artificial over-elaborate character of Peruvian architecture.

The essential materials used for building in Peru—at least in the coastal towns—were the adobe brick and stucco. As for stone and marble, even if their use had not been contra-indicated for security reasons, it would have been impossible to procure them, since there was no quarry near Lima, without carting them from very far afield at great expense.

Adobe was a mixture of moist clay, kneaded together with straw and animal excrement, which was poured into wooden moulds to harden and then dried in the sun. What the Peruvians called 'stucco' was a coating imitating marble and generally made of slaked lime, marble dust and chalk. As soon as the mixture was the right consistency, it was given the desired shape and then it hardened as it dried. When dry, it was polished. Fragile, but flexible, these materials made up for their apparent lack of solidity by great malleability. They were much easier to work than stone or marble, so that architects had no difficulty in supplementing the dearth of materials by a frequently extravagant affectation of shapes. This explains the superadded ornamentation, a constant need for un-expected ornamental details, which gave Peruvian architecture a 'sham' style, the bizarre character of which was further accentuated by a superfluity of mouldings, bossages, small columns, cornices, pedestals and balusters.

Consequently, there was a striking contrast between the com-plication, indeed, the mannerism, of the architecture and the primitive nature of the materials used, which were more or less the same as in the Inca period. In the same way methods had changed little. That was why the beams that supported ceilings and terraces, as well as the timber-work, were held in place, not by nails and hooks, but by leather thongs. Moistened in advance, the leather contracted as it dried, stretching the fastenings to the maximum and forming a ligament that was both solid and elastic. The same held good for internal partitions, which were made of a framework of reeds attached to wooden uprights by leather thongs, the gaps being filled with dry earth. This kind of light isolating wall was called the *quincha*. It was in common use. There is no reason to be surprised by the fact that the materials and technique of building should have changed little since the Inca period. They satisfied a concern that was more practical than aesthetic, and quite natural in a geographically unstable country. This concern was to produce supple—one might almost say cartilaginous—buildings that might perhaps bend in case of seismic shocks, but would never break.

THE EXTERIORS OF THE HOUSES

Built of the same materials, the houses of Lima resembled each other closely, whether they were palaces or humble dwellings. They adjoined each other in rows, usually with one storey, more rarely with two, as if they formed a single wall of uneven height, broken up by portals, grilles and balconies. All of them, as we have seen, were topped with terraces (*azoteas*). As it never rained in Lima, there was no roof in the real sense of the word, only a simple piece of matting, spread out on the floor of the terrace and covered with a thick layer of ashes to absorb the humidity of the fog, the *garúa*. In many houses, the terraces served as wash-houses and the washing was hung out to dry in the sun on clothes lines. Alternatively, the owners installed hen-coops on them. Sometimes they were used as an open-air lumber-room. Miscellaneous, worn-out objects accumulated there, covered with dust.

The terraces were surrounded by a cornice, moulded onto the last course of adobe tiles, or by a balustrade of turned wood. Sometimes, too, rising above the flat line of the terrace one saw a sort of dormer-window called a *teatina*. It looked like an air-shaft, with the vertical rectangle of its opening facing the prevailing wind, and its enclosed sides resting on the roof. These dormer-windows gave light and air to rooms situated at the back of the houses and which consequently had no opening onto the street or the *patio*. *Teatinas* were numerous in the populous districts, built on narrow pieces of land where the houses were jammed against each other, without openings for air or sun.

The doorways were always rectangular—the archway was reserved for church doors—and of vast dimensions, in order to allow carriages and men on horseback to pass. Big iron and bronze nails and studs gleamed on the wooden leaves, flanked on either side by two broad pillars surmounted by a more or less richly decorated entablature. The family coat of arms (the *solar*) was placed in the centre of the lintel or sometimes slightly to one side on the upper part of one of the pillars. Stone doorways were rare; only a few palaces had them. They were generally made of good-quality bricks, so that they could be embellished with mouldings and reliefs. But the simplest ones were of adobe, moulded and worked by hand.

The windows, which were protected, as from the middle of the seventeenth century, by grilles of turned wood and later by iron bars interlaced with elegant iron fittings, were low and projecting. They were called *ventanas de reja*, windows with grilles. Resting on consoles, they were topped by a sort of small round or pointed calotte. These windows were greatly appreciated by indolent and curious ladies, for they enabled them to watch the passers-by while remaining invisible themselves.

Balconies were generally of wood carved with varying degrees of affectation; they were enclosed and projecting. They were most frequently placed on either side of the main entrance, but asymmetrically, one of them being nearly always larger than the other.

Sometimes, there was only a single, very wide balcony. All these balconies were like galleries suspended above the street in which coolness, darkness and intimacy reigned and which allowed the occupants to see without being seen, a place where, while staying at home, they still felt as if they were in town.[1]

I should add that the façades were painted in warm, light colours (blue, pink, yellow, ochre) obtained by distempering directly on to the rough surface of the house.

That is how the houses of this period still appear to travellers today. Some of them are veritable models of their kind, for example, the palace of Torre Tagle. Built in 1690, finished in 1735 and completed later by an embellishment of *azulejos* specially made in Seville, this palace belonged to the Marquis of Torre Tagle, a prosperous ship-owner, whose fruitful expeditions on behalf of His Majesty had earned him the title of Marquis, as attested by the carved wooden figureheads attached to the walls of the patio. This palace is in the pure colonial style, with Sevillan and Moorish influences. The ceilings of turned wood are in the Mudéjar style, as are the patio balconies and the lattice-work balconies giving onto the street, the latter of cedarwood and the wood of the cinnamon tree.

At Cuzco, the former capital of the Incas, situated to the south at a height of 11,143 feet, at the foot of the desert tablelands of the *puna*, the architecture differed somewhat from the architecture of Lima. Firstly, the basic material was no longer exclusively adobe, but stone. Unlike Lima, which the Spaniards had built from scratch on an empty site, Cuzco was built right on top of the traces of the Inca city, followed the same street lay-out and rested on the same foundations. So it would be accurate to say that the lower part of the buildings was Inca and the upper part Spanish.

So the majority of the houses at Cuzco had for their foundations ancient Inca walls, made of enormous blocks of dressed stone, interlocking with each other, and which, in spite of the absence of cement, had resisted the earthquakes. This had been decided by Pizarro at the time of the Conquest. To save time and manpower, he had limited himself to removing the top of the old edifices and

---

[1] *Arquitectura peruana* by Héctor VELARDE, p. 87. Everything I have written about Peruvian architecture is taken from the remarkable works of Héctor Velarde and, more particularly from his *Arquitectura peruana (Fondo de cultura económica)*, Mexico, 1946. *Tierra Firme* series.

adding new storeys to them, so that the town, which was Catholic and modern on top, remained heathen at its base.

The style of the houses at Cuzco was also rather different from that of the Lima houses. It was heavier and more massive. The edifice, an enormous square mass, was entered by a monumental studded door that gave onto a court of honour paved like a street. A vast staircase led from the courtyard to the first storey, around which ran a wooden or stone gallery. Off this gallery opened the reception rooms and bedrooms, the doors of which had only a judas-hole with an iron grille or a ventilation hole to take the place of a window. Outside, a balcony, supported by projecting beams, often completely enclosed, but chequered with holes shaped like hearts, squares and diamonds, enabling its occupants to see what went on in the street, completed the physiognomy of these dwellings, which had tiled roofs.

The Cuzcans decorated the sides of their entrance courtyards with granite vases in which bloomed *yerbabuena* (mint). Others preferred a garden planted with green myrtles. Great clumps of dahlias, asters, stocks and streaked carnations glowed cheerfully against this background of greenery.[2]

The most curious (and the most typical) houses of Cuzco were those that had been built more than two centuries ago by the *conquistadores* of Peru and more recently by rich Creole landowners. They would have looked rather austere had it not been for the cheerful note introduced by the balconies of carved wood painted in bright colours, especially blue and green. They were protected from the rain by overhanging eaves.

THE INTERIOR OF THE HOUSES

Nearly all the interiors of the houses were distributed along a longitudinal axis and arranged like Graeco-Roman dwellings. A curious survival of a Mediterranean tradition (like that of the chess-board plan) which had come to Lima from Athens and Rome by way of Spain. This tradition had found a more favourable terrain in Peru than in Spain, the drier climate making it possible to erect flimsy buildings that the Spanish winters would have destroyed.

[2] Paul MARCOY: *Voyage de l'océan Atlantique à l'océan Pacifique á travers l'Amérique du Sud.*

After going through the doorway of the house, one entered a vestibule which gave access to the various rooms on each side and which were separated from the patio by windows with iron lattices. The patio, which was always rectangular, opened onto a suite of rooms, salons or bedrooms. Then, at the far end and parallel to the entrance, there was generally a vast salon called *el principal* or *la cuadra* in the largest houses. This reception room was the equivalent of the Graeco-Roman *tablinum*. The *principal* gave directly onto the patio; it was topped with a covered gallery formed of small delicate wooden columns. A central path paved with stone or marble, with side paths leading off it, divided the patio into equal rectangles. Plants and flowers in tubs were common. Arches were rarer, except in the patios of noble houses.

When the houses consisted of two storeys, the arrangement of the patio galleries was repeated on both floors. The staircases were nearly always outside, built either onto a sidewall or in a corner. In the palaces, the staircases formed an integral part of the construction and were situated inside the main building.

THE HOUSES OF THE MOUNTAIN INDIANS

These formed a marked contrast with the palaces of Lima and Cuzco, and even their more modest dwellings. In fact, in the mountain country the Indians were housed in the manner of primitive tribes. They built their houses round, like a cone, or rather like igloos are made, with a door so low that it could only be entered by bending double, the idea being to keep warmer inside. As wood was very scarce there, they only burnt the dried dung of mules, *guanacos* and llamas.

Sometimes, the Indians owned several houses, one acting as kitchen, the second as bedroom, the third as granary. Sometimes, too, they had both a 'summer residence' and a 'winter residence'. In summer, during the rainy season, they took refuge on the heights, away from the marshes. In winter, they went down again to the plateau, which had become one vast pasturage. These adobe houses had the advantage of storing the sun's heat and preserving it during the night, so that even when temperatures were at their lowest it was never very cold inside the houses. The roofs were of thick straw, solidly attached and protected from the wind of the plateaux by a trellis of cords pulled very tight. Windows and doors were reduced to a minimum. A hole in the roof served to get rid of the smoke from the fire. There was only one fire, the kitchen fire, because of the scarceness of fuel on the Andean table-lands. A small garden completely enclosed by walls surrounded these groups of houses. Small orange and red flowers added a note of gaiety to this rather melancholy scenery of the Andean *sierra*. There was no furniture in the houses, but a sort of low platform covered with rugs, furs and *ponchos* served as a bed into which the Indians climbed fully dressed. Spare clothes were hung any old how from lines stretched from one wall to the other. Their hats and all the usual objects were hung on the walls. There were no chairs; everyone sat on the floor. There were no tables. The loom was the only piece of furniture in these more than rustic dwellings. Its form was rudimentary. Four posts stuck in the ground supported the weft wound on two wooden uprights. It took twelve days to weave a medium-sized *poncho*.

THE CHURCHES

It was customary to say, when speaking of Lima, that there was a chapel, a church or a convent at every corner of the street. This was, of course, a sarcastic remark that nevertheless had an element of truth in it. In reality, there were sixty-seven churches at Lima, taking into account, besides the cathedral and the five parish churches, the chapels of the numerous monasteries and communities.

In the religious buildings of Lima we again come across the general characteristics of colonial architecture: superposition of styles, ornamentation that was often overloaded—a striving for the grandiose, accumulation of Andalusian, Moorish and Churrigueresque motifs.

The most representative monument of religious architecture at Lima was its cathedral, almost entirely rebuilt after the earthquake of 1746. The people of Lima were particularly proud of it. The façade had a width of more than 150 yards. At its two extremities rose two towers of the Tuscan order, 39 feet wide by 162 feet high. Seven steps taking up the whole width of the façade led from the square to the parvis of the cathedral. The frontispiece comprised three distinct sections. The first consisted of four Corinthian columns decorated with sculptures and friezes. Four large niches

8. Portrait of the Viceroy Amat

9. a. Peruvian Indians (drawing of 1837)

b. La Perricholi in her carriage (drawing of 1837)

placed between these columns housed the statues of the four evangelists. The second section of this frontispiece also bore columns forming niches in which appeared the statues of St Peter and St Paul. Above the keystone of the main door and between the two sections of the frontispiece there was a statue of the Virgin. The third section formed a semicircular fronton, which bore the escutcheon of the royal arms of Spain. Lastly, the statue of St John the Baptist, the cathedral's patron saint, surmounted the whole. The church was entered either by the big portal—the door of the Pardon—or by one of the two side doors which opened onto the side-aisles.

Inside, the cathedral consisted of a nave and two aisles, each divided into three bays. The choir contained seventy-five mahogany stalls. A wrought-iron grille situated at the entrance to the choir opened onto the high altar, raised on five steps and topped by the tabernacle, the pedestal, columns and dome of which were solid silver.

Silver . . . It was, like gold and precious stones, the main feature of the interior decoration of the churches. One of the preoccupations of religious builders was to make as luxurious a show as possible. The hierarchy encouraged them in this, seeing in the accumulation of precious shining materials not only the tangible exaltation of the glory of God, but also the costly, but effective means of making it visible to the eyes of the 'simple souls' who could not fail to be moved by it. To reach the soul by moving the senses, to lead it from emotion to faith, this form of apostolate, practised on many occasions by the Catholic church, had proved itself a long time ago.

The luxury of the altars, tabernacles and ecclesiastical objects was at its height towards the middle of the seventeenth century. All one saw in the main churches of Lima were Churrigueresque reredoses, covered with gold leaf, varnished *azulejos* from Seville, silver candelabra with crystal bowls, mirrors of gypsum, veneers of exotic woods . . . This accumulation of riches was not always in very good taste. It gave the churches a theatrical flashy look that was ill suited to religious meditation. This striving for luxury was not peculiar to the churches of Lima. For example, the cathedral of Cuzco, whose high altar, as well as the reredos, was solid silver, contained a veritable treasure in the cupboards of its sacristy: reliquaries, monstrances, pyxes, chalices, patens, studded with

97

diamonds, rubies, topazes and emeralds. They were taken out of their caskets for the big holidays of the year, the most impressive of which was that of the *Señor de los Temblores*, Christ of the earthquakes, protector of Cuzco. A gaudy and mysterious cathedral, since the Indians asserted that there was a lake beneath its foundations, the water of which, calm and somnolent throughout the year, swelled, seethed and beat dully against the flagstones of the choir on the anniversary of the conquerors' entry into Cuzco on November 13, 1532. To the visitor passing through this display of luxury and the vast excess of ornamental details became boring in the end. He began to think that all the churches, monasteries and chapels in Peru looked more or less alike, with only a few variations. He was not entirely wrong and this conviction helped him to remember the essential features of their architecture. Outside, a façade—sometimes of stone, at Cuzco, generally of adobe bricks —whitewashed or distempered with brown, white or ochre, flanked or not by towers with bell-turrets. At the foot of the façade and along its whole length a flight of a few steps leading to the parvis. A central portal. Often two side portals surmounted by a niche housing the statue of a saint. Above the main portal a more or less elaborately decorated frontispiece; or a simple triangular pediment supported by small coupled columns and dominated by a sort of small box pierced with square windows or an extraordinary jumble of stucco sculptures—bas-reliefs, friezes, cornices, mouldings—covering the whole frontispiece. Sometimes, but rarely, the façade was bare.

Inside, one nave taking the shape of a Latin cross, the arms of which, prolonging the transept to left and right, ended in a rotunda chapel. A wooden or wrought-iron grille separated the transept from the choir. Sometimes, another circular grille, taking the same shape as the curves of the apse, enclosed the sanctuary and the choir, which were thus shut in on all sides, isolated from the rest of the building, like a second church enshrined in the first one.

FURNITURE

As in all countries, the quality and variety of the furnishing depended on the wealth of the owners.

This, according to Ricardo Palma, is how the house of a countess living at Lima in the time of la Perricholi was furnished:

'The most luxurious salon of the period was furnished with very long sofas, covered with Cordoban leather, and armchairs, also of leather, with large nails showing. A candalabrum with five lights was suspended from the middle of the ceiling, with dusty glass and candles dripping tallow. On the walls there was almost always a picture of St John the Baptist or Our Lady of the Seven Sorrows and the portrait of the head of the family, with his wig, his ruff and his short sword. The real luxury consisted in the china and the jewels . . . One climbed into bed up a short ladder. In fact, these beds were so high that in case of earthquakes one ran the risk of breaking one's neck when jumping to the floor. The fashion for separate beds, which was beginning to take hold in France, had not been introduced into Peru, where households continued to observe the Spanish and patriarchal custom, and there had to be a very serious reason for the husband to go and bury himself in a separate set of sheets.'

Some French travellers of this period paint a rather unflattering picture of Peruvian houses and their furniture. Frézier, for example, has this to say:

'The housing of the Spaniards in Peru bears no comparison with the magnificence of their clothes. Outside of Lima where the houses are handsome enough, nothing could be poorer than their houses; they consist of a ground-floor fourteen to fifteen feet high. The most magnificent lay-out is to have an entrance courtyard decorated with timber porches the length of the main part of the building . . . The first room is a large hall about nineteen feet wide and thirty to forty feet long, from which one enters two or three rooms in succession: the first is the show room with the dais, and the bed situated in a corner in the form of an alcove, which is spacious within, and the principal convenience of which is a false door to receive or dismiss company by without its being noticed on entering, even by surprise. There are few beds in the houses, for the servants sleep on the bare floor on sheepskins. Nevertheless, the height and extent of the rooms would give them an air of grandeur, if they knew how to make regular openings in them, but they make so few windows that the rooms always have a gloomy dark air; and, as they are not accustomed to use window-panes, they close them with open-work wooden panels which considerably lessen the daylight. The furniture does nothing to relieve the poor lay-out of the buildings, only the dais is covered with a carpet and squares of velvet for the women to sit on. The chairs for men are covered with leather stamped in half-relief. The only tapestry consists of a large number of villainous pictures made by the Indians of Cuzco. Lastly, as a general rule, there is neither wood nor tiles on the floor.'[3]

Paul Marcoy, speaking of Arequipa, is less harsh:

'The luxury of these houses is rather indifferent ... All dwellings have their walls whitewashed and decorated with Greek key patterns and calligraphic flourishes in red ochre or indigo blue. The few pieces of furniture that they contain are in the Spanish manner, carved out of the wood, as if with an axe, painted white or sky blue, dotted with roses and marguerites and a few gilded fillets. Here and there, lost in the shadow or relegated to some corner, the eye picks out a delicately carved cabinet, a black oak sideboard, worked like lace, an abbatial armchair trimmed with *cordobán*, whose vermilion and gold flowers are almost worn away. These pieces, which date from the Spanish conquest, seem to protest against the wretched taste of their neighbours. The walls of the salons are decorated with smoke-blackened pictures representing decapitations, crucifixions, and *autos-da-fé* of martyrs, works painted by the artists of Quito and Cuzco, such as Tio Nolasco, Bruno Farfan and Nor Egidio. Good paintings of the Spanish school hang beside them.'[4]

And he adds:

'The interior of the houses at Arequipa consists of two courtyards in line, paved with gravel and lined with broad walks (*veredas*); the walls of the first courtyard are whitewashed and sometimes ornamented with cameos of a primitive style and an even more primitive design. The family's reception rooms and bedrooms are arranged along the two sides of this entrance court. In the majority of bedrooms the bed is placed beneath an arch which is four to six feet thick. This arrangement, which may seem strange, is a measure of precaution dictated by fear of earthquakes. These apartments have no windows, but massive double doors with a spy-hole, which

---

[3] FRÉZIER, *op. cit.*, p. 460.
[4] Paul MARCOY, *op. cit.*, p. 106.

lets in light and air. Beyond the courtyards is a garden lined by the arches of an enormous tiled or flagged room used as a dining room.'⁵

Lastly, Paul Marcoy does not forget Cuzco:

'The houses have kept furniture of Spanish manufacture carved and sculptured out of the solid wood, painted in bright colours, heightened with golden brown fillets and a sprinkling of roses or tulips—few or no curtains, but plenty of carpets to alleviate the coldness of the ground, covered, in the absence of parquet flooring, with a layer of *argamasa*, a sort of cement . . . Grey paper or distemper decorated the walls of aristocratic salons. There are tables and pier-tables with octagonal mirrors in steel frames. Oil paintings, painted by the artists of Cuzco, adorn the salons of the old aristocracy . . . In spite of the steady fall in the temperature, the use of chimneys, stoves and heaters, or even *braseros* is unknown in these houses. The *señoras* envelop themselves in their shawls and the *caballeros* drape themselves in large cloaks.'⁶

Generally speaking, the furnishing of even the luxurious houses, apart from the palaces, was very rudimentary: a bed, a horsehair sofa, a few chairs, some stools, a pedestal table, a number of mirrors —in short, the minimum.

At first sight, it is rather surprising to note the discrepancy—or at least the difference in tone—between the evidence of Peruvian or Spanish chroniclers and that of foreign travellers, especially Frenchmen. The things which are a constant object of admiration to the former inspire the latter with frequent reservations.

These divergencies are explicable. It was natural for the Hispano-Peruvians to be inclined to praise their achievements. As for the French travellers, if some of their descriptions dealt with dwellings that were poor or exhibited a sham luxury, it was probably because those were the only ones they saw. In fact, it is doubtful whether these 'tourists', with the possible exception of scholars or politicians on missions, were received in the noble houses and the palaces of important administrators. And then it was good form for a Voltairian Frenchman of the end of the eighteenth century to display, vis-à-vis the declining Spanish viceroyalty, the somewhat disdainful sympathy of 'enlightened' peoples for countries still subject to the prejudices of old Spain.

⁵ *Ibidem.*   ⁶ *Ibidem.*

PART THREE

PRIVATE LIFE: THE STAGES OF LIFE

CHAPTER ONE

SOCIAL LIFE: FROM BIRTH TO DEATH

In spite of the good will of jurists and the sincere solicitude of the Crown, the social inequality passionately denounced by Las Casas nearly two centuries before the reign of Charles IV was still evident. Although in principle there was no racial discrimination, it was discrimination that really determined the condition of the man of the New World from birth. The colour of his existence depended on the colour of his parents' skin, which was one of the seven hues that made up the palette of the Amerindian gods. The *white* of the Spaniard descended from the *conquistadores*, the *brown* of the Creole, the *red* of the Indian, the *olive shade* of the half-breed, the *black* of the negro, the *grey* of the mulatto, and the *chocolate* of the *Zambo*. And these colours, far from being complementary, were violently opposed to each other. Whites and Indians continued to repudiate each other. The only point on which they were agreed was on pouring scorn on the negroes.

THE SOCIAL CLASSES: IMPORTANT OFFICIALS, NOBILITY, MIDDLE CLASS, SLAVES

Thus, although in principle all the inhabitants of Peru were not only equal before the law, but all, for the same reason, subjects of the King of Spain, the social classes were very clearly differentiated by three essential elements: race, wealth and position.

The viceroy was at the summit of the social pyramid. His prerogatives were considerable and on many occasions he took pleasure in reminding people of the fact in case they might be tempted to forget them. He had under his direct authority the presidents of the audience and their assessors, as well as the senior magistrates who existed in large numbers: the *fiscales*, the *regidores*, the *juges*, all 'pure-blooded' Spaniards.

All the other officials, from the lowest to the highest, were of course subordinate to him, but he only had direct dealings with the men in the most responsible positions in the administration.

The officials lorded it over the rest. But they did so more by virtue of the importance of their office—of the practical power it gave them—than the size of their salary, which remained comparatively low, at least as far as officials of the middle group, i.e. the majority, were concerned.

In fact, there was a great difference between the salaries of officials in the higher and lower grades. The 'fixed' endowment of the viceroy was 40,500 pesos, to which was added an allowance of 20,000 pesos, a total of 60,500 pesos per year, or more than 43,000 pounds sterling. This figure, impressive at first sight, was not excessive when you come to think of it in comparison with the 'civil lists' of European sovereigns and the emoluments of certain officials of the British Crown at the time.

Naturally there was no common yardstick by which the emoluments of the viceroy and those of the officials could be measured. However, an auditor received 4,860 pesos per annum, an *alguazil mayor* 3,645 pesos and a *contador* 2,025 pesos, which represented a monthly salary of 289, 217 and 120 pounds sterling respectively.[1] As for officers, their pay was relatively modest compared with that of the officials. A colonel earned 1,800 pesos per annum (108 pounds a month), a captain 1,440 pesos and a lieutenant 960 pesos. Moreover they were regulars and belonged to the company of the viceroy's household cavalry. A simple captain of halberdiers only received 600 pesos per annum (thirty-six pounds a month), which represented the average salary of minor officials.

Thus, although they were fairly badly paid, the officials belonged to the privileged social class, almost on an equal footing with the nobility. Many officials, incidentally, were also noblemen, either because they were descended in a direct line from the *conquistadores*, or because they had obtained nobiliary titles as a reward for good and faithful service. Such titles were numerous, 505 to be exact. We can imagine how useful such a range of titles was when those in authority wanted to stimulate the zeal and reward the services of their officials. All the titles were greatly coveted, from the title of duke to that of *vecino* (or notable) granted to families who played an important role in the *cabildos*. It was the

[1] *Memoirs of Viceroy Amat*, pp. 361 and 369.

dream of big businessmen and wealthy industrialists to obtain a nobiliary title, even a modest one, once they had retired from business. For money was not everything. The 'true' nobles made fun of these *nouveaux riches* who lacked the coveted parchment (*el ansiado pergamino*) to satisfy their vanity completely.

The clergy also belonged to the *distinguida* class, not only because of their spiritual power, but also because of their wealth. The clergy were rich. At the time of the expulsion of the Jesuits, Amat had ordered an inventory of their assets to be made. In the inventory taken in 1767 in the eight Jesuit colleges at Lima, the four at Cuzco and the colleges of Guamanga, Huancavelica, Arequipa, Yca, Pisco and Trujillo, figured more than 173,000 silver and gold pesos, equivalent to 125,000 pounds sterling, which incidentally represented a minute fraction of the Company's fortune, which mainly consisted of real estate.[2]

In short, the upper class comprised the viceroy and his entourage, senior officials, businessmen and the clergy. This boils down to saying that one was 'someone' in Peru in the time of la Perricholi so long as one held an important office or was rich and worth so many pesos.

Peruvian society also had a large and active middle class. Its place was between the rulers and the common people. From it were recruited the owners of small industries, and assistants in commerce, the government, law and teaching. These people, intermediaries between the upper classes and the people, were generally Creoles and half-breeds. They represented the most useful sector of the population.

The people, too, had their hierarchy. As for the Indians, the *'miserables Indios'*, as the viceroy Amat calls them in his memoirs, and the negroes (the two largest groups), they performed the hardest tasks. *'Sobre el indio desheredado vivia la gente del arrabal,* the people of the suburbs lived on the disinherited Indian.' Street porter in the towns, agricultural worker in the fields, miner in the mountains. And yet, all things considered, the lot of the Indian was less distressing than that of the negroes traditionally destined to be slaves since their fathers had been imported from Africa by the first conquerors.

For there were slaves in the viceroyalty of Peru, as we have said. The condition of slavery still seemed so natural that slaves figured

2 *Ibidem*, p. 135.

under the heading of livestock in the tax declarations of taxpayers. This, for example, is in the inventory of slaves belonging to the big colleges of Peru and their *haciendas*:

College of San Pablo	1,848
Provincial	476
College of Cercado	402
College of the Novitiate	597
Professed house at Lima	13
College of Bellavista	296
Grand College of Cuzco	385
College of Quamanga	222
College of Arequipa	137
College of Moquegua	56
College of Yca	219
College of Pisco	274
College of Trujillo	191
Mission	108
	5,224

In addition to these slaves there were 270 negroes from Chile 'lent' to the viceroyalty of Peru by the captainry of Santiago, a total of 5,494.

BIRTH: BAPTISM, LEGITIMATE CHILDREN, BASTARDS

The differentiation between social classes was such that it is impossible to speak of a uniform 'daily family life'. It varied according to whether a child was born in an Indian hovel in the *sierra* or in some palace on the Alameda. Social inequality began in the cradle.

That is why the sketch of daily social life that follows only concerns a comparatively modest fraction of the population of Peru. In point of fact, only the upper and middle social classes —aristocracy and bourgeoisie—are well known to us; the others did not interest travellers.

Paternal authority, based on the 'idea of caste', determined the family's upbringing. Religious principles and the law guaranteed it a legal and moral foundation. But, in fact, the concept of the family was somewhat altered by the large number of illegitimate children.

Salvador de Madariaga writes:

'. . . The illegitimate child was generally brought up in a home without a father; this inconstancy had incalculable effects on the half-breeds, rich and poor, and consequently on the whole society in which they were so numerous. We speak of the absent father, because being of a different colour and blood and a different class from the mother, the instructions and news he sent were inevitably received as coming from a different world . . . from a world on which the secret resentments of the despised children were bound to converge. As, in nearly every case, there were also legitimate children, who enjoyed all the advantages of family, social prestige, class and colour of which the half-breed was deprived, the concentration of psychological tension was particularly serious. Illegitimacy was even more frequent among the mulattos than among the half-breeds. The rich Creoles rapidly discovered the outstanding qualities of the negress as priestess of Venus . . . The beauty and lasciviousness of the negresses had a great influence on the white man.'[3]

Frézier, as a typically caustic Frenchman, saw things more philosophically:

'Even if the Spaniards are sober when it comes to wine, they show little restraint as regards continence; in the matter of love, they yield to no nation, they freely sacrifice the greatest part of their property to this passion and although mean enough in all other encounters, they are boundlessly generous to women . . . They rarely marry within the Church, but to make use of their own phrase, they generally marry behind the Church, *detrás de la Iglesia*, that is to say they are all engaged in open concubinage, which has nothing scandalous about it, in their eyes; far from it, it is a disgrace not to be *amancebado*, i.e. attached to a mistress, whom they keep on condition that she is for them alone . . . It is even quite common to see married men leaves their wives to attach themselves to mulatto women and even negresses, which often causes disorder in families . . . and the public is only scandalized by this to the extent that jealousy intervenes . . . The laws of the kingdom seem to authorize it, for bastards inherit more or less like

[3] Salvador de MADARIAGA: *Le Déclin de l'Empire espagnol d'Amérique*, p. 129.

legitimate children as soon as they are recognized by the father and there is absolutely no shame attached to this birth, as there is in our country . . .'[4]

Legitimate or not, the arrival in the world of a child gave rise to rejoicing, proportionate, naturally, to the wealth of the family.

In prosperous circles, the father and mother, as soon as the child was born, hastened to inform their parents and friends, by telling them that they had 'one more servant at their orders'. Baptism took place as soon as possible, and the godfather was, if not the hero of the day, at least its organizer and above all its financier. So, far from aspiring to the title of godfather, people feared it as a catastrophe. The godfather (*padrino*) had first of all to give a substantial present to his godchild, to the child's mother and to the godmother, his fellow-sponsor (*comadre*). Each member of the family was also entitled to a present of less value, but substantial all the same. That was not all. When he came out of the church, the godfather was assailed by a mob of shouting children, who immediately began to praise his generosity. If he had remembered to bring with him baskets full of sweetmeats and maravedis, that he distributed in handfuls, he was blessed. If not, he was called *padrino cochino* and his lovely church-going clothes were in great danger of being soiled by the spittle of the youthful band.

When night came, it was time for the family banquet, at the godfather's expense. And if he did not want to be considered a *padrino cochino,* he did not forget to attach to the coat or corsage of each guest, suspended from a rose or blue favour according to the sex of the baby, not a maravedi now, but a peso.

When the last guest had gone, there was nothing more for the godfather to do but balance his accounts and bitterly regret not having had the presence of mind or the opportunity to refuse such a costly honour.

FAMILY LIFE AND THE GIRLS TO BE MARRIED OFF

Ricardo Palma has depicted family life in a Creole background:

'At eight o'clock the family assembled in the drawing-room to say the rosary, which took a good hour at least, with the addition of litanies, a novena and a whole string of orisons and prayers for

[4] FREZIER, vol. II, p. 446.

the souls of dead members of the family. Of course, the dog and cat were present at prayers . . . The mistress of the house and the young women then supped off a cup of porridge with verjuice or cinnamon cream and went to bed, into which they climbed up a short ladder. In those days, it was the custom to rise when the cocks began to crow, the reason why there were not so many chlorotic or consumptive young women as there are today. Let us not talk about neurasthenics; fits of hysterics had not yet been invented, those fits that are the despair of present-day fathers and fiancés; in short, if a female patient was subject to the vapours, the matter was settled by taking her off treacle or marrying her to a Catalan wine merchant. For, as a remedy for women's indispositions, there was nothing, it seems, like a husband in a good situation.'[5]

In the Peru of la Perricholi, as in all countries and at all times, it was easier to bring up boys than girls. When very young, boys were put into colleges where vigilant and inflexible masters were responsible for their education. Pedagogical methods were extremely harsh. 'Only the bravest children could stand up to them.' But when they left college those children were considered to be men.

As for the girls, they mostly stayed at home. Nobody worried seriously about their upbringing.

'The education of young women (writes Ricardo Palma) could not have been more absurd. A little sewing, some notions of washing, plenty of cooking and not even a suspicion of social life. Some old man, an intimate friend of the family, and the reverend confessor were the only men they saw. A large number of them were not taught to read for fear they might learn sinful things in forbidden books; and, if some of them managed to spell out the *Christian Year* more or less fluently, they were not allowed to trace their cramped writing or incoherent scribbles on paper, for fear that they might exchange some correspondence with their admirers as time went by. Did a young man come to visit the master of the house? The young ladies flew from the drawing-room like doves at the sight of a sparrow-hawk. Which did not stop them, of course, from making a detailed examination of the visitor through the keyhole. They protested against paternal

[5] Ricardo PALMA: *Le Divorce de la Comtesse* (French translation by Mathilde Pomès).

tyranny, for after all had not God created them for men, and
vice-versa? So they all had a frantic desire to get married, aggravated
still more by the ban on speaking to men, except cousins, who,
in the eyes of our ancestors passed for beings of the neuter sex,
in spite of which—o scandal!—they gathered the first fruits from
time to time or permitted themselves some other little act of
"cousinry".'[6]

Parents were in a hurry to marry their daughters off, for, as
Ricardo Palma says:

'In spite of paternal vigilance, there was not a single girl without
her gallant in attendance. For there was not a damsel, however
timid she was, who did not know more about such things than
books told her and more than St Augustine, St Jerome and all the
venerable fathers of the church, whom I for my part suspect to have
been well versed in naughtiness in their youth. So there was no
young lady of Lima who did not find the favourable moment for
an amatory conversation through the Venetian blinds of the
window of the ground or first floor.'

It was the father and not the girl's heart that chose the husband.
Such matters were arranged autocratically. In the person of its
head each family had a tsar more despotic than the ruler of all
the Russias. And woe betide the little demagogue who dared to
protest! Depending on the seriousness of her rebellion, she had
her hair cut off, was shut up in a dark room or even sent to a
convent.

Thus paternal tutelage was harsh, but the girls knew perfectly
well that it would not last long. Their intuition and the confidences they received from their married friends whispered that
one did what one wanted with a husband when one knew how to
manage him. Marriage was a kind of liberation for these young
ladies.

What sort of matches did fathers seek for their daughters? To
tell the truth, the fortune and social position of their future son-
in-law worried them less than the colour of his skin. Once again
we come across the capital importance of the *limpieza de sangre*.

'As the families who were really entitled to be considered white
were rare in America, the simple fact of being white took the place

[6] Ricardo PALMA: *Le Divorce de la Comtesse*, pp. 146-153.

of gentle birth among them.' This made all the whites who had come from Spain bold enough 'to seek the hand of the greatest ladies in the country'. The Creoles, in their turn, 'while flinging abuse at the Europeans because they envied them their success, thought it very honourable in the Indies to give their daughters to these Europeans in marriage' . . . even if they were, as they said, 'in rags'. But on the occasion of the slightest disagreement the humble origin of the son-in-law from Spain was thrown in his teeth.[7]

The young ladies who have just been mentioned belonged to the 'upper class' of Lima. Consequently it was always easy to find them a husband. Sometimes even, the fathers, because of financial and social position, had only too many to choose from. On the other hand, some families that were of humble rank or whose daughters had misbehaved were forced to place them in charitable foundations set up specifically to marry off poor or 'compromised' young ladies.

There were many of these foundations. There was a 'House of Charity' for 'poor women' on the Inquisition Square. In it girls were married off or became nuns. In the College of Santa Cruz de las Niñas, they brought up a certain number of 'found girls' to whom the Church gave a dowry when they married. A priest had left a foundation of more than 600,000 piastres, under the direction of the dean of the cathedral and the prior of St Dominique, to marry off twenty young women and give them 500 piastres each. There was also a foundation, with the title of Our Lady of Cochar-cas, for the poor girls of Caciques, and a college for bringing up the boys. Lastly, 'repentant girls' also had available a retreat 'that I do not think is very full, considering the lack of zeal shown by the public authorities in suppressing libertinage', as Frézier ironically remarked.[8] These girls were called *amparadas de la Concepción*. The protégées of the Conception—no pun intended.

MARRIAGE

Weddings generally took place at night, during a reception given in the house of the betrothed girl. As soon as the first guests

[7] Jorge JUAN and ULLOA: *Noticias secretas*, pp. 419–425. Quoted by Salvador de Madariaga in *Le Déclin de l'Amérique espagnole d'Amérique*, p. 571.
[8] FREZIER, vol. II, p. 398.

arrived, the banquet began, about seven o'clock. At half past nine or ten o'clock the priest arrived to bless the marriage. He made his way with difficulty through the company, which was already feeling very merry after a few *copitas* of *chicha*. When silence had at last been restored, the priest proceeded to celebrate the marriage. The formality was soon over, in a quarter of an hour at the most. The priest withdrew and the party continued.

In rich families which were in the public eye, the marriage ceremonies took on a more solemn note. The religious ceremony took place in the morning in the parish church, attended by a large congregation of relations and friends. Before entering the church, the engaged couple stopped under the main portal where they were given the church's blessing. Then they advanced slowly to the choir where they seated themselves in chairs prepared for the ceremony. After the priest had joined them in matrimony, high mass was said. Then everyone went off to the house of the bride's parents where everything was ready for the wedding breakfast and the ball that followed it. The reverse of the medal was that the newly-weds were required to pay as many visits as there were guests at the ceremony, which sometimes took almost a year. These visits were not supposed to take place until a month after the celebration of the marriage, the young bride staying cloistered at home during the first month and seeing nobody. Indeed, it would have been the height of immodesty for the virgin who had become a woman to expose herself to the curious gaze of her friends and acquaintances.

There were good and bad households in Peru, as in all countries, in all ages. In rich circles, where temptations were frequent, money easily come by and idleness common, infidelity on the part of the husband was by no means rare. But we should not imagine that legitimate wives cheerfully accepted seeing themselves deceived by their husbands. They either paid them back in their own coin or brought an action against them. Ricardo Palma relates, in this connection, the differences between an outraged marchioness and her flighty husband.

'. . . Doña María Josefa Salazar, wife of her first cousin Don Gaspar Carillo, Marquis of Valdelirios and Colonel of the Huara Regiment, complained that her husband had intercourse with her maids and after she had described, in all their coarseness, the details of certain occasions when he had been caught in the ʲ she concluded by demanding annulment of the marriage, alleging that the libertine husband had turned his back on her during all the years that he had slept in the same bed as her. The Marquis of Valdelirios, for his part, denied sinful intercourse with the maids, and maintained that his wife, afflicted with a slight limp before the marriage, having thrown all pretence to the winds after the blessing, began to limp "frightfully". Moreover, he showed that he was jealous of a "personage in a red cape" who always appeared just at the right moment to give the Marchioness his hand when she was getting out of or into her carriage. In conclusion, the Marquis declared that, in spite of the Church's order, he could not live with a woman who smoked cigars from Cartagena of the Indies . . .'[9]

Marriage, in Peru as in Spain, was exclusively the affair of the Church, which kept the registers of births, marriages and deaths. A religious marriage was the only one possible. It was not until the nineteenth century that competence as regards births, marriages and deaths was transferred to the civil authorities. Consecrated and celebrated by the priest, marriage in the time of the viceroys was consequently considered as indissoluble. But it could be annulled by the ecclesiastical authorities in the same conditions and for the same reasons as in European countries, if one or other of the spouses could prove its nullity. The procedure for annulment was lengthy and tricky. It took a long time to materialize and often it did not materialize at all. Even if the examination of the case and the final judgment rested with the ecclesiastical tribunal, the procedure proper was carried out by the judiciary administration, as in any ordinary trial. In other words, the Church settled the question and the Law looked after the preliminaries.

When the marriage was duly annulled, there was nothing to prevent the spouses from contracting marriage again, once they were 'released'. Cases of remarriage seems to have been quite common if we are to believe Frézier who notes: 'Every day one sees people "unmarry" themselves as easily as if the marriage was purely a civil contract, on simple grounds of disagreement, poor health or consent; and what is even more astonishing, they then marry others . . .'

[9] Ricardo PALMA: *Le Divorce de la Comtesse.*

However, Frézier's indignation should not be taken too literally. Whatever he may say, it was not easy to get 'unmarried'. And hope of a new union was restrained by the complications and slowness of the procedure.

One of the cases of this kind at the time that caused the greatest stir was that of Marianita Belzunce, which is amusingly reported by Ricardo Palma:

'Marianita Belzunce was thirteen. She was an orphan and under the guardianship of her aunt and godmother, Margarita de Murga y Munatoñes. The latter had got the idea into her head of making her marry the Count of Casa Dávalos who was over sixty and "uglier than a bull of excommunication". Our angel was in despair, but there was nothing to be done. Her aunt insisted, the priest came, the little niece said yes to the old millionaire and *laus tibi, Christe!*

The old couplet had no meaning to our ancestors!

> "The old man who marries
> A young girl
> It is he who tends the vine,
> Another who gathers the grapes."

Once in the conjugal dwelling and alone with the Count, the young girl said to him:

"My husband, Your Grace may well be my lord and master, but I have taken an oath by God and my soul not to be yours until you have succeeded in touching my heart; for Your Grace doubtless wants a companion and not a slave. Therefore accept the test for a year; that is time enough for me to see if what my aunt said is true, namely that love may come to me."

The Count resorted to prayers and threats, and invoked his marital rights. It was in vain, there was no way to make Marianita give in. So that His Lordship—may God keep him among his saints!—underwent a whole year's ordeal, that is to say rivalling Job in patience, and jealous even of the flies in the air, having heard in his youth the popular couplet:

> "Don't marry an old man
> for his money
> Money, money disappears,
> but the old man remains."

On the eve of the time-limit fixed by the young lady, she fled from the conjugal dwelling and took refuge under the protection of her cousin, the Abbess of Santa Clara. The Count flew into a temper. The ecclesiastical powers and the civil authorities took part in the dispute; many a piastre was spent on stamped documents and Don Pedro Bravo de Castilla, the best lawyer in Lima, took over the defence of the deserter.

Her case was one of the great events of the period. A good half of the town was in favour of the rebel. Especially the young people, who could not look favourably on such a pretty creature in the power of a decrepit old man. Out of resentment, really. For wretched men like our old fogey are often dogs in the manger.

One fine day, the superior of the order appeared in the parlour of the convent and had with the mischievous young lady, whom he urged to return to the conjugal home, the following little conversation:

"Tell me frankly, father, have I a figure like a plate of porridge?"

"No, my child, you have the figure of an angel."

"All right, if I'm not a plate of porridge, I'm not a dish for an old man; and if I'm an angel, I cannot marry the devil."

The superior was nonplussed. The little countess's argument seemed indisputable.

Time went by, writs came and went, and no one could foresee a date for the declaration of validity or nullity. The name of the worthy count was the object of slander and the pretext for licentious couplets, according to the custom prevalent in Lima of composing verses on scandalous subjects. Here are some of them which figured in the case:

> "With a rusty sword
> that has neither point nor edge,
> there's nothing to do, dear count,
> but to keep quite calm.
> All your valour fails
> When you put it to the test:
> your sword, which is no longer new,
> neither penetrates nor cleaves in twain.
> I give you some good advice:
> turn hermit,
> for dainty dishes are bad
> for the stomachs of old men.

For Marianita to have obeyed
your rights and privileges
you should have been armed
with a good Toledo blade."

When these manuscript verses circulated from hand to hand, the man they held up to ridicule was so enraged by them that he began, either to take his mind off his troubles, or to show his detractor that he was still capable of burning incense on the altar of Venus, to lead a dissolute life and make conquests not through the attraction of his personal charms of course but by using his money. And this dissoluteness promptly led him to the tomb and put an end to the litigation.

Marianita Belzunce left the convent, a virgin and a widow. Young, beautiful, rich and independent; I presume—although my papers say nothing about it—that she must have found someone else to perform, to her great satisfaction, the functions of husband and to know the happiness that was refused the deceased.'

If the Church proved comparatively severe when it was a question of maintaining the indissoluble character of marriage in the upper classes (had not they to set an example?), it exhibited considerable indulgence with regard to the mountain Indians, because it had stated, categorically and with good reason, that their 'understanding' was not on a level with the white man's. Consequently a custom of trial marriage continued to exist in the villages of the *sierra*. When a girl and a boy liked each other, they were legally authorized to live in concubinage for a year. If, on the expiry of this period, experience had shown that they were made for each other, they proceeded to get married. If not, the 'fiancés' separated on good terms. When a child was born of this probationary union, its fate varied depending on its sex. If a girl, she was taken in by the mother's family. If a boy, he was brought up by the father's parents. But in nearly every case the provisional spouses preferred to regularize their situation, as if there could be no better preparation for marriage than the habit of living together.

As the evidence of the chroniclers about matrimonial morals is completely at variance, it is difficult to form a definitive opinion. However, it seems that the average household conducted itself well—apart from some indiscretions kept as secret as possible—

that notorious concubinage was the exception and that marriage remained a generally respected institution, and one to which Church and state paid particular attention to maintain their laws.

DEATH AND BURIAL

However, the people of Peru reserved their greatest pains for death and its ceremonies, rather than birth and marriage; at the same time they considered it as one of their favourite distractions, especially when it was a question of the death or interment of a man of quality, a noble, high official or big businessman.

The spectacle began before death, the signal for which was given by the ringing of a handbell in the street in the vicinity of the parish church. It was the priest, who was taking the viaticum to the dying person. He walked beneath a canopy, surrounded by choristers and churchwardens, some carrying candles, others lanterns on the end of long poles. It did not take long for quite a crowd, hastening up when they heard the sound of the bell, to form a procession around the priest and his servants. They arrived in front of the dying man's house. The priest entered the room, followed by his escort, who alternated between groans and funeral hymns. Extreme unction was administered. The procession left the house and returned to the church where it disbanded. Such was the curtain-raiser to the melodrama which was to be enacted.

As soon as the dying man had drawn his last breath, the room was completely emptied. Not a mirror, no furniture, no pictures. It was absolutely bare. Then they proceeded to lay out the corpse. Previously someone had fetched from a neighbouring monastery a monk's robe (*mortaja*), pepper-coloured or dark blue, according as it came from the discalced brotherhood or the Franciscans. The deceased was dressed in it and then laid on the floor on a white sheet, spread over a straw mat. At the four corners of the sheet were candles, whose wavering light scarcely revealed the rigid corpse in its monkish robe, girded with a cord with big knots, the hood turned down over the ghastly face. Throughout the rest of the house, mirrors, windows and galleries were hung with mourning crape. The lights were turned down low. People spoke in hushed voices.

Sometimes, when the dead man was a person of great importance—an auditor or a general—his body was placed on a catafalque erected in the main room of the house and surrounded by a great number of lighted candles. He remained thus for twenty-four hours or more and during this time the doors of the house stood open, so that all those who wanted could enter and leave as they wished. In general, all the women of the lower classes were accustomed to come and weep for the dead. They were semi-professional mourners. They arrived dressed in black, usually at the end of the day or during the night, entered the room where the body lay in state and approached it, at times kneeling, at others standing upright and in the majority of cases as if they were going to embrace it. Then they began their wailing with a plaintive air, intermingling it with terrible howls. They called the dead man by his name and after a few exclamations, without changing their tone or attenuating their cries, they began to enumerate all the qualities that the deceased possessed, not forgetting in this lamentable inventory all the lewd habits and weaknesses with which they knew him to be afflicted 'with complete accuracy and mentioning all the details and circumstances possible'. When the women who performed this task were tired they withdrew to a corner of the room where the family in mourning put spirits and wine at their disposal. But as soon as they moved away from the body other women arrived and took their place. When they stopped coming the servants and friends of the house continued the sinister cantata.

Then the moment came when the body had to be removed from the house. It was ten o'clock at night, for it was forbidden to transport the dead during the day. The bier was carried by four mutes, wearing long black robes. The family and their friends followed, with measured tread. The coffin was deposited in the parish church, where it spent the night, waiting for the religious service that would take place next day.

Then came the deceased's last 'great day', the one when he received the last homage of his peers, his subjects or his customers. The walls, columns and galleries were covered with black velvet, with silver fringes and dotted here and there with escutcheons bearing the dead man's initials or his coat of arms. In the middle of the nave was the catafalque, flanked by four large candles (*cirios*), vases full of glowing resins that gave off fragrant fumes and bluish flames. Around the catafalque were the parents, friends and guests, wearing black. The monks of the parish community were assembled in the choir and their blue, grey, chestnut and white robes introduced a bright note into the black and silver symphony of the funeral trappings.

Then the body was taken to the newly-built cemetery, or *Panteón,* of which the people of Lima were very proud. After passing through the suburbs of the town, the procession left Lima by the *portada* of Manillas. It soon reached the cemetery. Immediately behind the wrought-iron gate rose a chapel, behind which a long gravelled avenue opened up, covered in by an arbour of clematis, wistaria and Virginia creeper. It was lined with tombs of varying degrees of ostentation, some of which were veritable mausoleums. The procession stopped in front of the family tomb of the deceased. At Lima the dead were never buried in the ground, but placed in niches (*nichos*) elevated above the ground and separate from each other. These niches were arranged in three superimposed rows in walls built of brick and which, laid out in parallel lines, formed a number of corridors called 'departments'. The *nicho* was big enough for the coffin not to be in contact with the walls. The bier was placed inside it and then a flimsy partition was put up with a few bricks and a little plaster; later a pane of glass was set into the partition. In this way, the family, when it paid a visit to the cemetery, could cast a compassionate eye on the deceased's coffin, while a marble plaque the width of the niche was inscribed with his names and titles in letters of gold.

When funerals were over, those who had been the chief mourners remained at home for nine days, it being clearly understood that members of the family must not move from the room where they received everybody's condolences. It was even traditional for those who had ties of friendship or relationship with the family to keep them company during these nine days, from sunset to sunrise.

Is there anything else to say about death? I cannot close this gloomy chapter without mentioning the death of small children, which—contrary to what one might think—was a cause for rejoicing by the family and their friends. A dead child, in effect, was one more angel who had gone to rejoin his brothers in heaven —an *angelito.* Blessed are the pure in heart! The little corpse was exposed upright in the finest room in the house in a coffin lined with velvet or pale coloured silk. It was dressed in a white robe, surrounded by flowers and lights. The lips were made up, the eyes opened and the hair carefully tended. The hands were joined and the forehead had a crown of roses on it. The funeral service was nothing like the service for the old dignitary. There were no black hangings, but flowers everywhere. No *De profundis,* but dance tunes. No death knell, but cheerful chimes. Those who attended were given bunches of carnations and jasmine. Everyone congratulated each other. They complimented the mother, who tried hard to smile.

However, among the advanced classes at least, the parents showed some restraint in such circumstances. The *angelito* was certainly very lucky, but it was sad that he had been taken away from you all the same! This was not so with the mountain Indians, who were more hardened to ordeals or simply fatalistic to the point of indifference. For these Indians, the funeral of a child was an occasion for dancing and entertainments. As soon as the child exhibited alarming symptoms, they began to lay in supplies of *chicha* and warn the neighbours that they would soon be sharing with them the guinea-pig reserved for grand occasions. Once dead, the *angelito* was hung by the neck from the top of a ladder, cardboard wings were attached to his shoulders and his face was daubed with red, blue and yellow. And the feast began. The Indians danced, ate and drank. Then each one in turn went to pour a draft of *pisco* or *chicha* into the mouth of the dead infant.

HYGIENE AND DISEASES

It was under the government of Viceroy Amat that the municipal authorities began to take an interest in urban hygiene, for the first time since the Conquest. Thus to the duties of the 'alcaldes who were commissioners of quarters' were added those of supervising the cleanliness of the streets and the incineration of refuse. The *encapotados* were responsible for verifying that the orders of the *alcaldes* were carried out.

A solution—at least a partial solution—had been found to the problem of water and more particularly the irrigation of the towns. At Lima, for example, the waters of the Rimac had been canalized, and once that had been done the townspeople were able to wash themselves. But of course the installations still left much to be desired.

'At this period it was not the fashion to have marble baths and the mains did not distribute water to all the houses. People had to be satisfied with washing in wooden tubs. The streets of Lima were not fitted with conduits, but traversed by irrigation channels. To stop the staves drying out and coming loose from their framework, the inhabitants of the town used to soak the tubs in the channels for a couple of hours.'[10]

Which was equivalent to saying that the people of Lima washed in dirty water.

Although this progress in the field of hygiene—modest though it was—had not succeeded in removing the threat of epidemics, it at least had contributed to lessening the violence of their manifestations. Terrifying epidemics like the one which had caused 60,000 victims among the natives during the viceroyalty of Caracciolo, from 1716 to 1720, were no longer seen. From the end of the century onwards, the ravages of epidemics were less extensive, due not so much to the improvements in hygiene as to the introduction into Spanish America of vaccination against smallpox which was the most deadly disease, apart from yellow fever.

It was in 1796 that the English doctor, Jenner, made public the discovery that he had made twenty years before. If a man was inoculated with the serous liquid from a pustule that developed on the udder of a cow suffering from cow-pox, he was assured of immunity from smallpox. The Spanish government was not slow to profit by Jenner's discovery. As from 1797, less than a year later, the practical inoculation that led to the discovery of vaccination had been systematically adopted in Mexico and Michoacan, considerably lessening the fatal effects of the epidemic during that critical year. Whereas 9,000 victims had perished in the capital alone in 1779, at Valladolid, principal town of Michoacan, in 1797, only 170 out of 6,800 people who caught the disease succumbed. The civilian and ecclesiastical authorities conducted the struggle with a courage to which Humboldt paid a well-deserved tribute. At Caracas, too, where the mortality caused by smallpox in 1766 had been terrible, Humboldt found the practice of inoculation widespread, sometimes even without the help of a doctor. In 1804 vaccination had been introduced into Mexico by the United States on the initiative of 'a *respectable* citizen' (in

[10] Ricardo PALMA: *Tradiciones peruanas*, p. 723.

French in the text), Don Thomas Murphy and made available everywhere thanks to the arrival of one of the ships of the Royal Spanish Navy specially fitted out to distribute the vaccine to the Spanish dominions in Asia and America.

The viceroyalty of Peru soon benefited by this valuable assistance. Vaccination Committees were set up in the principal towns. The senior medical officer of the expedition obtained the vaccine from cows in the surrounding district, according to the technique current at the period. Humboldt describes the moving ceremonies that took place when the ships arrived in certain ports.

'The bishops, military governors and persons of the highest rank assembled on the shore; they took in their arms the children responsible for bringing the vaccine to the natives of America and to the Malays of the Philippines; followed by the acclamations of the crowd, they deposited the precious containers of this providential remedy at the foot of the altars and thanked the Most High for making them witnesses of such a happy event.'

If the viceroyalty was well defended against smallpox, thanks to vaccination, it was powerless against yellow fever—or 'the Siamese sickness'—which worked havoc, especially on the Pacific coast. There was one curious phenomenon; the negroes were refractory to yellow fever, which, incidentally, claimed more victims among the Indians than among the whites.

As for syphilis, it raged with nothing to check it. Recalling the consequences to the health that certain sensual allurements can entail, Frézier notes:

'Misfortune is not the only punishment of those who succumb to them, they often lose the inestimable treasure of their health, which they rarely recover, not only because little notice is taken of venereal diseases in these temperate climes, but also because of the scarcity of doctors who are only to be found in three or four big towns, and so cannot give the victims the opportunity of being cured.'[11]

An attempt was made to treat venereal diseases, but cures were not obtained for the simple reason that the specific agents of these diseases were still unknown. The gonococcus was not discovered until 1870 and the treponeme until 1905. Consequently, syphilis

[11] FRÉZIER, *op. cit.*, vol. II, p. 276.

remained for both patients and doctors a disease as mysterious and tenacious as in the time when, it is said, Christopher Columbus's sailors contracted it and brought it back to Europe—hence the name 'the American sickness' which was current both in Spain and Peru. In fact, and in the majority of cases, the treatment of venereal diseases consisted in letting them run their course. Some women palliated the maladies with *zarzaparilla*, infusions of mallows and other native herbs, but particularly by cauteries (or blisters), which were regarded as specifics. Both men and women resorted to them and women made so little secret of them that they asked each other at society gatherings for news of their *fuentes*, which they used to bandage for each other.

Another fairly common disease with women was cancer of the uterus, the origin of which Ulloa defined as follows:

'This dangerous disease is attributed to two causes, among others: to the abundance of perfumes with which women are always supplied, which may, indeed, contribute greatly to it, and to the continual motion they are subjected to in their barouches ...'

As can be imagined, the decoctions of herbs prescribed by the doctors were not the sort of remedies that could put an end to such cancers nor hold up their inexorable development.

Of course, belief in miracles and the intervention of the Virgin or the saints was, if I may say so, one of the elements of the therapy. In the markets one could buy *ex votos* representing miniature silver models of hearts, lungs and brains, corresponding to the diseased parts that celestial intervention was supposed to have cured. These *ex votos* were hung up in the churches, at the foot of statues or pictures representing the presumed agent of the miraculous inter- cession. Not until they had exhausted all the resources of quackery and superstition did the afflicted decide to go to hospital.

The general administration of the hospitals devolved upon officials of the Treasury. Each hospital was managed by a 'major- domo' or 'administrator of property' who gave an account of his stewardship to a governing body itself controlled by the Treasury of the viceroyalty.

That was the principle. But in practice the hospital services were the object of continual quarrels between the archbishopric of Lima, which pleaded its ancient privileges, and the viceregal government, which would have it that Public Assistance came under the *Real Patronato*.

The hospitals of Lima were comparatively numerous for the period. The first, called St Andrew, was a royal foundation and reserved for Spaniards, that is to say for whites. The hospital staff consisted of four priests. The hospital of San Diego, intended for convalescent patients from St Andrew, was run by the brothers of San Juan de Dios. The hospital of San Pedro had been founded solely for priests by Archbishop Toribio. The hospital of the Holy Ghost was intended for sailors and maintained by contributions and alms levied on ship-owners. Viceroy Amat had taken part personally in the construction of this hospital, acting as carpenter. The hospital of St Bartholomew had been founded for the negroes by Father Bartolomeo de Vadillo. Lepers and syphilitics were treated at the Hospital of St Lazarus. It was a 'Royal Foundation' intended for those who were afflicted with epilepsy and lunatics. The hospital of St Cosmo and St Damian, founded by the inhabitants of Lima, admitted exclusively Spanish women. The hospital of St Ann, established by the first archbishop Jerome for the Indians, was subsidized by the Treasury of the viceroyalty. I should also mention the hospital for incurables, run by the Bethlehemites, those for convalescent Indians and numerous houses of rest available to all, whether rich or poor, black or white.

So there were plenty of hospitals in Peru, mainly in Lima, but the hospital problem was not solved for all that. The number of beds was minute in comparison with the number of patients, doctors were scarce and hospital staff ignorant or brutal. Moreover, not just anyone was admitted to hospital. In this field, as in many others, there were the privileged and the rest.

MATERIAL LIFE: FOOD AND CLOTHING

Eating, drinking, dressing themselves, perfuming themselves and amusing themselves . . . Those were the main things that preoccupied many of the people of Lima. It was also in this sphere that the most distinct social differences appeared. People were judged and 'appraised' by the luxury of their clothes and the standard of their table.

FOOD

The national dish of Peru was *puchero*, a complicated one that made a meal on its own, owing to the variety of the ingredients. The recipe was to put into a pot a large piece of beef, then pork, smoked mutton, cabbages, American sweet potatoes (*camotas*), sausage meat, pigs' feet, *yucas*, sweet corn, bananas, quinces, black puddings and chick-peas, the whole highly salted. Water was poured into the pot and the mixture was cooked over a slow fire for four or five hours, until this animal and vegetable mixture had become a sort of jamlike and fragrant mass that only needed serving to the guests. The *yuca* was a long, white, flowery root, like a sort of turnip. *Camotas* were tubers larger than potatoes and sweet. They were abundant in the vicinity of Lima.

Next to the *puchero*, the favourite dish was *chupa*, which was easier to digest. It consisted of potatoes cooked in water or milk, to which were added big prawns (*camarones*), fried fish, eggs, cheese, lard and salt.

The *cazuela* was a very clear soup in which floated chicken giblets cut into tiny pieces, as well as bits of beef. The *estofado* was meat stewed without seasoning and rather insipid, whereas *sancochado* was a piece of mutton cooked very rare and garnished with *yucas*, *camotas*, cabbages and rice. As for *chicharón*, it was pork simply fried in its own fat. Lastly, *anticuchos* were made of small pieces of beef heart marinaded in vinegar, stuck on slivers of bamboo or iron skewers and cooked over a charcoal fire. *Anticuchos* were generally eaten with corn on the cob and sweet potatoes. There were also *anticuchos* of veal, fish, shrimps and mussels or a pleasant mixture of them all.

All the above-mentioned recipes were the most common main dishes on Peruvian tables. But they were also fond of less nourishing but spicier dishes that were called *picantes,* containing hot peppers. Generally speaking, these were pre-cooked dishes that were bought in the *picanterías* run by the Indians. Among these highly seasoned dishes were *ajiaco,* a mixture of meat, fish and red pepper, and *cebiche,* cold raw fish cut up into small pieces and marinaded for several hours in the juice of a green lemon. This dish was eaten with slices of raw onion, hot peppers and boiled corn.

Also very spicy were *tamales,* ground corn seasoned with hot pepper and mixed with bits of pork or chicken, hard-boiled eggs, grapes and almonds, the whole cooked by braising, wrapped in the green leaves of banana trees or ears of corn.

The sweets, of which the women were fond, were numerous. There were sweets for all tastes and all purses, from the popular *zango de nanjú,* a kind of sweet porridge made of cornflour and raisins, to the *turón* of *Doña Pepa,* a pastry made of flour, eggs and butter, fried in fat and served with *chancaca* syrup. But the favourite dessert was the *empanada,* a kind of marzipan pastry made of cornflour sprinkled with *anis.* Unless the consumer preferred *pan de dulce, pastelitos* made of ground *yuca,* fried and sprinkled with sugar after cooking, *manas,* yokes of egg with sugar, *mazamorras,* cakes made of honey and cornflour, or the creams of lemon juice and milk that were called *champuz de agrio y de leche.*

As pastry-cooks and confectioners had not yet found their way to Peru, it was the religious communities which held the monopoly of sweetmeats, cakes and set pieecs. They took orders for balls, banquets and weddings and spared no pains to satisfy the public and increase the number of their customers, not so much for love of money as for the pleasure of getting the better of another community, for there was permanent rivalry between these convents as attested by the pin-sticking indulged in by the nuns and the verbal duels, or even blows, which were even more common among their servants when they met in the street.

Each of these communities had its own special dainty which recommended it to the public esteem. Santa Rosa had its *mazamorra* with carmine, a kind of gruel that was exposed during the night on the roofs of the convent, where the frost gave it its special qualities. Santa Catarina excelled in the preparation of small cakes, preserves of chicken with almond milk and the *manjar blanco*, blancmange. Lastly the Carmelites had their honey fritters sprinkled with rose petals and gold dust.

But the most economical and basically the best desserts were the fruits, particularly *chirimoyas, paltos* and *plátanos.* It has been said of the *chirimoya* that it is a 'purse of green velvet full of frozen cream'. In fact, good to look at and good to eat, the *chirimoya,* the size of a coconut, is pale green with black markings. Inside, a milk-coloured cream contains big pips shaped like broad beans. The flower of the tree, reminiscent of that of honeysuckle, is very fragrant. It was put in wardrobes, where it perfumed linen and clothes. *Paltos* or avocados contained a savoury vegetable butter which was eaten with sugar or salt, depending on one's taste. As for *plátanos,* they were bananas which were eaten very ripe, almost overripe, like jam. There were many other fruits, some of them like those of Europe—apples, Barbary figs, grapes, quinces—others peculiar to Peru, such as *granadillas,* a kind of gooseberry, guavas, pineapples or *piñas,* watermelons and several varieties of lemons.

The national drink was *chicha.* It was made from corn, used at the moment when it was beginning to germinate, the *jora.* After being ground, the *jora* was cooked in large bowls for a certain time. The result was a decoction that fermented and then became *chicha.* It was sold in *chicherías,* where it was kept in glazed earthenware receptacles or glass vessels. The mountain and coastal Indians were very fond of *chicha,* but even more of *aguardiente,* the white spirit distilled in the valley of Pisco, from which its name *pisco* came. It was stored in stoneware pots called *botijas.* As for the negroes, they preferred *guaropo* to *chicha* and *pisco. Guaropo* was made from the remains of the canes used for making sugar.

Wine was also drunk, especially with desserts. The *dorado cabello* and the wine of *Elvira Rosa* were drunk at the end of a meal or accompanied snacks. The ladies preferred syrups which comprised many varieties: *frescos* of *piña*, *cereza* and *limón*, *emolientes* (infusions of barley and marsh-mallows, prepared with gum arabic and linseed) and, most of all, *'ante con ante'*, the cry to which was sold in the streets of Lima an iced drink in small glasses, composed of wine, syrup, almonds, cinnamon and an assortment of slices of lemon and small pieces of mixed fruits, something like Spanish *sangría*.

The commonest drink was an infusion of maté. Maté was also called Jesuits' tea and Paraguay tea. It was indeed the Jesuits who were the first to cultivate maté in Paraguay and recommended its use to the natives. The dried and pulverized leaves of maté produce a powder with which an infusion is prepared. Like tea and coffee, it contains caffein. Frézier, as a true French wine drinker, was very surprised by the Peruvians' liking for a drink that seemed insipid to him.

'They use a great deal of the herb of Paraguay, which some call the herb of St Bartholomew (whom they claim visited these provinces . . .) Instead of drinking the tincture separately, as we drink that of tea, they put the herb in a cup made of a gourd with silver bands, which they call *maté* . . . They use a silver tube, at the end of which is a bulb pierced with several little holes; this tube is called a *bombilla*.'

Obviously the townspeople did not eat like the country folk, nor the rich like the poor. To realize this, it would have been enough to glance into the home of a mountain Indian. The walls of the kitchen were impregnated with soot. The Indians cooked small girdle-cakes of *quinua* flour in an oven crudely built of *ladrillos*; they also roasted grains of corn. That was the basis of the Indians' nourishment, together with gourds (*zapallos*) and haricot beans. Fresh meat, which was rare, was only eaten on holidays; the rest of the time it was cut into strips, dried in the sun and hung from the ceiling of the granary. Out of frozen and dried potatoes they made a sort of flour which was kept in reserve for hard times.

They ate better in the *haciendas* on the coast where the *peones* licked their lips over fish soup containing a poached egg or boiled beef with *papas fritas* (fried potatoes) and rice. Or else they had *choncholies*, ox tripe seasoned with a sauce of onions, garlic and peppers. On holidays, they caught a guinea-pig, cut it in half, kept it in shape with skewers, spread it out over an open fire and roasted it. It was a dish for feast days.

In the majority of wealthy families in Lima, the mistress of the house was in a position to cook and prepare the most complicated dishes. She had skilful cooks and all the necessary material at her disposal: kitchen utensils, ovens and ranges. In poor, or simply modest, families, on the contrary, utensils were scarce and rudimentary; the cooking was done over a simple fire and there was hardly any variety in the menus. Rather than cook themselves, many of the poor people of Lima found it cheaper to buy ready cooked food from the itinerant merchants who went through the streets of the town. There were many of these street sellers and it was their peculiarity to announce themselves by different cries. Their timetable was almost invariable, so that even if one could not set one's clock by the hour when they passed, one could at least work out what time of day it was.

The milk woman was the first to pass, about seven o'clock in the morning, soon followed by the woman selling different infusions. One hour later, the sour milk man shouted: 'Curds and whey!' At nine o'clock, 'the canon's hour', as it was called, the man who sold cinnamon sweets came by, followed closely by the *tamale* seller. On the dot of eleven came the woman who sold melons and the mulatto woman hawking her *cocadras,* coconut jam, her *chancaquitas,* little balls of sugar candy mixed with coconut and toasted corn, and her purée of haricot beans. At noon, the fruit seller and the cake man, at the same time as the woman with *ante con ante* and the man with honey cakes. Around two o'clock in the afternoon, the *picaronera,* selling *picarones* (Peruvian fritters made of *yuca,* flower and eggs fried in fat and served with a syrup of molasses), and the man with *humitas,* a cornflour pastry, prepared with sugar and cinnamon, appeared in their turn. At three o'clock came the *melcochero,* selling a pastry of flour and warm honey, the *terronera,* a woman with lumps of sugar, and the *anticuchero,* who sold *anticuchos.* At four o'clock it was the turn of the *picantera* with her spices and of the *pinita de ñuez* with small nuts. At seven in the evening one heard the sweet seller, the woman with *mazamorra* and the one with *champuz,* a sort of corn gruel mixed with pieces of apple, pineapple and other fruits. Lastly, around eight o'clock, came the icecream man and the wafer man. No sooner had these itinerant vendors uttered their cries at the corner of the street than all the inhabitants of the neighbourhood were on their doorsteps, with various kitchen utensils in their hands to hold the merchandise.

It must be admitted that most of these dishes were rather nauseating. In any case, they were only tit-bits or crude hors d'œuvre, good enough for the people. In the wealthy classes, the people did not pick at their food, they ate solidly, three times a day, as Frézier observed: 'They have two meals, one at ten o'clock in the morning, the other at four in the evening, which takes the place of dinner at Lima, and a snack at midnight; otherwise, they eat as in France . . . They drink a lot of the herb of Paraguay.'[1] Obviously, this 'herb of Paraguay' held no attractions for the engineer from Saint-Malo.

Table manners depended on the degree of education of the guests and especially on their racial origin. For example, Frézier was very shocked by the way some Creoles ate:

'They (the Creoles) are temperate in their use of wine, but they eat greedily and dirtily, sometimes out of the same plate, usually in portions, like monks. At a special meal, they serve each of the guests with several dishes of different stews in succession and each of the guests then hands them to his servants and the people who are not seated at table, in order, as they say, that everyone may have their share of the good cheer . . . As they do not use forks, they are obliged to wash at the end of their meals, which they all do in the same basin . . .'

The whites, on the contrary, had more customs—in particular, the use of forks—although some of them did not encourage good table manners. For example, there was the custom of the *bocadito* (mouthful of food). If a husband was invited to dinner without his wife he filled a plate with one of the dishes he liked best and had it sent to his wife by a servant, with a message to eat the *bocadito* which had 'stuck in his throat'. This custom, which was comparatively common, forced the mistress of the house to provide double rations or only to invite bachelors. Another variation of the *bocadito* was widely practised. A choice morsel was chosen from the communal dish. A male guest stuck it on a fork and passed it to a neighbouring lady who, when she had eaten the

[1] FRÉZIER, *op. cit.*, vol. II, p. 441.

bocadito, returned the fork to the kind donor, accompanying it with a smile. In her turn, the lady, following the same procedure, passed the gallant guest a *bocadito* of her choice on the end of her fork. Anxious to emulate them, every guest did the same and there was a sort of general post of forks which was picturesque, but spoilt the formality of the meal. Besides, how could one recognize one's own fork among all those which were passed round in turn?

There was a custom as traditional as the *bocadito* from which one could not escape without seriously offending the person concerned. When a guest wanted to honour another guest, he caught his eye, winked, raised his glass and drained it in one gulp, gazing at his partner all the time, who was required to return the compliment. If this gesture was repeated frequently in the course of the same dinner and the drink was alcoholic, one can imagine what state of drunkenness the guests must have been in at the end of the evening. Other rather unrefined habits were current even in the best families in the country. For example, the habit of taking snuff or smoking between each course. The guest took out his snuffbox or extracted a pinch of snuff from it, blew on it to eliminate the dust, then inhaled deeply, even if he sneezed a few particles of it onto his neighbour's shoulder. Or else he lit a cigar, without worrying about making the air stink. This habit was so widespread that a spittoon was placed at the feet of each guest and was frequently used by the smokers. Lastly, it was good form at the end of a meal to express one's contentment and satiety by a salvo of belches politely muffled by one's cupped hand.

There was one last custom which was very civil. On the day after a special dinner, the mistress of the house always made a point of distributing to her friends the cakes and sweetmeats that had been spared by her guests' appetites the night before. She accompanied these 'left-overs' by a piece of the *empanada* which inevitably figured on the menu of a gala dinner. Sometimes, when it was a question of a birthday or wedding dinner, for example, the guests returned to the house the next day uninvited (the day after a banquet was called the *corcoba*) to finish off the *empanada*.

WOMEN'S CLOTHES

The Frenchman Frézier, travelling to Lima at the beginning of the eighteenth century, did not conceal his astonishment at the elegance of its inhabitants:

'It is the most celebrated, the largest and the most magnificent town in the whole of Peru . . . Men and women are both addicted to sartorial magnificence; the women, not content with choosing the finest materials, decorate them in their manner with a pro- digious amount of lace and are mad about pearls and precious stones for their bracelets, earrings and other jewellery, whose making, which absorbs them, ruins husbands and gallants. We have seen ladies who had on their persons more than 60,000 piastres' worth of jewels, that is to say more than 240,000 *livres*.'[2]

This was quivalent to some tens of thousands of pounds.

Juan and Ulloa went one better about the extraordinary luxury of the jewellery:

'They wear on the chest a very large round piece of jewelry as loaded with diamonds as their bracelets and other ornaments, so that when one of these ladies is wearing her very best, when lace decked with pearls and diamonds replaces lawn, it is easy to believe what is universally said in these parts, that she sometimes wears on her person clothes to the value of 30 to 40,000 *pesos*.'

And they add further on:

'The habit, among the women, of dressing themselves in lace, by reducing the quantity of cloth, however fine it was, to the minimum necessary to support the lacework, was general in all classes and castes "with the single exception of negro women of the lowest extraction". Moreover, the women of Lima showed them- selves finicky about the quality of the lace, accepting nothing but Flanders lace, the dearest and the best made in the world.'

This was also the opinion of Frézier, who notes at roughly the same period: 'The women are the principal cause of men's ruin (at Lima). Vanity and sensuality make them insatiable when it comes to ornaments and good living.' And he describes their costumes in great detail:

'Although the make-up of their clothes is simple enough in itself and not very susceptible to changes of fashion, they like to be

---

[2] FRÉZIER, *op. cit.*, vol. II, p. 381.

magnificent, regardless of cost, in the most hidden places. It is not only the shift and the linen petticoat worn underneath, called *fustán*, which are dripping with lace; prodigality goes so far as to put it on slippers and bedclothes. The skirt, called *faldellín*, that they normally wear, is edged with a triple row of lace, of which the centre one is gold and silver, exceptionally broad, sewn on silk braids which terminate their hems. Their doublet, which they call *chupón*, is of rich cloth of gold, or, in hot weather, of fine linen, covered with a great mass of lace arranged in confusion; its sleeves are large and have a pouch which falls to the knee, like those of tiny tots, and are sometimes open like long tails, very much in the style of those that were worn in the time of Henry IV. But in Chile they are beginning to suppress the pouch and cut them in simpler shapes. They have a little apron or *delantal*. It consists of two or three bands of cloth of gold or silver, joined by bands of lace. In the cold countries they are always wrapped up in a *rebos*, which is nothing more than a piece of woollen cloth, not made up, a third longer than it is wide, one of the corners of which falls in a point on their heels. The most magnificent are of rich materials, covered with four or five rows of broad and unusually fine lace.

Their dress clothes are the same as those of European Spanish women, i.e. they wear the cloak of black taffeta that covers them from head to foot. They also make use of the *mantilla* instead of the *rebos* when they want to dress more modestly.

It is a sort of mantle rounded at the back, dark coloured and edged with black taffeta. Their full-dress clothes consist of a mantle of black taffeta and a *saya*, which is a close skirt, musk-coloured with little flowers, beneath which is another close skirt which is made of cloth of the colour called *pollera* (hen house). In this outfit they go to church with solemn step, their faces veiled, in such a way that generally all that can be seen of them is one eye.

To go by appearances, one would take them for vestal virgins, but one would be making a big mistake. They wear absolutely no ornaments on their head, their hair falling down behind in plaits; sometimes they make themselves a head band with gold and silver ribbons, called *valaca* in Peru and *haque* in Chile; when the ribbon is wide, trimmed with lace and covers the forehead with two turns, it is called *vincha*. Their breasts and shoulders are half bare, unless they are wearing a large handkerchief which comes half way down their legs behind, which serves in Peru as the small cloak called *gregorillo* (gorget). Moreover, they are not committing any sin against the proprieties when they reveal their breasts, which the Spaniards regard with indifference; but, owing to a ridiculous peculiarity, they are much enamoured of small feet, which they set great store by; and for this reason the women take great care to hide them, so that it is a favour to show them, something they do with great skill . . .'[3]

One would not have expected such a wealth of details from a seafaring man and military technician, who was rarely called on by his profession to be a fashion critic.

Jorge Juan and Antonio de Ulloa confirm the impression of luxury and wealth that the women of Lima gave:

'Their clothes are of silk and lace, *faldelliness* of velvet with ornamented and precious fringes, doublets and *armillas,* filmy shifts and ornamented aprons; not to mention the earrings, necklaces, rings, pearl and diamond bracelets, sprays, *polisones* in the hair, white silk stockings and the very small shoes . . . One of the things to which these ladies pay the greatest attention is the size of their feet, and those who have the smallest feet consider themselves more perfect than the others.'

In fact, the majority of the women of Lima had small feet. They wore light shoes of precious satin or velvet, only the soles of which were made of a piece of supple leather. No heels. For ornaments, diamonds or pearls embroidered on the uppers. Shoes of light-coloured satin were the great luxury of Lima women, even the poorest. As the dust in the streets rapidly tarnished them, some women wore out one pair a week. Legs were encased in white or coloured silk stockings, fine enough for the flesh to be visible.

The same Jorge Juan and Antonio de Ulloa prove, by the following description of the costume of the women of Lima, that they were just as accurate as the French travellers when it came to fashions:

'The costume demanded by fashion comprised shoes, underwear, a shift and a full white petticoat, a short full skirt and in summer a white bodice; in winter, a woollen bodice; some, but not many, wear a small vest as well; the short skirt only falls to half way

[3] FRÉZIER, *op. cit.,* vol. II, pp. 456–457.

between the knee and the foot, and from the hem of this skirt to the ankle a flounce made of the finest lace hangs all round: as it is transparent this lace sometimes enables one to catch a glimpse of the end of garters embroidered with gold and silver and sometimes dotted with pearls, although this is not always the case. The short skirt is made of velvet or any other rich material, trimmed with a wide braid of lace or ribbon. The sleeves of the shift, which are six feet long and more than six feet wide, are made of bands of lace sewn together and whose design is alternated in order to form a charming symmetry. The bodice is worn over the shift; it has a very wide sleeve forming a circular pattern, and it too consists of bands of lace. The body of the shift is drawn in behind by ribbons and as the circular sleeves of the shift and the bodice are also turned down over the shoulders, the whole forms four wings which fall down to the waist. Over their skirt, they wear an apron of the same style as the bodice. No one is surprised to learn that one of these shifts costs a thousand pesos or more. (About seventy-two pounds sterling.)'[4]

Such then were the clothes that an elegant woman of Lima wore at home and which can be summed up as follows: over a linen petticoat (*fustán*) a short flared skirt (*faldellín*), edged with a triple row of lace. In front a small apron or *delantal*. Over the shift a bodice (*chupón*) with wide sleeves, over which was thrown a shawl or mantilla. Flat slippers, like ballet shoes. And as many jewels as possible.

The appearance of the woman of Lima when she went into the town or to church was quite different. Then she covered her dress with a *saya*, a sort of overskirt with several stiff pleats which covered her from waist to feet. The complement of the *saya* was the *manto*, a small sleeveless hood, enveloping the head and the bust, and falling to the waist where it was fastened. The *manto* concealed the face and the woman who wore it could, as she wished, by clutching and holding together the extremities of the cloth, show only one eye, half an eye, or even a quarter of an eye, depending on the situation or the needs of the moment. Thus *tapada* (covered) or *enfundada* (hooded), the most virtuous or

---

[4] Antonio de ULLOA and Jorge JUAN: *Relación histórica* . . . , quoted by Salvador de MADARIAGA in *L'Essor de l'Empire espagnol d'Amérique*, pp. 250–251.

reputedly virtuous woman of Lima could practise all the tricks of coquetry at her ease. The *saya* and the *manto* were something like the domino of Venetian masked balls. Sure of not being recognized by her friends and acquaintances, there was nothing to stop her taking certain liberties, from a simple lingering look to a note slipped into the hand. One can imagine the mistakes to which this costume gave rise. Sometimes, a man thought he saw a young and charming woman in the lady so strictly veiled, when he really had to do with a *zamba* who laughed at his error and enjoyed deluding him. Was it not enough for the arm which held the hood to be well shaped to arouse the gallant curiosity of the men of Lima, who then burned with desire to know more about the mysterious unknown?

The tradition of the *saya* and the *manto* are amusingly recalled by Ricardo de Palma:

'When one wants to leave the beaten track and speak about the origin of something very old, this phrase springs to one's lips: it is lost in the mists of antiquity. When one wants to write about the *saya* and the *manto,* one notes that they have never figured among the clothes of any province in Spain or of any European country. They grew up at Lima as spontaneously as mushrooms in a garden. In what year did this mushroom grow? I have done a lot of research, but have been unable to find out. However, I dare assert that the shawl and skirt came into existence in 1560. Now let us look at the reasons on which my assertion is based. I hope that the reader will not find them too advanced. Lima was founded on January 18, 1535, and there were no more than ten native Spanish women who came to inhabit the capital. One could almost name them. So it is clear as crystal that only from 1555 to 1560 could there have been women of Lima, daughters of Spanish fathers and mothers, capable of forming a nucleus that could produce a fashion like that of the *manto* and the *saya.*'[5]

Having become part of the customs of Lima at an early date, the fashion of the *manto* and the *saya* persisted for a long time. When Admiral Dupetit-Thouars put in at Lima during his cruise round the world on the frigate *La Vénus,* during the years 1838–1839, his attention was attracted by this 'singular costume, only in use in

[5] Ricardo PALMA: *Tradiciones peruanas*, p. 156.

the town of Lima', and he gave a description of it showing that
it had not changed since the days of la Perricholi:

'This original costume is the one that is worn to go to church or
pay calls in the morning. It is called the *saya manto*. This costume
is composed of two main garments: the one which is the skirt
(*saya*) fits the body closely at the waist and falls to the ankle. This
skirt is pleated from top to bottom; the pleats are held together
by threads which hold them in place, without however interfering
with the elasticity of the garment, which is very narrow and takes
the shape of the body so exactly that the legs look as if they were
attached; the pleats are so close together that the skirt needs pushing in order to move the foot forward and walk. The second part
of this costume is the mantle, *el manto*. It also fits closely at the
waist, where it is held by a cord running through a hem and gathering it; it runs up behind, over the head, which it envelops, as well
as the upper part of the arm; each hand holds one of the edges of
this part of the mantle, which acts as a veil and is crossed over the
face, so that only one eye is left visible. The *manto* is always of
black silk, whatever the colour of the *saya*. Women in this costume
cannot be recognized; there is a sort of perpetual masquerade, for,
in this disguise, one can speak to them without their taking offence;
they seem to be wrapped up like the figurines that are found in
Egyptian tombs; they can only walk with very short steps and when
they walk quickly this gives them a look and a gait which are
most extraordinary, and highly amusing to travellers who have
just arrived and do not yet know about this singular outfit.'

After this detailed description, the Admiral's secretary
concludes:

'At first this fashion seems rather inconvenient to foreigners;
later it shocks them less; and after they have stayed here for some
time, all they notice is the gracefulness exhibited by some women
beneath this costume.'

Only the women of Lima were called *tapadas*, the *saya* and the
manto not being worn outside Lima. It was not even seen in Callao,
two leagues away from the capital. Everywhere else in Peru, the
women went about the town in the same clothes which they wore
in the house.

The question of the wearing of the *saya* and the *manto* not only

139

provided a topic for the chronicles, but also came before the highest courts of the viceroyalty in the past. Indeed, one of the proposals discussed by the third council, that met in 1601 under the presidency of Archbishop Torribio de Mongrovejo, had in view the abolition pure and simple of the *saya* and the *manto* under penalty of excommunication.

In fact, the Church considered that this costume, which guaranteed the wearer the impunity of anonymity, made debauchery easier for light women, and encouraged the others to become debauched. Undoubtedly the archbishop had forgotten in 1601 that since 1590, the date when Dona Teresa de Castro, wife of Viceroy don Garcia Hurtado de Mendoza, Marquis of Canete, had come to Lima, the numbers of skirt and shawl lovers had increased considerably. Including the chamber-maids, lady's maids and maids-in-waiting, Dona Teresa had brought with her twenty-seven Spanish girls, whom she installed in her palace. All of them found husbands at Lima within the year. Moreover, in the viceroy's suite there were forty 'budget-eaters' with their wives, their daughters, their sisters and their maids. Because of the novelty and in order to get into the good books of the women who were natives of Lima, they all began to cover their heads with the hood. Dona Teresa was one of the first to wear the *manto* and the *saya*, perhaps on the advice of her husband, for the story goes that the viceroy was always quarrelling with the archbishop. So the damage was done and could not be repaired without implicating the highest notabilities in Peru. It was an awkward situation. The council realized this and did not come to any decision.

Viceroys Guadalcazar and Montesclaros also tried to abolish the *manto* and the *saya*, but they got no further than thinking about it. There was one viceroy, more daring than the others, who merely 'recommended' husbands not to allow their wives and daughters to wear 'such a garment'.

The costume worn by Cuzco women was rather different from that worn by the women of Lima. The women of Cuzco's skirt was called the *saya angosta* or 'narrow skirt'. It was pleated, quite short and adorned with fringes or a lace flounce. The petticoats or *enaguas* were of wool, not cotton, undoubtedly because it was colder at Cuzco than at Lima. They were dyed certain favourite colours: flaming red, sky blue, Chinese pink, Veronese green and chrome yellow. The ladies of Arequipa did not dress like their

140

counterparts in Lima and Cuzco. In addition to their town costume, their indoor négligé (a simple dressing gown with a triple flounce, orange or flaming red shawl draped like a peplum, a rose in their hair) and their special costume for riding on horseback, they had a church-going costume, invariably black, which consisted of a silk skirt and a mantilla of the same material, trimmed with velvet or lace that they closed over the forehead. Since the use of pews and prie-Dieux was unknown in the churches, the ladies made their maids follow at a discreet distance, carrying a mat on which they knelt. For an elegant woman of Arequipa, the height of fashion was to have as carpet-bearer a little Indian from the *sierra* 'as big as one's fist' and wearing his traditional costume. In addition, the women of Arequipa wore on their heads either the round or triangular *montera* (a sort of cap very fashionable in Spain), or the *lliclla*, a piece of woollen cloth measuring about four square feet which they arranged over their heads like a sari or covered their shoulders with, by pinning it in front with the *tupu*, a pin shaped like a soup-spoon, whose use went back to the earliest days of the Incas. This combination of features borrowed from Spanish tradition and Indian folklore formed a curious whole that was not without charm.

As the Peruvian women were superstitious, they wore round their necks amulets which generally consisted of unstamped medals and a small hand made of jade or the wood of the fig-tree. They attributed to these amulets the power of preserving them from the evil that their admirers communicated to them, as they thought, merely by looking at them. They called it the *mal de los ojos*, well known in the East under the name of the 'evil eye'. This superstition was familiar 'to ladies and the people', but there was another almost universal one that was of great importance when it came to avoiding the ordeals of the other world; it was to be careful to procure, during this life, a monk's robe in which to be buried. For people were convinced that if they were wearing a habit so respected here below, they would be welcomed to the abode of the blessed and no one could banish them to outer darkness. It was another way of averting bad luck.

The Indian women of the *sierra* were very simply dressed; they wore a dark blue woollen dress, terminating a little above the knee and leaving their legs and feet bare. This dress, cut low at the neck, had short sleeves, leaving the arms bare to above the elbow.

A small red fringe sometimes brightened up this drab garment. The Indian woman also wore a sort of open sandal, held on only by the toes. Her over-garment was a piece of thick, long-piled cotton; it was very full and garishly coloured, and fell half way down her legs, but not being made to measure, it was not a perfect fit at the shoulders and did not envelope her completely. She wore a coarse straw hat on her head.

COIFFURES AND PERFUMES

The women of Lima paid the utmost attention to their coiffure. They had extremely thick, generally black hair, whereas the women of Guyaquil often had blonde or light brown hair. Long and loose, it fell to their knees. They made six plaits of it, rolling them up into a coil at the neck. The coil was held in place by a long pin ending in two balls of diamonds. Buckles hung down to shoulder level from this coil.

The attraction that jewels had for Lima women had not eradicated the primitive liking of all southern women for flowers and perfumes. On the contrary, the chroniclers attribute to them an 'immoderate love' of flowers and perfumes. Once again, let us leave the floor to Ricardo Palma, who takes us to the famous bridge over the Rimac, a rendezvous for lovers:

'On moonlit nights, one had only to see Mariquita walk backwards and forwards over the bridge in a dazzlingly white cotton dress, with a little neckerchief of white tulle, in tiny size four-and-a-half shoes fit to revive the dead, and her head covered with jasmine . . . During the colonial period, it was practically impossible to cross the bridge on moonlit nights. It was the place where everybody met. Both pavements were occupied by elegant young men who, while recovering from the fierce summer heat by partaking of the light breeze from the river, rested their eyes by watching the women of Lima who had come out to enjoy the cool of the evening, and who perfumed the atmosphere with the sweet scent of the jasmine they stuck in their hair.'

In fact, to a Lima woman, 'to be in the fashion' meant not so much wearing valuable jewels as being adorned with the flowers in season. Fathers and husbands had no complaints about this custom, which put no strain on their pockets. As for the gallants, they knew at once who they were dealing with, for married women wore flowers on the left side of the head and unmarried girls wore them on the right.

Every summer afternoon, a band of young boys went through the streets of Lima and when the cry '¡El jazminero!' was heard you saw young women appear at the iron grilles of their windows and buy a couple of leaves of the banana tree, on which there was an armful of the blossoms of ordinary jasmine, the flowers of Arabian jasmine, orange blossom, chirimoya flowers and others, all equally fragrant. The woman of Lima of this period sought her adornment in nature and made no demands on art.

And this is the moment for Palma to recall certain details of the Lima women's toilet:

'The woman of Lima did not use special liquids or powders for her teeth, and yet their whiteness and regularity were remarkable. In those days people did not know that it was possible to hide a whole California of gold and that it was possible to make ivory mandibules which need fear no comparison with those that God had not given you. Do you know to whom the Lima women owed the whiteness of their teeth? To the *raicero*. Like the *jazminero*, he was another industrious street seller who sold certain white juicy roots which the young women enjoyed chewing and rubbing their teeth with . . .'[6]

The Lima women did more than look after their teeth, if we are to believe Juan and Ulloa:

'Words cannot describe their absolute cleanliness. Cleanliness approaching exaggeration is a quality widely found among all women (that is to say the noble and the humble, women of the white race and negro slaves); so that they are always dressed in immaculate white beneath the flowering of their lace, and their main preoccupation is cleanliness, a cleanliness that can be observed equally well in their houses, which are the object of their most scrupulous care.'[7]

The ladies in Cuzco society made up their faces with ceruse and vermilion red, after having previously covered them with white of egg. The latter was very good for the skin which was easily

---

[6] Ricardo PALMA: *Tradiciones peruanas*, p. 541.
[7] Juan and Ulloa. Quoted by Salvador de Madariaga in *L'Essor* . . . , p. 250.

chapped by the altitude. But it was also customary at Cuzco for the women to give a sheen to their hair with mutton fat which was good for the hair, but had an unpleasant smell. Hence the use of jasmine and perfumes that were often very strong.

The women of Peru's passion for perfumes did not escape Garcia Ventura Calderón, who includes the following dialogue between Amat and his mistress in his *Perricholi*:

'It seems that you women of Lima have the habit of perfuming your ears and even a certain secret part with amber ...'

'You make me blush, sir.'

'Tell me, is it true that you all have the habit of perfuming flowers, even carnations and roses, not finding them fragrant enough—and yet people also say that you add *palillo* (a myrtaceous tree with fragrant leaves) to your mixture, perfuming it too. It's extraordinary! As for me, you understand, I have been used to African women, who smell like wild beasts, when they do not smell of musk.'

MEN'S CLOTHES

Men's clothes also varied depending on their social class, although everyone, even among the poorer classes, was bent on rivalling the rich in elegance. 'It is not surprising to see a *mulato* or other manual labourer wearing a rich cloth of gold or silver so fine that a person of the highest rank could not have found a better to uphold his dignity,' wrote Juan and Ulloa. There were plenty of little clerks who strutted proudly down the Alameda, trimmed with satin, but with empty stomachs. They had to choose between clothes and food. The important thing was to create an impression. However, the high price of materials and the even higher price demanded by good tailors restrained the humble classes' appetite for elegance. Male fashion remained the privilege of the rich and the aristocracy.

'The fashionable man (of Lima) had his head wrapped in a silk scarf set off with Chinese ribbons, attached by a gold clasp set with diamonds, and his neck protected by a silk handkerchief embroidered in black. He wears an enormous felt *sombrero* on his head. His cape is of blue Carcassonne plush and his jacket of black velvet with gold buttons. His breeches are of the type called

10. Peruvian native types
    a. Traditional dress

b. Folk dancers of Huarochin

11. Peruvian native types
   a. Traditional Indian
      dress

b. Indian flute player at Cuzco

tapabalazo (gun case), also of velvet and ending at the knee in a garter of gold braid three fingers wide. The stockings are made of the finest Philippines' silk and his shoes of the best Cordovan leather, with double soles with little gold stars on the uppers. On his hand flash six or seven rings of great richness, and from one of the buttonholes of his jacket hangs a big chain with emeralds as links. His shirt is made of the finest batiste with three rows of Quito braid and trimmed with Flanders lace. He takes snuff from a gold box which weighs at least a pound and a half.'[8]

Not all the men of Lima were so sumptuously clad. Generally they were dressed '*à la française*', although out of national pride they did not like to admit that they had borrowed this fashion from France. The legal profession wore the *golilla* (bands) and sword, as in Spain, excepting the presidents of audience. For travelling, they wore a jacket, slit under the arms on both sides and whose sleeves, open above and below, were fastened by buttons. It was the *capotillo de dos faldas* (small cloak with two skirts).

When riding, the animal's trappings were more important than the horseman's costume, and he paid great attention to it. His stylishness resided in his horse's harness, the separate items of which had their own characteristics. The reins and straps that held the bit and supported the stirrups were not flattened and of one piece but finely plaited. This gave them great flexibility and a rounded shape. They were encircled at intervals by chased solid silver rings. The saddle was also richly worked. But two items of harness were especially important: the stirrups and the *pellón*. The stirrups were not made of metal but of carved wood. They could be described as two pyramidal mountings, about eight inches high by ten inches wide, square at the base and open on one side to admit the rider's foot. In fact, his foot disappeared almost entirely into these cell-like apertures, which left only the large rowel of his silver spur visible. These stirrups were very expensive and people assessed the financial position of the horse's owner by the finish of their workmanship, the chasing and the inlays of ivory, tortoise-shell or silver. The *pellón* was a horse-cloth used to cover the saddle, a veritable fleece that fell down to the animal's flanks. The indigo silk pile which made up the *pellón* was thick and lustrous. It went perfectly with the horse's tail and mane. The

---

[8] Ricardo PALMA: *Tradiciones peruanas*, p. 575.

rider sat on this double saddle. He wore soft boots, a broad-brimmed hat and the traditional *poncho*.

The mountain Indian was poorly clad. He wore baggy trousers. His feet were protected by sandals and the lower part of his legs to the knee was roughly wrapped in pieces of cloth that took the place of gaiters. Above his legs he wrapped round himself a thick cloth in the shape of a sack, which served as a mendicant monk's scrip and impeded his progress. He wore a *poncho* that went down to his knees. The *poncho* was the main item of the Indians' clothing. It was a simple square of wool, in the centre of which a hole had been made to enable the head to pass through. Clad in this envelope, the Indian's shoulders, back and chest were protected from dust, rain and sun. He kept his freedom of movement, for the *poncho* was not fitted to the body, but simply draped over it, although its special cut and the heavy cloth it was made of did not allow the wind to get a hold on it. To all intents and purposes, it was stuck to his shoulders. *Ponchos* were striped in gaudy colours on a more or less dark buff background. The stripes were blue, red or green—or all three at once.

Lastly, in the Arequipa region, Indians were to be seen wearing curious costumes that recalled both seventeenth-century Spanish fashions and Inca garments. They wore a suit with three square tails, a full waistcoat and breeches coming below the knee. Contrasting with these European-style clothes, they affected a long cloak (*llacolla*) like that worn by the Incas, rawhide sandals and a sort of diadem holding in their hair, which fell on either side of the face in two plaits.

CHAPTER THREE

AMUSEMENTS

There were many ways of amusing oneself. And ways to suit all purses, from a walk, which did not cost a *centavo*, to the *corridas* (bullfights), where the seats in the *sombra* (shade) were sold to the highest bidder. But the Peruvians—and especially the men of Lima's—fondness for idling their time away was so great that one of the most appreciated distractions was the 'promenade' on foot or on horseback.

THE PROMENADE

Lima men were lazy. The inveterate lack of vigour that made them shun work and the apathy that made them dread the slightest fatigue were connected with the mildness of the climate, at least on the coast and in the plains. So, rather than walk, they preferred to let horses do the work of conveying them.

Compact, small of stature, with thick tail and undulating mane, the Peruvian horses had a gait that was both graceful and noble. They proceeded at a foot-pace, which gave them the name of *caballos de paso,* as opposed to the European mounts known as *caballos de trote* (trotting horses). Their step was long, even and fast, which enabled them to cover the ground quite briskly without their riders being jolted in the slightest. However, like their masters, they suffered the debilitating effect of the climate. Good tempered and docile, they were not in the least skittish, easily adapted themselves to both draught and saddle work and never bolted. It was common to see riders stop outside a house, dismount, enter the building and leave their horse outside the door for hours, without it moving an inch from the spot where its master had left it. Sometimes, at a simple sign from its master, a horse would even make its way obediently back to the stable all by itself. It was on this peaceful steed that the men of Lima allowed themselves to be conveyed nonchalantly through the avenues of the capital.

And what of the promenade on foot? On Sunday afternoon, people went to the *portales* situated, as we have already seen, in the Plaza Mayor, which extended from the Calle del Correo to the Calle de los Mercaderes, and from there to the Calle de Bodegones, thus forming the *portal de Escribanos* (Arcade of the Notaries) and the *portal de Botoneros* (Arcade of the Button Sellers). The *portales* were most frequented towards three o'clock in the afternoon. Flower-girls set up their fragrant stalls there. The *señoritas* came there to buy flowers and *misturas,* a mixed bunch of small sweet-smelling flowers wrapped in a cornet of leaves, and, above all, to show themselves off. The *portales* were the rendezvous of fashion and sometimes of gallantry.

There were other objectives for strollers. The Alameda de Acho, in the lower part of the town, which ran from the Stone Bridge to the Balta Bridge, and led to the Plaza de Acho where the bull-fights were held. Shaded by American willows, it had three carriage-ways, the middle one for carriages and horsemen, the other two reserved for pedestrians, and it followed the Rimac for 300 *varas* (275 yards). The Alameda (Avenue) or Paseo (Promenade) de los Descalzos (of the Discalced), so called from the name of the Carmelite convent to which it led, was also situated in the lower part of the town. On either side of the central avenue, flower beds nine feet wide were arranged, full of flowering plants and shrubs. Alongside these clumps of blooms were one hundred iron urns, standing on columns of the same metal, painted white with dark green reliefs. Twelve marble statues represented the signs of the Zodiac. At the end of the avenue was the famous Paseo de Aguas built by Amat. Unfortunately, the attractiveness of the Alameda de los Descalzos suffered somewhat from being near the convent, whose daily distribution of victuals drew a great number of beggars. The beggars, summoned daily by the monks' charity to the porch of their church, then spread out in its vicinity, invaded the seats to eat their meal and introduced a depressing note into the scenery with the spectacle of their misery.

CAFÉS AND TERTULIAS

The indolent Lima man who objected to both walking and riding was content to stroll through the streets in the centre of the capital. He leant against the shops for hours at a time, stared out the young ladies and lavished compliments of varying degrees of polish on them. He hailed the passers-by he knew, gossiped with some, argued with others and sometimes followed a *tapada*, although he never left the space comprised between the Calles de los Espaderos, de los Mercaderes and de Portales. Often, too, he went into the shop of someone he knew and engaged him in an interminable conversation that kept him from his business and sometimes sent potential customers away. Some shopkeepers, tired of these too frequent meetings, put a large sign on their counters, where it would be most in evidence. On it these words were written:

'*No se admite tertulias, Tertulias* not allowed,' or '*Perjudice la tertulia,* The *tertulia* is harmful.' Then the only remedy for the talkative idler was to go to a café.

The first café had been opened in Lima in 1771 in the Calle del Correo Viejo. So great was its success that soon there were scores of cafés. This sudden enthusiasm for cafés had nothing to do with the quality or the originality of the drinks consumed in them. Often people drank nothing more than a glass of sugared water. But the café was a comfortable place to hold a *tertulia.*

The *tertulia* was a meeting of men—women were rarely admitted to them, at least in cafés—at which both topical events and gossip and private affairs were discussed. Hitherto *tertulias* had taken place in private drawing-rooms or in the open air. People could be seen sitting on benches all along the Alameda de los Descalzos and talking animatedly far into the night. This new habit of meeting in a café to talk of this and that—but especially politics—came from France; and if the cafés were so firmly established at Lima, it was because people strained their ingenuity to copy Paris and famous cafés such as *Le Procope,* where the French talked more than they drank. I should add that at Lima, as in all the 'cultured' capitals of South America, a taste for discussion was very marked, as Juan and Ulloa pointed out:

'Moreover, because of the vivacity and penetration of their minds, the inhabitants of Peru, men and women, are very cultured and their culture is all the more flourishing because they are in constant contact with the people of importance and talent who arrive from Spain, and a political atmosphere prevails everywhere, so that discussions being frequent, every social gathering among the citizens of this country becomes a school for their minds.'[1]

The reader will realize the importance of the *tertulia* and the café by following almost hour by hour, the week of a fop at Lima, about 1790, as reported by Ricardo Palma.

'*Sunday:* North wind. From nine to ten o'clock, I took my chocolate, dressed, washed and combed my hair. I left home at eleven and went to the parvis of the cathedral. I don't know what's got into Doña Pancha, she frowned at me. I dined at half past twelve. The food was too salty. This cook is not turning out well, she gets worse every day. From three to four, siesta, then a walk in the Alameda with a friend. At eleven o'clock, *tertulia*. I supped off a stew and went to bed.

Monday: I got up at half past eight. I slept well. The north wind continues. I washed my hands, but not my face, the water was ice-cold. My day for the barber's. The barber was dumb as a carp, he doesn't know any news. If he doesn't change his mood, I shall leave him for another one. At ten o'clock, to the office. I wrote two letters and cut my nails. It's not a life to make one grow old! We left at half past twelve; dinner at two o'clock. The wine had gone sour. Siesta until three. Perico came to wake me. From three to five, promenade. Impossible to know what the means of existence of the lady living opposite are. I see a Dominican brother going in. Is he her confessor? Tomorrow I shall ask for Don Fabricio. *Tertulia* at seven. Don Jaime did not come and we were short of news. I said goodbye at eleven. The supper was burnt. I complained and gave the cook the sack. I am going to bed to read a little so that I shall sleep.

Tuesday: The north wind continues. I got up at eight, I had slept very badly. The affair of the woman opposite kept me awake. At nine, I took my chocolate, brushed my teeth and combed my hair. At half past ten, to the office. The *Gaceta* has nothing special to say. Don Celio bought some greaves and we ate them avidly. At noon, calls. At three, dinner, there was no salt pork in the stew. At four, to the café. They say that the grand vizier is ill with gout. At seven, *tertulia*. Doña Felipa sang well . . . I took my chocolate at

[1] JUAN and ULLOA: *Relación histórica* . . . , pp. 79–82.

eleven, read one act of the *Magician of Palermo*, wound up my watch and went to sleep.

Wednesday: East wind, a very unusual thing in this country. At ten o'clock I went to the office. Little conversation, I smoked seven cigarettes, I wrote a letter and left at noon. A duty call. I ate on the way and enjoyed myself quite well. The wind disturbed me and I took shelter in the Genoan's shop. *Tertulia* from eight to eleven at night. The mulatto girl Dolores has taken orders. They say she is very scatter-brained. Supper at half past eleven. I went to bed on the dot of midnight.

Thursday: South-east wind. Chocolate, shaved and combed my hair as usual. There was no office today. From ten to eleven I sat in the balcony. Two women from the mansard opposite look suspicious to me. From eleven to noon, in the G. café, I dined at the inn. I learnt a thousand and one bits of news after the meal. From three to five, billiards: item, two calls I did not pay in the morning. I am not very well, I spent a moment at the *tertulia*. I made four reversis, I said goodbye at ten. I rubbed myself with tallow and at eleven I went to sleep.

Friday: North-east wind. I slept well. Tallow is marvellous. Marshmallow water instead of chocolate. I did not shave so as not to catch cold. At half past ten, the office. I wrote a letter for the Cuzco. I bought a bar of soap. A small spot has come out on my nose. Dona Jacinta noticed it at once. Frugal meal at half past twelve. At three, promenade. I ate a supper of pigeons at half past eleven.

Saturday: South-east wind. From ten to one, at the office. We read the *Diario* and Don Lope bought half a ring biscuit. I cut pens and folded paper so that they will be ready when I have to write. I received my month's salary. At one, calls. I dined at two. The new cook cooks very well. Please God it may last! Conversation with my neighbour instead of siesta. *Tertulia* until eleven. Doña Jacinta sang a new song. At eleven, account of expenses for the week. Total, thirty-three and a few reals, *caramba*! I supped in bed and fell asleep . . .'[2]

A pretty easy time of it for this official who spent two hours a day in his office—and then only to cut his nails!

[2] Ricardo PALMA: *Tradiciones peruanas*, pp. 706–708.

CIVIL AND RELIGIOUS FESTIVALS

We must not conclude too readily from this diary that public office was always a sinecure. Even though a few government posts, reserved for young men of good social position, were purely honorary, the majority called for application and assiduity on the part of their holder. Civil and religious festivals alternated in this viceroyalty that emphasized its 'civil' character without having broken its links with the Church, and almost all of them were compulsory holidays. This meant a large number of days when no work was done. The malicious concluded that Lima was on a perpetual holiday and that its inhabitants, as a certain viceroy jokingly remarked to the king, did nothing 'but ring bells and set off fireworks'. He was exaggerating, but it was a fact that any kind of auspicious event was an excuse for noisy and ostentatious civil or religious ceremonies: kissing of hands, processions, cavalcades, marching past and illuminations. The whole of Lima took part in the solemnities on the great occasions—celebrations of victories, births, princely marriages, enthronements of viceroys and canonizations. In the crowded streets, beneath the balconies crammed with women, the spectators watched the passage of brilliant formations of militia companies and their cheerful bands, the viceroy's mounted guards and halberdiers in blue and red uniforms, the municipal kettledrummers and buglers in crimson cloaks trimmed with silver fringes. The religious communities followed, recognizable by the different colours of their habits, the college students wearing blue, green, red or brown tunics and breeches; the judges and presidents of the audience mounted on horses harnessed with black saddle-covers, the mayors and the municipal magistrates dressed in scarlet, the corps of nobles followed by their lackeys in different liveries, the 'gentlemen at-arms' and the ladies of the aristocracy in their ceremonial carriages.

One of the biggest civil festivals of the year was the almost pagan feast of the *amancaes*, which has already been mentioned. It took place in June, at the time when the yellow flowers of the *amancaes* began to bloom in the *lomas* (hills) around Lima. St John's Day was the moment when the tops of the hills near Lima—particularly that of St Cristobal four miles north of Lima, also called *Lomas de Amancaes*—were covered with these yellow flowers, a kind of narcissus. On this occasion the people of Lima of all classes flocked to this plateau that had become one vast golden meadow. The itinerary was always the same. People assembled in the Paseo de los Descalzos, then, on horseback, in a carriage or on foot, they took a rather tortuous route that began at the convent of los Descalzos and finished on the plateau of the Amancaes. There were no surprises along the road. Two *chacras* (farms the rent of which is paid in kind) broke its monotony, one situated at the gates of Lima, the other at the half-way mark, beyond a steep slope. A small channel three feet wide ran parallel to the road the whole way and its moisture nourished a luxuriant growth of giant watercress on its banks. After an hour's rather hard going over rocky slopes where nothing grew but enormous cactuses with sharp spikes, vulgarly known as *mojones de gigantes* (giants' turds), the crowd reached the top of the plateau from which they could see Lima on the left and the Pacific on the right. It was one vast meadow spangled with flowers. The large dark yellow ones were the *amancaes*. The other smaller ones were all colours of the rainbow. Among the latter, the flower of San Juan, so called because it began to appear around St John's day, was a chestnut colour. On this day, the 24th of June, the slopes of the hills and the plateau were invaded by the crowd. A crowd so boisterous and so numerous that careful or aged people, afraid of being jostled, made only a token pilgrimage by walking up and down to Paseo de los Descalzos. Throughout the day the festival was in full swing. Flowers were picked; the men put them in their buttonholes, the women stuck them in their hair. Groups of dancers performed their numbers on a stage of green grass, while street vendors offered all kinds of highly spiced foods, pastries and drinks. On their return, the whole crowd, drunk with fresh air and *pisco*, flowed down the Alameda and over the Stone Bridge where their behaviour often caused a scandal.

The tradition of the feast of the Amancaes was one of the most tenacious in Peruvian folklore. Flora Tristan, a Frenchwoman, daughter of a Peruvian and grandmother of the painter Paul Gauguin, described it as follows in her travel diary, *Pérégrinations d'une Paria*, when she took part in it in 1834, fifteen years after the death of la Perricholi.

'On St John's Day the promenade of the Amancaes begins—a sort of Longchamp, to which I went with Doña Calista, one of our friends. There were more than a hundred barouches containing magnificently dressed women; there were also numerous cavalcades and an immense crowd of pedestrians. During the two winter months of May and June, the mountains are covered with yellow flowers called *amancaes*. The road that leads to these mountains is very wide and the prospect that unfolds at a certain height is enchanting. In several places tents are set up where refreshments are sold and highly indecent dances performed. During the two months of the season, fashionable society frequents these parts; and the rule of fashion, the desire to see and to be seen overcomes the many inconveniences that they present.'

Nothing had changed since the period of the viceroy.

Another semi-civil, semi-religious festival was the carnival.

The diversions to which Lima society devoted itself during the three days before Ash Wednesday were every bit as gay as those which took place in the towns of Spain on this occasion. Lima added a literally incredible vulgar exuberance and lack of restraint. Perhaps simply because the carnival festivities surprised the inhabitants of Lima in the month of February, one of the hottest of the year, in the very middle of the southern summer, licence giving itself free rein more easily when it is hot.

As from the Saturday evening of the last week of carnival, it was impossible to venture into the streets without exposing oneself to a soaking, the game consisting in throwing water at each other, or more accurately the men throwing it at the women and vice versa. Throughout the year people laid in an ample store of eggshells. The egg was emptied through a hole made in one end. They preserved the shell, which they filled with water that was sometimes scented or with a mixture of gum dyed indigo or carmine. They blocked up the opening used for introducing the liquid with wax and thus they obtained a light and fragile projectile which the men threw at the women and the women at the men. Sometimes the eggshell was replaced by a more resistant and heavier wax container. This was known as the *cascarón*. This weapon could be thrown further, but being harder and heavier than an eggshell, there was a danger of its wounding the man who received it in the face.

From dawn on the first day, men and women dressed in white from head to foot, then the earliest risers ran to the bedsides of those who were asleep, their pockets full of eggs of different colours. These eggs were squashed on the sleeper's face, which was immediately sprinkled with flour. He got rid of his mask of paste as best he could and hastened to avenge the insult. The masters in the drawing-room and the servants in the kitchen were hard at it bombarding and 'flouring' each other. The Shrove Tuesday egg respected neither age nor sex. This day was one of the few when the iron grilles of the balconies were removed. As from midday a battery of injection tubes was installed on each one and people soaked each other from one balcony to the next, while eggs and *cascarones* described white trajectories through the air. Sometimes buckets of water were poured on the heads of passers-by from the balconies. In the afternoon, couples armed with umbrellas to protect themselves against the showers from the balconies went round the town to the sound of guitars and, stimulated by several drinks, sang and gesticulated. At this moment, troops of emaciated horses were brought in from the country and sold at ridiculous prices. In a flash detachments of 'cavalry' set out to lay siege to those balconies whose liquid artillery had caused most damage. Each horseman, a basket of eggs on his arm, posted himself opposite a balcony generally defended by ladies armed with syringes, watering-cans and pumps. They answered the enemy's eggs with torrents of water. The men, drenched to the skin, and the dishevelled women vied with each other in deeds of valour.

From time to time a patrol responsible for preventing brawls passed down the street. For there were some people going about their own business who did not appreciate a soaking. If they made the mistake of showing their dissatisfaction too keenly, they merely excited the fury of their assailants, who bombarded them more than ever. The patrols themselves were not averse to contributing to the general sousing and it was common to see *serenos* and *encapotados* throw eggs at the *ventanas* (windows) when they caught sight of a lady inside. No one escaped from these practical jokes, not even the old and the sick, or the priest carrying the *viaticum*. Even staying at home to seek shelter from this kind of aggression was no use, for bands of young people roamed the streets armed with portable pumps and big syringes with which they sent jets of water into the interiors of the houses.

There was still another, more harmless distraction. In a firmly stitched cloth sack was placed a metal box full of bits of glass, stones, broken china or any similar rubbish that came to hand. A very strong cord was tied to the upper part of the sack and the other end of the cord was attached inside the window. When some rash pedestrian ventured under the balcony at night, the inhabitants let the sack go. It fell and remained suspended about twenty inches above his head, but making a frightful noise, as if hundreds of plates had fallen and broken. The victim jumped, leapt to one side in fright, but at the moment when he turned to look at the sack that dangled above his head, he received a balloon of gold-beater's skin containing several pints of water on his head. He was unwise to complain, for if he was in a district remote from the centre, he ran an even worse risk. Some Indians and negroes took advantage of carnival to demand money from passers-by; if they refused, they drenched them in dirty water, or dye, or put vases full of thick, sticky glue upside down on their heads.

These practical jokes in bad taste only amused their authors. They mainly took place in the street and were perpetrated by the lower classes.

During these three days fashionable Lima men and women were knowledgeable enough to avoid mingling with the populace too much. But they celebrated carnival just as gaily in their own homes and in their own way.

It was customary for neighbouring and friendly families with young men and women to invite each other to spend these days of gaiety together. They assembled in one of their houses. They lunched there, dined there, wet each other there and dried there. For good society resorted to the same procedure as the people to amuse itself, i.e. reciprocal drenchings.

Young women, so reserved during the rest of the year, dressed lightly for the occasion. They had an excuse; it was very hot. A shift and a transparent dressing-gown generally composed their whole costume. The game began. At first they only wet each other with a few perfumes, but gradually the game became more animated. Both sides warmed up and water took the place of perfume. Soon the game became a struggle, at first at a distance, then hand to hand, between the combatants of both sexes. The idea was to see who could hurl his adversary into a barrel of water, for naturally the barrels had already been prepared and filled with water. What happened then to the fine shift and filmy dressing-gown of the unwilling naiad? They stuck to her body. She escaped, someone tried to restrain her, she ran, someone pursued her, she ran away, someone followed . . . Out of breath, she slipped into a corner. Her pursuer caught up with her. And then there was an impassioned set-to. To restore the combatants' forces, *copitas* were lavishly distributed. They drank and drank and drank. Everybody became intoxicated, even those who were most sensible normally. The game began again more strenuously than ever. Night fell; they dried themselves, changed their clothes and danced until they were exhausted. And everybody went to bed to rise at dawn and begin this game which lasted for three days all over again.

At dawn on Ash Wednesday, the majority of houses were in a sorry state. The furniture was soaked, streams still flowed in the patios, the windows were broken and the carpets stained. What did it matter! They had all enjoyed themselves. Now the time for contrition had come. At the first stroke of the Angelus, young men and women—with their parents—hastened to kneel at the feet of a monk, who, after having marked their foreheads with a grey cross of ashes, while reminding them that they were only dust, absolved them for their sins.

Without being irreverent, it is possible to classify the religious feasts among the distractions, if not the amusements, for they were the occasion of spectacles that were very popular with the people. Some of them, such as the processions, were rather like the poor people's theatre, in which they were both actors and audience.

Processions were numerous, especially at Lima. Among the most picturesque were those of Our Lady of the Negroes and those which left the Church of San Agustin on Maundy Thursday and the Church of la Merced on Good Friday. (The latter was known by the name of *Procesión del Santo Sepulchro*.)

In the first of these processions, a band of the faithful, dressed as devils, followed the procession. Some with tattooed faces and heads surmounted by a pair of horns, others covered with feathers or snakes' tails attached around the waist. Some, rigged out in bear skins, uttered fearful groans. All were armed with sticks, shields, tridents, pitchforks, bows and arrows. They dyed their bodies red and blue and made a tremendous din by banging stones together. The Maundy Thursday and Good Friday processions included, in addition to the devils, cardboard giants carried by negroes and *papahuevos*, cardboard heads of monstrous dimensions, which children dressed up in. Everybody indulged in contortions and grimaces that were quite unsuitable to the pious character of these

festivals. That was why, on several occasions, the viceroy had tried
to restrain these masquerades, especially by forbidding the *papahuevos*. But each time an edict was issued to this effect, petitions
flocked in, begging that the procession of devils and *papahuevos*
be allowed again. The petitioners were often priests, such as this
one, in charge of a parish at Lima, who protested to the viceroy
in these words:

'The priest . . . Doctor of Sacred Theology of the most illustrious
Royal and Pontifical University of San Marcos has the honour to
point out respectfully to Your Excellency that it is a gross offence
and a blow obviously aimed at the Majesty of the Divine Shepherd,
of the Redeemer and Saviour of generations, to have forbidden by
an authority that was not competent the participation this year of
giants and devils in the public processions at Quasimodo (next
Sunday). The measure is strange and ill-timed:

a because these devils form a harmless escort to the Divine
Majesty and the people see with joy that they prostrate themselves
before God;

b because the giants, without frightening the children, attract a
larger crowd to follow God; without which the holy processions
would be completely deserted.

It follows, therefore, that the applicant begs of Your Excellency
and his pious court that, next Sunday, my faithful parishioners may
leave my church disguised as devils and giants. *And he added as a
PS.:* Moreover, I demand that there will be *papahuevos*.'

We must believe that the viceroy was touched by the naïve con-
fidence of this missive, for notwithstanding the decree he replied:

'Considering the petition, its author is allowed to send out four
giants to accompany the Divine Majesty on the following Sunday
of Quasimodo. In addition, I give permission for there to be
papahuevos.'

In addition to the general and 'official' processions there were
many parish and conventual processions which normally took
place on the holiday of the patron saint: San Marcelo, San Sebastian, San Agustin, Santo Domingo, etc. But, regardless of the importance of the procession, its ceremonial—its staging, one might
say—varied very little. The preparations began the evening before
the day fixed for the procession. The parish or conventual church

had to be decorated in anticipation of the next day's ceremony. To this end the members of different confraternities, aided by devotees in the district, shared the task. Some hung gaudy cloths over the façade. Others attached painted paper fringes round the small bells, or sometimes small pieces of glass which, shaken by the wind, made tinkling music. The front and sides of the church were decorated with lanterns of coloured glass.

Then came the day of the procession. Since dawn, chiming bells (*repiques*) and the loud reports of fire-crackers (*cohetes*) had kept the inhabitants of the quarter awake. The church square had been transformed into a fair. Indian women had come during the night to put up their stalls, on which they had placed the usual titbits: *chicharrones, empanadas, camarones,* not to mention the *turrones,* corn roast with brown sugar, and the *butifarras,* small rolls split and containing cold meat, a lettuce leaf and a red pepper.

The hour of the procession approached. The faithful had been assembled inside the church for a long time. The members of the different confraternities arrived, enveloped in large white, red or blue robes and carrying big lanterns surrounded with strips of glass that tinkled with every step they took. All those present were given a lighted candle. It only remained to open the double doors of the church. The procession went out into the street, divided into two files. In the middle, the servants of the parish advanced, hands clasped around the banners of the saint whose holiday was being celebrated. Then came the notables of the quarter, carrying standards. Lastly, the members of the confraternities and the women, loaded with baskets of flowers with which they strewed the ground in order to honour the saint who was going to pass. He was generally represented by a rather crudely painted wooden statue, but his vestments were sumptuous. He was attached to a stretcher carried by six or eight Indians, who disappeared almost entirely beneath the curtains arranged around the pedestal. The parish priest came last, covered with a velvet canopy and followed by the *beatas,* devout women belonging to the confraternities, in black, white or violet robes, drawn in at the waist by a broad patent leather belt. Then there were the *mistureras* carrying plates full of rose petals, the *zahumadoras* (women of the people) and sometimes young society women holding *braseros* (braziers) on which they sprinkled incense or perfumes. Last of all, a band brought up the rear of the procession.

159

That was the usual arrangement for processions. However, some of them followed a ceremonial peculiar to the feast that was being celebrated. For example, on Palm Sunday, after the palms were blessed, the so-called procession of the *borriquito* (ass) re-enacted Christ's entry into Jerusalem. The ass destined to carry Jesus was only used on this occasion and during the rest of the year the greatest care was lavished on it, as if it was a sort of sacred bull like Apis.

The procession *del Señor de los Milagros* was intended to avert earthquakes. Its origin went back to one of the most serious earthquakes that Lima had suffered, in 1654. Many houses had been completely destroyed, including that in which a negro confraternity customarily held its meetings in the quarter of Pachacamilla —with the exception of one wall on which a freed slave had painted the image of Christ crucified. During the years that followed, the quarter was rebuilt and the wall whitewashed by the new owners. However, in spite of the layers of whitewash and paint, the image reappeared, bright and as if freshly painted. An oratory was built and then a church—the *Church de las Nazarenas*—where the miraculous image and its reproduction on a canvas painted in 1747 could be seen behind the high altar.

The procession took place on October 28th. Enclosed in a shrine of solid gold, placed on a silver litter weighing almost a ton, the Christ of the Miracles—or rather a copy—was carried on men's backs. The procession made its way to the sound of funeral music. It set out at eight o'clock in the morning and did not finish until midnight. During the halts, every ten or fifteen minutes, old ballads were sung.

On the day of her feast, August 26th, the statue of Santa Rosa, patron saint of Peru, was also carried in procession, surrounded by a forest of candles and holding a bouquet of roses in her hand. This procession was as popular as the one organized on October 4th by the Dominicans in honour of St Francis. Ten men carrying the statue of St Dominic went to pay a visit to St Francis. St Francis went to meet him half way, in the main square of Lima, in front of the palace gates. There was an exchange of compliments, then the reception of the two saints at the entrance to the Church of St Francis by a white man, a negro, a mulatto and an Indian, who came to dance ahead of the procession. They wore giant masks made of baskets covered with paper. Between the giants was a

12. a. The devil dance of Guayaquil c. 1830

b. Lima street scene today

13. a. St. Blaise's Hill,
     Cuzco

b. Street scene in
   Cuzco

monster from local mythology. The procession entered the church. When night fell, there were fireworks and the town was illuminated by lanterns. Then the monster and the giants were set on fire. The next day, there was mass set to music and a sermon. The cloister was open to women. In the evening, St Dominic was taken home by another procession.[3]

Those were the main processions which passed through the streets of Lima on fixed dates, attracting a considerable crowd composed of the curious rather than the faithful. In fact, they were an excuse for lounging about and meetings. At these times the *tapadas* had the chance to make eyes, and the young men had an opportunity to try to discover who they were. The *beatas* (sanctimonious old women) were sure of a good day of pious rejoicing. Thus everyone got something out of them without paying a penny. For one of the advantages of the religious ceremonies and promenades on foot and on horseback was that they were free. One could say much the same of the cafés where people talked more than they drank.

SPORTS AND DISTRACTIONS

Walking, going to the café, following processions and keeping the saints' days or celebrating national anniversaries were rather monotonous distractions. Only the rough rejoicing of carnival introduced a more exciting note into the uniform cycle of the calendar. Fortunately there were sports and games, in the front rank of which came *corridas* and *peleas de gallos* or *lidas de gallos,* that is bullfights and cockfights.

The people of Lima had always been very fond of bullfighting. There had been famous *corridas* at Lima, such as those given on the accession of Charles IV or when the viceroys O'Higgins, Aviles, Abascal and Pezuela took up office.

The first *corrida* was held at Lima on Monday, March 28, 1540, in the Plaza Mayor. Francisco Pizarro himself killed the second bull on horseback with a spear (*al rejonazo*). As from 1599 the Cabildo authorized four *corridas* a year. In 1701, for the first time, posters were put up with the names of the bulls and the *ganaderías* where they were bred, which formed their pedigree, as it were. In

[3] Camille PRADIER-FODÉRÉ: *Lima et ses Environs* (la Procession à Lima, p. 191).

1790, on the occasion of Charles IV's coronation celebrations, Terralla y Lalanda published a book entitled *El sol en el melodia* (The Sun at Noon), which gives the best description extant of bullfights in Peru.

Since the Plaza Mayor had proved inadequate to house the crowd of bullfighting enthusiasts (*aficionados*) as the years went by, Viceroy Amat had a ring of colossal dimensions built at a place called Hacho away from the town. In 1768, the Plaza de Hacho—it became the Plaza de Acho from losing a letter—was finished. Its construction had been entrusted to Don Agustin Hipolito Landaburu. This ring, which took three years to complete, cost nearly 100,000 pesos. It was in the shape of a fifteen-sided polygon and could easily hold 10,000 spectators. For size and luxury, it bore comparison with the best plazas in Spain. However, in spite of the construction of the Plaza de Hacho, bullfights were still held, as before, in the Plaza Mayor on the occasion of royal feasts and the reception of viceroys. The last to take place there was in 1816 for the reception of Viceroy Pezuela. Wooden galleries and tiers of seats, which were sold to the spectators at high prices, were set up all round the square.

In the time of la Perricholi, the *corridas* took place on Sunday, which greatly annoyed the Church, for the *aficionados* were in such a hurry to reserve their seats and to get one in a good position that they went to Acho at daybreak, joined the queue and once they had their ticket did not bother to return to the city. They found it more convenient to stay near the ring until three o'clock in the afternoon, when the fight began. So they missed Sunday mass owing to their passion for bullfighting. The ecclesiastical authorities, disturbed by this situation, made repeated representations to the viceroy asking for the bullfights to take place on a weekday. They did not obtain satisfaction until the end of the eighteenth century, when a royal *cédula* of October 6, 1798, decided on Mondays for bullfights. Then it was public business that suffered. For although the attendance of the faithful at Sunday services was assured from then on, work on Monday suffered. Many offices and shops closed on Monday to enable the employees—and their bosses—to go to the *toros*. The courts closed their sessions at one p.m. so that the magistrates could go to the *fiesta*. The colleges interrupted their classes, for neither teachers nor pupils would have put up with being deprived of their national distraction.

In short, whether it was on Sunday or Monday, the *corrida* caused inconvenience in public life, but this in no way prevented the whole town rushing to see it.

Animation began with the first hours of daylight. From dawn onwards, there were large crowds in the Plaza Mayor in front of the posters put up by the municipality with the name of the *toreros* and the details of the bulls. People estimated the chances of both. The prices of the seats were also given. Even the cheaper ones were still dear for the poorer classes. But there was not a single citizen of Lima who would not have saved a few *centavos* to treat himself to the spectacle of a *corrida*, even if his seat was so bad that he only saw half of it. From the day before, the quarter of Acho was invaded by the inevitable itinerant stalls piled with food and drink that sprang up at all the popular gatherings. The avenues leading to the ring were sprinkled with water to reduce the clouds of dust that would soon be raised by the riders and carriages going to the *corrida*. Towards noon, the number of the curious increased. The Stone Bridge and the Balta Bridge gradually filled with a dense crowd which came from all parts of the town. Exclamations rang out when a *torero* passed on his way to Acho or when the *aguadores* responsible for watering the bullring went by.

Sometimes the *corrida* was preceded by a sort of 'dummy run' reserved for a few *aficionados*. Two or three bull-calves with their horns already shaved were released into the ring. The enthusiasts made passes with these young bulls and teased them, without risking anything but a few bruises. This was what was known as the *encierro del ganado* which meant both the action of shutting the bulls up in their pens and this game preparatory to the *corrida*. If the bullfight assumed exceptional importance owing to the fame of the *toreros* and the quality of the bulls, or because it fell on a holiday, the viceroy was present. At two in the afternoon, he left his palace, surrounded by a crowd of notables, all mounted on superbly harnessed horses. The people, who had massed on the parvis of the cathedral and beneath the *portales*, did not spare their applause.

As soon as they entered the *plaza*, the spectators immediately looked at the doors of the *toril* (bull pens) opening directly into the ring in which the bulls which were to fight had been placed and kept safely since the early hours of the morning. Kept in total darkness, they were separated from each other and hobbled so that they could not make the slightest movement. From time to time, a well-placed jab with a goad kept them in the state of nervous irritation that stimulated their aptitude for combat. It was the custom for the well-known *aficionados* and owners of *ganaderías* to come to look at the *toril* before the fight. They measured the length of the horns, appreciated the power of necks and shoulders and estimated the cost of the *enjalmas* (velvet or satin covers, embroidered and fringed with gold and silver, which were put on the bulls' backs). During this period, the spectators beguiled their impatience in various ways. Some shouted to one another from row to row, yelled, sang and sometimes settled their quarrels with their fists. Others hailed the sausage and *butifarra* sellers and ate heartily. But then a fanfare of trumpets announced the arrival of the viceroy. The archbishop accompanied him, and a magnificently attired retinue. No sooner had the noble suite taken their seats in the reserved box than a second trumpet fanfare announced the arrival of the *cuadrilla*.

In composition the Peruvian *cuadrilla* differed little from the Spanish *cuadrilla*. It contained the *toreros* who fought on foot (*banderilleros, matadores*) and those who fought on horseback (*picadores*). But 'specialization' was carried further than in Spain. The men whose role was to arouse the bull had different names according as they used the javelin (*rejoneadores de vara corta*), the dagger (*cacheteros*) or the 'pike'(*garrocheros*). Moreover, a dozen *parlampanes* (characters out of carnival), and *mojarreros* (buffoons) performed in the ring throughout the *corrida*. Their grotesque evolutions, mimicking the different phases of the death of the bull, were somewhat reminiscent of those of clowns during acrobatic turns. This burlesque note, introduced into the sacred mystery of the taurine drama—as the Spaniards considered it—was what really differentiated Peruvian *corridas* from the *corridas* of the Peninsula.

The spectacle began with the presentation of the horsemen who performed exercises of virtuosity called *capeos* with their capes, while the matadores marched round the ring, their torsos draped in their scarlet, green, blue or pale yellow *capas* (capes). Then a third trumpet-call announced the beginning of the *corrida*. The viceroy tossed the gold key of the *toril* into the ring, crying: 'Long live the King!' A gentleman, chosen in advance, picked it up, walked to the *toril* and threw the double doors open wide. The bull, infuriated by the treatment it had suffered, dazzled by the blinding light of the plaza after the semi-darkness of the *toril*, bounded into the ring.

The crowd gave a wild shout. A shout of admiration, first of all, for the animal's formidable beauty. All the spangles on the short mantle that covered its flanks flashed in the sun's rays, and the numerous ornaments with which it was adorned, emphasized its nobility and pride even more. The bull rushed to the middle of the ring. It was dazzled by the broad daylight and deafened by the noise of the band. It stopped, looked at the crowd in terror and tried to return to the *toril* to seek shelter, but the door was shut. It returned slowly to the middle of the ring where the many-coloured pieces of cloth shaken at it put an end to its hesitation and revived its fury.

Before engaging the animal, the *toreros* advanced to the mayor's box, bowed and walked round the ring. The fight began with the *capeos* on horseback. These were executed solely by *zambo* and negro *picadores*, who enjoyed, among the people of Lima, a reputation for skill and agility of which they were very proud. Some owners entrusted them with extremely valuable horses on which they carried out the dangerous exercise which consisted in the horseman drawing the bull into the middle of the ring by showing it the *capa*; the infuriated animal charged at the motionless rider, but at the moment when the horns of the impetuous animal were about to hit him, he spurred his mount, making it rear and turn to the right or to the left. The bull plunged its horns vainly into thin air.

Then came the *toreros*, each doing his utmost to wound the bull with the weapon of his speciality, the cruellest of which was the *banderilla* fitted with fire-crackers which exploded when the metal pierced the animal's skin. Soon the bull grew mad with pain; it pawed the sand violently with its feet, its nostrils contracted and dilated under the goad of suffering. With lowered head it charged in every direction; its body was drenched with blood, its eyes were blurred, but it went on fighting.

But already the public was getting impatient. It wanted to see the bull fall and it shouted for the sacrificer. '¡Que muera! ¡Que Muera!' people yelled on all sides. The *matador* who was going to give the *coup de grâce* stepped forward, preceded by the applause of the spectators. He was draped in his cape; he carried a bared sword, the *espada,* in his hand. He approached the animal boldly and held out his *muleta* (red and yellow cloth) to it. The bull charged, the *muleta* fell, the animal was about to pierce its enemy with its horns, but the *matador* extended his arm and the flashing sword disappeared into the hollow below the shoulder to stick directly into the heart. The *matador* was the object of ovations and applause from the delirious crowd; a hail of gold and silver coins rewarded his courage and skill. Then four horses, harnessed to a sort of limber called a *carretilla,* trotted smartly into the ring. After describing a vast arc the horses approached the dead bull. It was tied to the *carretilla* by its horns and dragged out of the ring, leaving a broad trail of blood on the sand.

We can see, therefore, that in its broad outlines the Peruvian *corrida* respected the Spanish traditions. It only deviated from them in points of detail. For example, the barbarous custom of the *lanzada* consisting in placing a man in front of the *toril* beside a big lance resting on a plank. Blind with fury, the beast rushed on the lance and fell transfixed, but there were times when the bull avoided the lance and charged the defenceless man, who rarely emerged alive. Another peculiarly local custom was the performance of 'passes with *capeos*' on horseback. This exercise was considered so dangerous and so difficult that it was reserved for volunteers, generally men of quality.[4]

A very ancient origin has been attributed to cockfighting. In fact, it was Themistocles, in the course of his expedition against the Persians, who is supposed to have suggested to his soldiers that they should set cocks to fight each other to amuse themselves. Then the Romans were supposed to have adopted this sport in their turn.

Although it is difficult to fix the date on which the first cockfights took place at Lima, we do know that half a century after the town's foundation the streets, crossroads, gardens and even the cloisters of monasteries were the scene of cockfights.

The negroes and the Indians brought their birds to fight and boasted to each other of the strength and length of the spurs, the hardness of the beak, the force, size and superiority of their feathered bipeds. The spectators supported their particular champion passionately. They indulged in bets and the loyalty and good faith of the gamblers sometimes left much to be desired.

[4] Ricardo PALMA: *Tradiciones . . . ,* pp. 42–45.

Arguments broke out, people came to blows and it frequently happened that the fights begun between the cocks ended in a no less bloody manner between their owners and the spectators. The authorities had to intervene and prohibit them in the public thoroughfares. But, in the same way that on the eve of carnival a *bando* (decree put up on the walls) forbade the throwing of water from windows and balconies, and begging was also forbidden, but nevertheless one was soaked in the streets from Sunday to Shrove Tuesday and assailed by beggars of every description, in just the same way the authorities tried over and over again to prevent cockfights in public thoroughfares and they were continually ignored and the fights began again worse than ever.

The interest taken by the people in cockfights had become an absolute passion at the time when Amat assumed power. The viceroy's attention was drawn to the serious inconveniences occasioned by this popular frenzy. Not only did the people leave their work to watch this sport, but also they ruined themselves by it, the bets reaching enormous sums.

The viceroy showed his wisdom on this occasion. Instead of setting the population against him by suppressing cockfighting, he decided to bring it under regulation, in other words to make it official, and accepted the proposal made by a certain Juan Garial to build a *coliseo* in the little square of Santa Catalina. In return for the exclusive privilege he held, the impresario undertook to pay 500 pesos a year to the *cabildo* and 500 to the Hospital of St Andrew.

At first, Amat authorized cockfights on Sundays, holidays, Tuesdays and Thursdays. Later, this permission was extended to Saturdays, while the Coliseo became State property under the control of a 'judge of spectacles' with a salary of 500 pesos a year. In 1804, the *cancha de gallos* (cockfighting ground) was transferred to the Calle de Mármol de Carbajal.[5] The place where the fights took place, then, was called *el coliseo,* or *la cancha,* or simply *la casa de gallos,* the house of cocks. It was a miniature arena, painted blue and white. The spectators were seated in tiers. There was a mixed audience of whites, mulattos, Indians and negroes, all animated by the same passion: gambling. Bets were exchanged noisily; they were jotted down in notebooks as on racecourses. While this was going on, an official introduced the future combatants, presented

[5] *Ibidem*, pp. 608–614.

them to each other and then armed them with a spur fitted with a blade. An official inspector, *el juez de las navajas* (the judge of the knives), saw to it that everything was done regularly and that the chances were equal on both sides. The last bets flew through the air, then everyone was silent. The two champions approached each other slowly, pecking at the sand. Suddenly, as if they were moved by a single spring, they rushed at each other, combs bristling and eyes bloodshot. The fight was usually very short and nearly always ended in the death of one of the adversaries. Often both cocks lay dead on the ground and the (posthumous) palm went to the one which had expired last.[6]

One anecdote clearly illustrates the importance attached to this sport by the local authorities. There exists in the archives of the *cabildo* of Lima an appeal made on June 30, 1802, against the sentence pronounced by the 'judge of the knives'. The incident had occurred on the occasion of a cockfight that took place in the Plaza de Santa Catalina and involved two cocks famous for their victories. At the most stirring moment of the conflict, when its issue was still in doubt, a spectator at the cockpit was heard shouting: 'Cheating!' What had happened? The judge approached the combatants and discovered that one of the two cocks had a string round its neck to which was attached a little cross to bring it luck. The *regidor* to whom this case was refererd concluded that the cock's owner, by putting a cross round his champion's neck, had become guilty of both trickery and irreverence. As a result, the bets were cancelled and the cock's owner was sent to prison. What history does not tell us is whether the *cabildo* of Lima confirmed the *regidor's* decision.

Although it required as much muscle as feeling—at least that of rhythm—dancing was considered much more an amusement than a sport. The negroes had stamped it with their influence. Originally a favourite dance of the negro slaves, the *calenda* had penetrated into the best Lima society. This is what Father Labat says about it:

'The Spaniards have learnt it from the negroes and dance it throughout Latin America in the same way as the negroes. The French who own slaves have forbidden it, because the postures and movements of this dance are most improper . . . It is nevertheless

[6] Raul PORRAS BARRANECHEA: *Pequeña antologia de Lima*, p. 304.

popular with the Spanish Creoles of America and is so customary
among them that it forms the better part of their amusements and
even enters into their devotions. They dance it in their churches
and during their processions and the nuns never fail to dance it
on Christmas Eve on a stage raised in their choir, opposite the
grille, which is opened so that the people may share in the joy
that these good souls testify to for the birth of the Saviour.'[7]

In addition to the *calenda,* they danced the *huayno,* a sort of
bolero of Spanish influence, the *sicuri,* an Indian dance from the
region of Titicaca and the *zamacueca* or *mozamala.* The
zamacueca was the typical dance of Peru and especially of Lima.
To dance it well, one had to be a real woman of Lima, piquant
and arch. Depending on the couples who danced it, it could be very
pure or lascivious, for it 'disturbed both the heart and the senses'.
Everything depended on the *almea,* the state of soul. The story
goes that an archbishop saw this dance and asked what it was
called. 'The *zamacueca,* Your Excellency,' was the answer. 'The
name is badly chosen. It should be called "the resurrection of the
flesh".' This remark seems so surprising in the mouth of a prelate
that we may doubt its authenticity. But it is true that in Peru, and
other parts, dancing, particularly the *zamacueca,* was not always
innocent. People either thought only of shining by their grace and
agility or else they saw in it a convenient introduction to gallantry.

Gallantry went from simple flirting (*discreteo*) to concubinage
(*amancebamiento*), or merely to passing adventures to which
sequels were not desired, but which sometimes left painful traces.
The practice of gallantry was facilitated by the fact that the women
of Peru were freer than in Spain. They went out little by day and
preferred to pay their calls at nightfall, their face hidden in the
famous Lima shawl. 'Without it being possible to recognize them,
they make the approaches that men make in France,' remarked
Frézier, who, on this occasion, draws a charming sketch of the
gallant Lima woman:

'The charms that education gives Spanish women are all the
more touching as they are normally accompanied by good looks.
They are generally quite prepossessing. They have beautiful
complexions, but of short duration, owing to the lavish use they

---

[7] *Voyages du Père Labat,* vol. II, part 4, p. 53. Quoted by Salvador de
MADARIAGA in *Le Déclin . . . ,* p. 143.

make of rouge of *solimán,* which is a prepared sublimate. They have bright eyes and make vivacious conversation, enjoying frank attentions, to which they reply wittily and often with a turn that smacks a little of libertinage, according to our manners. The propositions that a lover would not dare to make in France, without deserving the indignation of an honest woman, far from scandalizing them, give them pleasure, although they would be far from agreeing to them, being persuaded that it is the greatest mark of love one can show them; they thank one for them as for an honour done to them, instead of getting angry as at a bad opinion that one has of their virtue. One recognizes in these simple and natural manners the pleasure and secret contentment that we feel when we see ourselves sought after. [*As a practical man, Frézier adds:*] Human prudence alone should suffice to prevent a sensible man from falling into the traps of the coquettes of this country, for their engaging manners are usually a result of their avarice, rather than a mark of their inclination . . . it even seems that having ruined several lovers is something for them to boast about . . .'[8]

Of course, everybody did not fall into the traps of gallantry. That old Spaniard of Lima who crossed himself and kissed his thumb when a pretty girl passed by was not the only one of his kind. Just a furtive glance . . . and then flight! Besides, many Lima women remained honest and reserved or else their wiles were confined to fluttering their eyelashes. So many debauchees found it more convenient, and often pleasanter, than vainly courting a society lady, to turn to their maids, generally negresses, who were reputed to be of easy virtue and with reason, for they benefited by such commerce, as Juan and Ulloa emphasized:

'If the negress was a slave, the children she had from a free man, in Spanish territory, were also free; naturally this was an encouragement to unions with white men . . . These half-breed or mulatto women of the second to the fourth degree gave themselves up to a licentious life, although they themselves did not consider it as such, for it was a matter of indifference to them whether they were married to one of their peers or lived in concubinage (i.e. with a man superior in rank or colour). But the corruption is so great in these countries that they esteem it more honourable to

<hr>

[8] FRÉZIER: *Relation* . . . , p. 453.

adopt the second course, when they can obtain advantages that they would not obtain by marrying.'

And Madariaga concludes: 'Irregular love led the three peoples to mingle their souls and thus, through the Indian native, rooted whites and negroes in the soil of America.'

Even less regular was a certain exhibition of homosexual gallantry, which severely shocked the people of Lima, if we are to believe the press of the period. This is what we read in a number of the *Mercurio peruano* at the end of the eighteenth century:

'*Un desorden tan monstruoso como el de los llamados maricones apenas podría creerse si, a cada paso, no se presentasen a la vista estos fenómenos,* An excess as monstrous as that of the men known as *maricones* would be scarcely credible if these phenomena did not meet the gaze at every step.'

This chapter on gallantry would have been incomplete if it had not recalled these 'phenomena called *maricones*' prowling through the streets of Lima. 'Scarcely credible', states the chronicler, but true, although it seems surprising that one met them 'at every step'. Journalistic exaggeration, no doubt.

PART FOUR

CIVIC LIFE: ECONOMIC LIFE: THE MUSES

CHAPTER ONE

CIVIC LIFE: THE ARMY, THE CHURCH AND EDUCATION

'This viceroy militarized the country and expelled the Jesuits.'[1]

Carlos Pereyra sums up Amat's administration in this singularly brief sentence. To reinforce Peru's defences and drive the Company of Jesus out of the country were indeed among instructions he received from the king and those which called for his closest attention when it came to carrying them out. But the first was by far the most important. In fact, Amat, like his successors and predecessors, was constantly preoccupied by military questions.

To tell the truth, by expelling the Jesuits, the viceroy was merely applying to the territory in his charge the royal orders applicable to the whole of Spanish America. At the same time he settled a personal quarrel with the Company, which he detested. Thus he gratified his spite while obeying the monarch, for he found that his duty coincided with his own desires. But this police operation formed only one episode in his administration. Military necessities, on the other hand, were permanent; they took absolute priority, for they controlled the integrity and security of Spanish Peru. Indeed, it was to be feared that the conflicts in which continental Spain was engaged would have their repercussions in the colonies and particularly in Peru. In August, 1762, when Amat had only just taken possession of his office, Havana fell into the hands of the English fleet, which sent twelve Spanish ships to the bottom. The following month, Spain lost Manilla and twenty-six vessels, while the British squadrons cruised quite close to Callao.

THE DEFENCE OF THE TERRITORY AND THE ARMY

The English threat to Peru, which was promptly averted, had a salutary effect. It forced the viceroy to turn his attention to the

[1] Carlos PEREYRA: *Historia de la América española*, vol. VII, p. 306.

problem of the defence of the territory, which hitherto his predecessors had rather neglected. In fact, the hostilities had taken Peru by surprise, at a time when it was totally lacking in fortified towns, troops and armaments, and absolutely without means of defence. Callao was only protected by a simple town wall on which it would have been difficult to instal a single cannon. It was an enclosure which seemed made to enclose the soldiers rather than to protect the kingship. And if the troops were counted, 'the few there were lacked military training'.[2]

Don Manuel de Amat devoted a large part of his reign to establishing personally and having carried out by engineers of his own choosing the plans of works intended to protect the coasts which lay wide open and defenceless, as if inviting attacks by pirates and enemies, who, at this period, were mainly represented by the English, omnipotent on the high seas, thanks to their fleet. He also had built, under his direction, other fortified works, intended for the Spanish land forces in Chile and Peru. This warrior had proved himself an excellent military architect, just as he had shown genuine qualities as a town-planner, as we have seen. The old fortifications of Callao had been almost entirely destroyed by the earthquake of 1746 and although the Conde de Superunda had planned their reconstruction, nothing had yet been done when Amat came into office. It was then that the new viceroy, with the idea of making Callao a stronghold and a safe port, ordered important works which were finished in 1774. In order to supply the fortresses and frontier posts with powder, he signed contracts with 'all those who could fulfil this obligation, compelling each of them to supply 40,000 pounds to the officers designated, at short notice'. He encouraged private efforts to build artillery engines and manufacture bullets, of which he had none. Lastly, to remedy the lack of raw materials, he made private individuals hand over to the army the antique cannons that adorned the entrance to certain houses and the walls of the town, arguing that they had no right to possess these pieces of artillery.

The problem of personnel was just as acute as the problem of material. The regular troops were few in number. Moreover, they had often shown their lack of combativity, especially during engagements with the rebels, who were seasoned and full of ardour.

[2] *Memoirs of Viceroy Amat*, Seville, 1947. *Estudio preliminar* (Ref. AHN Consejo de Indias 20,333 cuaderno 4° folio 263 and 264), p. XLVIII.

Then Amat hit upon a rather ingenious formula, which reconciled military necessities and pecuniary contingencies. He had the idea of putting the population on a permanent war-footing. To this effect, Amat instituted a general enrolment, separating the professional bodies, the different races and the social classes.

Then he established militias and to take over their command he promoted officers on whom he lavished both praise and rewards when they deserved them. In fact, they did not have much to do in between military operations, except stroll through the streets of Lima in their dashing brand-new uniforms. These officers, mostly born in the Peninsula, paid for their equipment and upkeep themselves, rather like the musketeers of the King of France in the past. The militiamen had to be prepared to take part in military exercises two or three times a week and to wear their parade uniform on the official feasts at which the viceroy was present. These assemblies of soldiers coming from different Spanish provinces sometimes gave rise to incidents that were rarely serious and often comic. One of the latter had lasting fame in Peru, for it inspired the viceroy to make a *dicharacho* (witty remark) that filled the Catalans with joy. The incident occurred on the occasion of a review of troops who marched past in the following order: the first company composed of Castilians and Estremadurans: 140 men. Second company, formed of Navarrans and men of Arragon: 128 men. Third company, Andalusians: 144 soldiers. Fourth company, men of Biscay: 130 places. Fifth company, Asturians: 118 men. Sixth company, Galicians: 120 soldiers. Seventh company of Catalans: 121 men. Eighth company formed of Canary Islanders, Majorcans, Valencians and other provinces of the kingdom: 147 places. The viceroy, accompanied by the Royal Audience, the Municipal Council and important authorities, presided over the march past from a balcony in the palace. The people, in the Plaza Mayor, applauded and acclaimed each company when it saluted the representative of the Crown by lowering its flag. To flatter the viceroy, who was a Catalan, the applause was greater and longer in honour of the Catalan company and its captain, who was none other than Don Antonio de Amat, His Excellency's nephew. An Andalusian gentleman who formed part of the small committee around the viceroy on the balcony, said under his breath to another Andalusian next to him: '*Para insolencia y p . . . Cataluña,* for insolence and whoring, Catalonia.' But Don Manuel had sharp ears. His Catalan blood boiled and, without turning round, he replied to the insolent fellow: 'For boasting, idleness and mendicity, Andalusia.'[3]

So Amat succeeded in forming a corps of militiamen, who, equipped and clothed without having cost the Treasury anything, 'were ready to defend the arms of the king with honour and glory in any invasion or attack that the kingdom might be confronted with', as the chroniclers pompously declared.[4] In reality, Amat, gambling on the prestige of the uniform, had found the means, without spending a penny, of setting up a sort of national guard which soon numbered 5,000 infantrymen and 2,000 cavalrymen. The example of the capital was rapidly followed and regiments of cavalry and armed companies sprang up in towns and provinces hitherto without military forces.

In his *Memoirs,* Amat gives a detailed description of the composition of his armed forces, their number and their uniforms. An infantry regiment of Spanish militiamen, for example, was divided as follows: 10 companies, 30 officers, 26 sergeants, 76 corporals, 566 soldiers. This was the strength of the second battalion: 9 companies, 27 officers, 26 sergeants, 70 corporals, 524 soldiers, i.e. a total of 1,347 men. Each battalion had its own staff, including a colonel, a sergeant-major, adjutants, officers carrying the colours, a chaplain and a surgeon. The uniform consisted of a cloak, tunic and blue breeches with a red band, silver buttons and, for the officers, a broad silver stripe on the cuffs.

The uniforms varied according to the units. That of the Battalion of Commerce was white with a green band and gold buttons. Of course, its owner had paid for it with his own money, and he kept it carefully in his wardrobe between parades. The uniform of the Infantry Regiment of militiamen, 'Natives of Lima', was white with a yellow band and silver buttons and that of the battalions of free mulattos also white, with a black band and gold buttons. White too was the uniform of the free negroes, with a red band and silver buttons—for although they were in the minority, there were also coloured militiamen. All these regiments represented eighty-eight companies, in all 5,251 men, with the exception of the members of the staff who formed a separate cadre and enjoyed the privilege of having a fife-player or trumpeter

---

[3] *Tradiciones peruanas,* p. 602.
[4] *Memoirs of Viceroy Amat,* folio 264 (p. 2).

at their disposal. As for drummers, only the crack regiments had them.

In all the countries of the world, the cavalry is the noble branch of the army. The cavalry regiment of Lima 'and six leagues round about' was called the regiment of the nobility. The staff officers wore a red uniform with a blue tunic, gold buttons and button-hole. Each of the companies of the cavalry regiment had its own uniform: the gentlemen of the lance were clad in blue, with a red band and gold buttons. The fusiliers had a green uniform with a blue tunic and band, and silver buttons. There were other cavalry regiments: the mounted dragoons, the mounted militiamen from the valley of Lurigancho, the mounted dragoons from the valley of Caraballo and the squadron from the valley of Bella Vista. Altogether, 47 militias comprising 170 officers, 86 sergeants, 2 adjutants, 172 corporals, 1,767 soldiers, a total of 2,197 persons, excluding the staffs.

The personnel of the militias were recruited from the wealthy classes. Indeed, to devote oneself to the service of His Majesty, it was necessary to have at one's disposal resources and leisure that were not within everyone's reach. That explains why the soldiers themselves were of 'good family' at least relatively well-to-do. In the same way the few free Indians, negroes and mulattos in the militias were chosen from among the best of their race, descendants of Inca dynasties, caciques or big businessmen. Considerations of the same order were involved when it came to forming the strength of the regular army. The military career was not open to everybody. Candidates of humble origin had little chance of taking it up, or in any case of making a success of it, for promotion more often went by favour than by merit. And sometimes the viceroy's signature at the bottom of a colonel's commission meant recognition of complete political submission and not a good record of service.

The real problem of the military personnel was to be found at the base of the hierarchy, i.e. at troop level. For although officers were not lacking—some corps had too many—there was often a shortage of private soldiers. The other ranks were recruited by means of drawing lots as and when they were needed. But in case of necessity or urgency, the brutal procedure of the levy or *leva* was adopted. In fact, it was a veritable man-hunt, directed against the Indians and the negroes. Everything was used: ropes, chains and *lazos* or lassos. It remained to set the traps. The authorities took care of that. An officer, accompanied by twenty men armed and equipped with everything necessary to master recalcitrants, suddenly appeared at the entrance to a street, blocked the exits and seized the passers-by, who could not escape from this mousetrap. Only those who by their appearance or their clothes seemed to belong to the upper or middle classes were allowed to go on their way. It was not the same for Indians and negroes. Knowing the fate that was in store for them, they tried their hardest to escape from the *leva,* but in vain. So as soon as the cry of *'La leva, la leva'* was heard, they could be seen taking flight, entering the courtyards of houses and seeking refuge on terraces. A large number of them sought asylum which was never refused them in the cellars of the *pulqueros* (dram shops) where they remained in the darkness, cowering behind the barrels and sacks.

Often the *leva* was carried out in the early morning, at the moment when servants were going to the market to do the shopping. Cast in these conditions, the net always made a good catch and masters could whistle for their major-domo. He would be returned to them in a few years' time! The man-hunt sometimes lasted two or three days. It was carried out methodically, district by district, in a town, and street by street, in a village. This levy was particularly painful to the Indian of the *sierra,* accustomed to live in his hut among his own people, in the midst of the vast silence of the Cordillera. It was heartbreaking for him to find himself shut up in the barracks (*cuartel*) where he was the butt of his leaders' brutalities, the mockery of his comrades from the town. If he had brought his rustic flute (his *quena*) with him, it was soon confiscated, for the plaintive notes of the modest reed were so many appeals to desertion. However, the Indian did not desert. He even made an excellent soldier, for he possessed, from the military point of view, valuable qualities. A tireless marcher, remarkably sober, satisfied with a handful of *coca* and a little corn, he was brave and disciplined. And then, to keep his morale up, he had with him his *rabona,* whom the military regulations, this time with singular mildness, allowed him to take with him.

The *rabona* was an Indian woman from the same province as the soldier, his fellow-countrywoman, who accompanied him on his marches and consoled him in his isolation. It would be inacur-ate to say that the *rabona* was always the legitimate wife of the soldier. On the contrary, it frequently happened that the Indian left his wife in his hut and set out for the regiment with a *rabona* taken from his village. During the marches, the *rabona* stayed in the rear-guard and carried on her back all their household goods, their clothes, their mattress, their children if they had any and almost always a dog to which she showed the most tender affection. Undoubtedly because dogs were supposed to have the property of curing certain fevers solely by bodily contact with the patient. Sometimes, the *rabona* carried most of the soldier's equipment, in addition to their baggage.

When the company was on the point of arriving at its destination and as soon as the last day's march began, the women separated from the troops, went ahead and prepared the soldiers' dinner and bedding. Like locusts, they invaded the place where the troops were to camp, forced their way into houses, made a clean sweep of what they found and turned the village upside down. Once she had arranged her soldier's billet in her own fashion, she lavished attention on him. She made his bed, did the cooking, washed his clothes and even washed him, not forgetting to delouse him carefully. I should add that she never left him, even on the battlefield, not hesitating to risk her own life to protect her soldier's, to look after him if he were wounded and bury him if he succumbed to his wounds. The only fault the *rabona* had was jealousy. Absolutely faithful to her soldier, she would not accept being supplanted by another *rabona*. So brawls between rivals were frequent. But the soldier concerned took good care not to intervene in these feminine contests, not even to separate the combatants. He was too afraid that they might turn their wrath on him. When they were tired of the battle, each solder pulled his *rabona* gently by the arm, took her away with him, dried her tears and tenderly plaited her long hair which was somewhat dishevelled by the struggle. Then they drank a big bowl of *chicha* together and the *rabona* and her soldier were reconciled.

The Memoirs of Viceroy Amat[5] give a detailed description of the armaments and munitions the 'Forces of the Kingdom' had at their disposal. It was an incongruous mixture to judge by some of the headings figuring in a list of war material put into the military storehouses at Lima on August 31, 1775: 12,026 'old and new' guns, 59 blunderbusses of various kinds, 9,654 cartridges 'with bullets', 28 'useless (*sic*) gun and carbine barrels, 671 old arquebuses, 6,686

[5] *Memoirs of Viceroy Amat.* Part IV, chapter 3, pp. 732–748.

swords of different kinds, 764 'useless' (*sic*) *machetes* and knives, 6 iron bars, 16 coats of mail 'with pieces missing', 8 'useless' (*sic*) iron axes, 70 old tools and 18 'useless' (*sic*) halberds. So the viceroyalty possessed armaments that were varied rather than effective and the majority of which were considered as 'useless' and kept as museum pieces. If we continue our inspection of the military arsenals in Amat's time, we come across much the same types of arms, plus some composite material, mainly for the artillery: sacks of grape-shot, iron and bronze cannonballs, grenades, 'chain-shot', mauls, cannon, wad-extractors, gun-sponges, linstocks, lanterns of all kinds, levers, suspension hooks, kegs of cartridges, poles, mortars, benches and planks for drying powder. So it seems that the viceroyalty disposed of armaments that were perhaps adequate in quantity, but very antiquated and of mediocre quality, if we compare them with those which were in use at the same period in European armies, particularly those of France and Prussia. Powder alone was not in short supply, for on September 3, 1768, Amat had concluded a commercial contract for four years with a 'mill master' to supply 50,000 pounds of powder during the first year and 80,000 during the following years. 'Powder and bullets.' There was no doubt that they would be more effective against the English and the Portuguese than *machetes* and bronze sledgehammers, even though the Indians performed wonders with them.

If the infantry were the shock troops and the cavalry the noble branch of the army, then the artillery represented the learned branch. It was almost entirely concentrated in the port of Callao and along the neighbouring coast. Indeed, it was the viceroyalty's vulnerable point. The authorities had not forgotten the attack in 1624 by the Dutch pirate, Jacques Ermite, who had very nearly succeeded in landing at the head of eleven ships and 1,600 men. Thanks to the composure of the then viceroy, the Marquis of Guadalcazar, who was warned in time, the pirate had weighed anchor after a short combat. Instructed by this precedent, Amat had turned his efforts to the defence of the coast and artillery was its main feature. Six ramps had been installed to place cannon on. 600 kegs of powder were stored inside each of these bastions, which were proof against bullets. Above the port rose two towers, serving both as watchposts and defence works, each containing twenty-four cannon, a reserve of powder and a small garrison. In addition, certain constructive words, including the impressive fort Real Felipe, made Calloa one of the best fortified towns in Spanish America. One gets an idea of the artillery material, considerable for the period, installed at Callao from consulting the list of the 'iron and bronze artillery . . . in the charge of Captain Don Pedro Antonio Bracho in the square of Callao at the end of December, 1775'. 109 bronze cannon, 7 bronze mortars, 760 essential spare parts for mortars, 100 iron cannon, 294 gun-carriages for cannon, 4 limbers, 66,239 shells with fuses, 10,188 case-shot cartridges and 1,200 cannon-balls. In the list of munitions the following objects stand out: pikes, iron keys, small 'Flemish' knives, hammers, bull's-eye lanterns, priming horns, primers and shell scrapers. It contains not only an exact statement of arms and munitions, but also their cost. For the notion of 'cost price' was inseparable from military accounting. For example: the cost price of a charge of grape-shot in terms of its calibre and taking into account the following elements: pounds of powder, price of powder, forge, leather and accessories, making, wad and fuse, iron bars, cost of iron and total cost. So we see that a charge of grape-shot of 24-mm calibre came to exactly 13 pesos, $1\frac{1}{2}$ reales.[6]

The attention paid by the viceroyalty to the land arms—infantry, cavalry and artillery—did not make it neglect the navy, whose role was of capital importance. Indeed, the fleet had always to be ready to face the greatest danger, that of an invasion from the sea. On the whole, the viceregal fleet consisted of three types of ships: the men of war with sixty-four cannon, the frigates with twenty-six cannon and those with twenty-two cannon. In addition, the fairway of Callao was under the permanent guard of a vessel called the *Astuto*, the Wily One, which had on board 150 cannon, 1,500 guns and as many bayonets. The crew of a man of war with sixty-four cannon was large. The staff consisted of a post captain, a commander, three lieutenants and five sub-lieutenants. A purser controlled the provisions and, assisted by the 'victualling master', commanded the 'water *alguazil*', the 'storekeeper', the cooper, the cook and the galley boy. The naval artillerymen included a chief artificer, a corporal in chief, a corporal, a bombardier and seventy-seven artillerymen. The navigation was in the hands of a pilot, two assistant pilots and an apprentice. Four carpenters, three petty officers, four caulkers, a sailmaker and a petty officer in charge of lights saw to the ship being kept in good trim. Two surgeons

[6] *Memoirs of Viceroy Amat*, p. 762.

attended to the sick and wounded. A barber shaved and bled the crew. Fifteen drummers and fife-players played for parade. Two chaplains heard confessions. 2 marines, 7 adjutants, 6 sergeants, 2 coxswains, 96 soldiers, 2 look-outs, 1 armourer, 98 sailors, 110 ship's boys and 20 pages completed the crew. The pay was not very high, since the post captain earned 150 pesos a month and his assistant 100 pesos, about 110 and 70 pounds a month. It is true that the former was entitled to six servants. The purser received 50 pounds, the surgeon 25—less than the senior pilot, who got 40 pounds. An ordinary seaman was paid about 8 pounds 15 shillings and a page rather less than 4 pounds. Thus, on the whole, naval personnel were badly paid. It should be pointed out that at sea their expenses were nil.[7]

So a man of war had 479 officers and men on board. As for the 26- and 22-gun frigates, they carried 267 and 231 respectively. The maintenance—pay and victualling—of the total crew of a man of war and two frigates, 977 in all, cost the Treasury of the viceroyalty an annual sum of 241,384 pesos, or about 174,660 pounds sterling. This figure, of course, only applied to expenses relating to the personnel, excluding general expenditure (munitions, amortization of material, etc.).

There are two conclusions to be drawn from these particulars of military life in the time of la Perricholi. First of all, the relatively vulnerable character of the Peruvian coast meant that it was both a duty and a necessity for the viceroys to maintain an army in a permanent state of alert. So that every subject of the viceroy, whatever his colour or social standing, was permanently liable to be called up. No one escaped this liability to military service, from the son of a president of the audience to the Indian of the *sierra* sought out in his mountain village on the occasion of a *leva*. However, we must distinguish between the soldier who was conscripted and brought to the barracks with his wrists bound, and the 'enlisted' soldier, i.e. the regular officer, non-commissioned officer and private soldier, incorporated into a permanent formation. For them, service in the army was a career. A career that was highly prized, incidentally, less for its rather modest material advantages than for the esteem attached to it. In Peru, as in other parts of the world in all ages, the prestige of the uniform compensated for the low pay.

[7] *Memoirs of Viceroy Amat*, p. 788.

However, it must be admitted that the prestige attached to soldiers by no means meant that the army was admired unreservedly. Its weaknesses and gaps were known to everybody. To be sure, the navy, well equipped and fitted out with a good fleet, manned by experienced personnel, played its role as protective shield of the Peruvian coasts very well. But the army, owing to its lack of manpower and the frequently mediocre quality of its officering, by no means lived up to the viceroy's ambitions. As proof—the virtues of an army being measured by the victories won—people quote the lack of success of the few military undertakings under the government of Amat, such as those against the Portuguese, who had occupied the gold mines of the Matto Grosso. But the viceroy undoubtedly felt that his expeditions had not been complete failures, for they had made it possible to explore unknown territories and to open up new ways to the Atlantic coast. Which was true, incidentally.

THE CHURCH

Pereyra's remark about Manuel Amat comes to mind again: 'The viceroy militarized the country and expelled the Jesuits.' We have just seen how Peru was militarized. What was the situation from the religious point of view?

Although he was not an unbeliever, Amat was not noted for his piety. However, he was present at all the religious ceremonies at which his presence was required in his capacities of first magistrate of Peru and representative of the King of Spain. But the scandal-mongers in Lima society would undoubtedly have been more indulgent about his private life if he had shown his repentance by practical manifestations of his faith.

The royal orders decreeing the expulsion of the Jesuits reached Lima on August 20, 1767, accompanied by the famous letter from the Count of Aranda and secret instructions. Amat himself said: 'The expulsion of the Jesuits was one of the most arduous events in my government.' He had the houses of the Jesuits occupied in great secrecy during the night of the 9th September. A few days later, the members of the Company of Jesus embarked at Callao or the southern ports. The operation had been carried out with severity and speed.

Amat's attitude to the Church echoed that of 'enlightened' Spain.

He did not deny its utility, knew perfectly well how to make use of it and even judged it indispensable in many fields, especially that of education, but he intended it to remain entirely subordinate to the temporal power, at least as far as its public activities were concerned.

'In the Church, there are two jurisdictions: one spiritual, deriving from the religion observed during the early centuries by its ministers . . . the other temporal, which the zeal and love of emperors and kings for the exaltation of the veritable divine cult have communicated to it, showering it with exceptions, immunities and privileges, in order to facilitate the exercise of its sacred ministry . . . but these privileges comprise and have comprised certain limits.' And he added that the Church cannot exceed these limits 'prescribed by the liberality of princes'.[8]

In short, in this territory of the Crown where religion formed one of the principal means of governing the Indians, there could be no question of suppressing the traditional privileges of the Church, but the viceroyalty had a tendency to restrain their practical application. Take this example referring to the right of asylum in holy places. 'The piety is highly to be recommended and the delinquents should be treated with consideration, but there are excesses which it would be impiety not to correct.'[9] Thus priests were 'recommended' to hand over to the Law common-law criminals who took refuge in churches. The same held good of the personal immunity which members of the clergy enjoyed. There were cases when it had to be lifted. Immunity did not mean impunity. The result was that the viceroy of Peru, in his capacity of representative of the king, exercised over the Church both the authority of *Patrón y Delegado* (Patron and Delegate) of the Holy See and that of *Real Patronato* or right of patronage. This was equivalent to saying that nothing could be done in the ecclesiastical domain without the viceroy's authorization, including the foundations of churches, parishes and pious establishments. In the same way, his approval was needed for all appointments to ecclesiastical posts of the creation of dignities, canonries and prebendaries. The secular clergy were less numerous than the 'anti-clerical' chroniclers of the period asserted. Let us look, for example, at the parochial

[8] *Memoirs of Viceroy Amat*, p. 7.
[9] *Ibidem*, p. 13.

organization of Lima. The town of Lima included eight parishes: the first was the cathedral, in which there were four parish-priests and two curates, contrary to canon law which only prescribed one parish-priest per church, 'because a body should not have more than one head'. The second was that of St Anne, which had two parish-priests and one curate. The third, St Sebastian, also had two. The fourth, St Marcellus, had one parish-priest. The fifth, St Lazarus, had a parish-priest-cum-curate from the cathedral. The sixth, Nuestra Señora de Antocha, an annex to the cathedral and dependent on it, also bore the name of *Los Huérfanos* (The Orphans). A parish-priest was at its head. The seventh was the Cercado, parish of an Indian suburb, in charge of a parish-priest. The eighth, established only a few years, was called San Salvador or St Saviour. A parish-priest was in charge of it.[10]

LIFE IN THE MONASTERIES AND CONVENTS

The right of patronage (*patronato real*) which the viceroy held was exercised not only over the regular clergy, but also over the secular clergy. And Viceroy Amat never failed to emphasize that the 'monasteries and convents of monks and nuns founded within the domains of His Majesty could never free themselves of the character of vassals forming part of the Body Politic'.[11] And in greater detail he added: 'As the monks must be useful to the State, which is the justification for their establishments, it is part of the viceroys' functions to render an account of the monks who are in their territory.' So the Church owed allegiance to the viceroyalty, which did more than merely control religious questions, it did not hesitate to settle them, if necessary. It even had to intervene in connection with the reform of certain monasteries where the monastic rule had relaxed until it was no more than a memory. Further on we shall see that these interventions by the civil authority were largely justified.

It goes without saying that the Church's subjection to the civil government infuriated the clergy. So they never missed an opportunity of checking the viceroy's authority, either openly or, more often, by clandestine threats. When Amat tried to expropriate certain monasteries and sell their lands so as to make new roads

---

10 FRÉZIER: vol. II, p. 395.
11 *Memoirs of Viceroy Amat*, p. 86.

through them, he had to give up the idea in the face of the vehement protests of the clergy, who were only too happy to find a valid excuse for rebelling publicly against their master, who was too inclined to sacrifice religion on the altar of town-planning.

The viceroyalty kept an accurate account of men and women's religious establishments. It is interesting to refer to it if we wish to have a correct idea of the importance of the religious world within the viceroyalty.

In 1775, there were nineteen monasteries at Lima, comprising 1,306 persons, including 639 priests, 251 novices and 416 lay brothers, distributed as follows:

	priests	novices	lay brothers
4 monasteries of St Dominic	182	55	54
3 monasteries of St Francis of Assisi	157	58	123
3 monasteries of St Augustine	109	63	45
3 monasteries of la Merced	144	37	47
1 monastery of St Francis of Paola	10	8	10
2 monasteries of St Camillus	32	5	26
1 monastery of St John of God	4	5	55
2 monasteries of Bethlehemites	1	20	46

Women's convents, in the town of Lima alone, numbered 14, containing 822 persons, distributed as follows:

	professed nuns	novices	lay sisters
Incarnation	57	6	39
Conception	81	3	59
St Catherine	49	6	25
St Clare	74	7	46
Discalced	35	3	16
Reformed Cistercians	41	3	26
Upper Carmel	20		
Lower Carmel	20		
Daughters of Nazareth	33	1	
St Rose	37	4	
Capuchins	32		
Daughters of la Merced	27		
Redemptionists	36		
Daughters of the Prado	34		

Daily life in the religious monasteries varied according to the order. Some were stricter than others. This was also true of the women's communities, which ranged from the 'nun in the world' to the purely contemplative. Let us see how they lived, for example, in a 'fashionable' convent such as that of the daughters of the Prado. The conventual rule did not allow the nuns to leave the convent where they had made their vows, under any pretext. A dispensation from the bishop was required before a doctor could treat them in case of illness. The gardener was the only male whose presence was permitted inside the cloister. But a gardener was not a man. Thus sequestered behind thick walls, the nuns, whom one might imagine limited to prayer, tears and mortification of the flesh, led a pleasant enough existence. Their cells were small, but pretty. They put tapestries in them and furniture commensurate with the wealth of their families, who paid for them. Each nun had her library, her own birds, her guitar and her little garden planted with rare flowers. Better still, each of them had a bosom friend, an adopted sister, who shared her secret troubles and received her confidences.

This friendship, which blossomed under the shadow of the chapel, sometimes assumed a passionate character. Nuns exchanged tender missives, eternal vows, bouquets of flowers and serenades. Innocent idylls, often broken by a terrible scandal—a smile bestowed on a rival! Perhaps without fully realizing it, the recluses played at the profane love which they had renounced.

Although the nuns of the Prado were forbidden to go out of the convent, they were allowed to receive there and even invite to dinner their parents and their parents' friends. The meals were served in the parlour, a large vaulted room with grilles let into the walls. The table was close enough to one of these grilles for the nun, seated on the other side of it, to be able to see her guests and converse with them. The conversation generally concerned the latest bits of gossip from the city. They ran the gamut of loves, marriages, births and deaths. This pleasant gossiping was interrupted by bursts of laughter and epigrams. The men, when there were any at the party, did not fail to season their jokes with coarse allusions. One might have thought oneself in some drawing-room, in the midst of one of the liveliest *tertulias*, except that guests and hostess were separated.

Sometimes the family invited a foreigner to one of these

conventual, but succulent meals. After the conventional compliments, the nun very soon enquired with interest about his fatherland and the parents who gave him birth. For she preserved a lively curiosity about the things of this world.

So, thanks to the troop of alert and knowing *cholas* which every nun maintained at her own expense in the capacity of domestic servants, kitchen boys and bank-messengers, and who walked the streets from morning to night, she knew what went on in the town and suburbs better than the inhabitants themselves. One could say of the living tomb in which Peruvian nuns buried themselves alive that its lid was left fairly wide open to the world.[12]

THE INQUISITION

The progressive taking in hand of religious affairs by the viceroyalty had had a salutary effect. By restraining the Church's autocratic tendencies, it had done it a very good turn. Nor was it a bad thing that the part it played in certain weighty proceedings, such as those of the Inquisition, was clearly defined.

In his *Memoirs* Viceroy Amat gives precise details of the Church's competence in this particular field. For example, common law crimes, especially bigamy, offences against honour and morality, no longer came under the tribunal of the Inquisition, which was to deal solely with 'sins against the Faith', i.e. cases of heresy and apostasy. This marked a singular and most auspicious restriction on the competence of this jurisdiction, which had long been far too inclined to encroach upon the judicial territory.

So the Inquisition still existed in Peru during Amat's viceroyalty. It was abolished in 1811, but even before then it had become much milder. The sentences it passed affected the guilty parties morally, but never called for the death penalty, and rarely for loss of liberty. And if the lack of faith was accompanied by some ordinary crime, the guilty parties were brought before the secular authorities. Admittedly, everybody was still amenable to the jurisdiction of the Inquisition, even the most highly-placed officials and the viceroy. But the powers of the Inquisitors were very theoretical with regard to the latter. The story is told that one day Viceroy Castelforte was accused and sent for by the Inquisition. He appeared before the tribunal, followed by his bodyguard, a company

[12] Paul MARCOY: *Voyage de l'océan Atlantique à l'océan Pacifique*, p. 104.

of infantry and two pieces of artillery, which he had trained on the gate of the prison. He entered, put his watch on the table and made it clear to the Inquisitors that if the affair was not rushed through within an hour, the house would be destroyed from top to bottom, for that was the order he had left with the commanding officer of the detachment. This threat was enough. The Inquisitors hastily left their seats and politely accompanied the viceroy to the door, 'only too happy when they saw the claws of His Excellency and his formidable escort'.

In other words, times had changed. There was no more torture. There was no more burning at the stake. The last person put to death was a woman called Castro, a native of Toledo. Before her and since the introduction of the Inquisition into Peru in 1570, forty individuals had been burnt at Lima, 120 of the condemned escaping the extreme penalty by a solemn recantation. Comparing this figure with the number of victims of the Inquisition in Spain, one would be tempted to write that this was scarcely one sacrifice every five years! In fact, the condemned were heretics, magicians and maniacs. A convenient way of ridding society of them!

Although torture had stopped, punishments continued, commensurate with the gravity of the offence committed and the delinquent's social position. These punishments, in addition to the canonical penalties and the humiliation of publicly confessing one's sins, generally consisted in being forced to wait on the sick in a hospital for a specified period of time—a sort of social service —or spending a few weeks in prison. Curious details about the Inquisition's famous prison are to be found in the works of the English writer Stevenson. Stevenson had arrived in Lima during the viceroyalty of Abascal, shortly before he received the act of the Spanish Cortès abolishing the Inquisition in the metropolis and overseas possessions. During his stay, the English traveller saw two individuals publicly punished by the Inquisition, one for having celebrated mass without having been ordained, the other for prophesying and practising sorcery. After serving their sentence —a few months in prison—they were condemned to serve in the hospitals 'for as long as it pleased the Holy Office'. Stevenson himself was called before the Inquisition for having quarrelled with a Dominican. Duly admonished by those gentlemen, he harboured bitter resentment against them. As soon as the decree abolishing the Inquisition reached Lima, he asked for and obtained permission to visit the prison, henceforth put to another use, in the company of some friends.

Stevenson describes the torture room with a great wealth of detail. In the middle there was a table eight feet long by seven feet wide; at each end an iron collar, opening in the middle, was intended to hold the victim's neck. On either side of the collar strong straps fitted with buckles held the arms along the body; on the sides of the table, more straps, also fitted with buckles, held the wrists. These fastenings corresponded to cords placed beneath the table and secured on the axis of a horizontal windlass; at the other end there were bonds for the feet with cords also attached to the windlass. 'It was obvious that it was possible to lay a man out on the table and, by turning the wheel, pull his limbs in all directions without fear of killing him, but with the certainty of dislocating all the joints.' Each new discovery drew a cry of indignation from him. A vertical pillory, placed against the wall, comprised one large and two smaller openings, with the help of which a condemned man, with his neck and wrists fixed in the holes of the pillory, his head and hands hidden in the wall, could be whipped without being recognized by the executioners. Whips of different kinds hung on the wall, some with knotted lashes, others of wire. Then there was a certain torture tunic, made of plaited wire. Each piece of mail was armed with points 'about one eighth of an inch long' and turned inwards. The outside was fitted with leather thongs for attaching the tunic round the victim's chest. Then there were the pincers for immobilizing the tongue, the thumb-screws for crushing the nails and cartilages—nothing was lacking for extorting a confession from the prisoners of the Inquisition. And Stevenson concluded his account as follows:

'After having visited all the nooks and corners of this mysterious prison, we withdrew towards evening, taking with us books, papers, whips, instruments of torture, etc. Several of these objects were distributed at the door. The next day, the archbishop summoned the faithful to the cathedral and declared excommunicated everyone who had taken and kept in his possession any object that had belonged to the ex-tribunal of the Inquisition. Frightened by this anathema, several of the looters returned what they had taken. As for me, I kept what had fallen into my hands, in spite of the infernal flames with which the holy archbishop had threatened us.'

This lugubrious account cannot be accepted in its entirety. We must not forget that Stevenson was English and Protestant, and so doubly inclined to denigrate systematically things Spanish and Catholic. So we can only give a limited credence to his assertions. Besides, on his own admission, the instruments of torture he described in such detail were rusted, twisted and had obviously been out of use for a long time. As for the cells, Stevenson himself admitted that some of them were very clean, sometimes preceded by a little garden, and that in any case their appearance suggested that they had not been occupied for many years.

Was it the progressive liquidation of the Inquisition or 'liberal' propaganda that was penetrating insidiously into every sphere? The religious spirit, or at least genuine piety, was declining. True, large crowds followed the processions, people recited the rosary and sang hymns. The 'zealots'—mainly Indians and negroes —assembled in confraternities, called *hermandades*. These *hermandades,* which had once existed in very great numbers and of which the main two were the brotherhoods of Our Lady of the Rosary and Our Lady of Carmel, were still important and all had a large membership. Violent disputes continued to keep the *hermandades* at loggerheads with each other, especially when it came to celebrating the cult of Our Lady of the Rosary. Thus there was one *Nuestra Señora del Rosario* for the whites, a second for the negroes, a third for the mulattos and a fourth for the Indians. Each *hermandad* was anxious that its Virgin should be distinguished from that of the others by the richness of its vestments on days when it was carried in procession and bloody brawls frequently broke out between the members of the various rival confraternities.

Devotion still had its fervent adepts in the person of the *beatas,* that is to say the category of women who were so to speak enrolled in the confraternities of the town. We should call them bigots. Their costume invariably consisted of a straight dress and a *manta* firmly held in by a broad patent leather belt. The details of the costume varied according to the brotherhood of which the *beata* was a member, or the religious order to which she was affiliated, while remaining a laywoman. At Lima some *beatas* were dressed in white, others in black, others in grey, others in violet and some in brown. Lastly, there were some, though not many, whose robe and *manta* were made of the coarse cloth of the discalced brothers. It was these shrill, fanatical women who accompanied the processions, burnt incense and bawled out the hymns. There were many of them and they came from all classes of society, but mainly from the women of the people.

However, religious fervour was no longer what it had been in the past. The rivalry of the *hermandades* and the noisy exhibitions of the *beatas* belonged to the theatre rather than the faith. People prayed less and there were many compromises with Heaven, as Frézier remarked in connection with fasting: 'Abstinence from meat is considerably alleviated by the use of *grosura*, which consists of the tongues, heads, entrails, feet and extremities of animals eaten on fast days, not to mention the use of *manteca* (lard or beef fat), butter and oil.' Lenten dispensations were more and more common, and on pretexts that were less and less valid. Yes, times had changed.

RELIGIOUS COSTUME

This did not mean that the number of nuns had diminished. Far from it. To be convinced of this, it was only necessary to stroll along the Alameda on any Sunday in Lima. That was also the best place for seeing the great variety of religious clothing, from the richest to the humblest. Let us begin with the richest and finish with the humblest. In fact, ecclesiastical costume was outstanding for its variety and luxury. Although the bishops in Peru, for example, wore more or less the same costume as in the Catholic countries of Europe, they used it differently. Thus, whereas in Europe bishops wore discreet and sober garments in the street, at Lima, on the contrary, they made themselves conspicuous by the luxury of their attire. As the bishops frequented the capital, which they preferred to their episcopal residences for more than one reason, they could be seen walking down the Alameda in a surplice of delicate lace, a cape of violet silk, with a flashing pectoral cross, in other words, in the costume which bishops in the Catholic countries of Europe only wear to take part in the ceremonies of the Church. They wore on their heads an enormous hat, like the one worn by Basile in *The Barber of Seville*. Its brim, turned up and attached to the top of the crown by gold braids, was lined with very pale green satin, which contrasted with the violet of the cassock and the surplice. They were escorted by several ecclesiastics and followed at a short distance by one or two lackeys wearing livery.

The costume worn by canons was also rather striking. They wore a black cassock with a satin front. The buckles of their shoes and garters were of silver, their very large hat—rather like the bishops —with turned-up brim, which gave it a narrow, elongated shape, looked like a felucca. It was called a *teja*. A long twisted cord, with black silk tassels, worn only by doctors of theology, hung down on their shoulders. They wrapped themselves in a full mantle (*capa*), lined with black satin in summer and velvet in winter, which kept them in a constant perspiration in a country where the coldest day of the year has a temperature of 82·4°F and the hottest day 89·6°F. In the cathedral the canons wore the costume of bishops, violet cassock, lace surplice and an enormous collarette, also of lace, covering the upper part of the cassock.

The other ecclesiastics wore the Roman hat and a less elaborate mantle. They had neither the satin robe nor the silver buckles. Their bands were replaced by a collar embroidered with blue and white pearls. The costume of the seminarists was picturesque. Their full black and 'Carmelite-coloured' (i.e. brown) vestment capriciously draped, the embroidery on the left side of their cassock and the scalloped cap in the form of a ducal crown which adorned their heads, gave them a distinguished air.

Such were the main costumes of the secular clergy. Those of the regular clergy were in no way inferior as regards variety. The Dominicans also wore a black and white costume. They wore the same hat as the Fathers of Mercy and sometimes a lace cap with a very elevated shape, a sort of Persian tiara, which they generally reserved for wear inside the monastery. The Augustines were more modestly clad. They usually had two costumes, one black, the other grey, but not cloaks, like the two preceding orders. Their robe had wide sleeves and a hood. A strap knotted round their waist fell to their feet. The Franciscans were dressed in a dark blue robe held in at the waist by a white knotted cord, which fell to the ground. The Order of Discalced Brothers (*los descalzos*) was the strictest of all the monastic orders in Peru. Consequently, scandal, always so quick to seek a victim, came to grief at the door of their community. Their wretched clothing exemplified their vocation.

As their name implies, they walked about barefoot, save for sandals. Their very full robe was made of coarsely woven grey cloth, the very sight of which aroused gloomy thoughts, for it was the *mortaja* in which the dead were clothed before being laid out and put on the bier. These monks wore nothing else on their bodies but this sinister robe. They were buried in it. So they never left it, unless it had become so worn and dilapidated that they had to change it. They had a big cloak falling to the ground, with a hood which they pulled over their heads in winter. In summer they wore straw hats. The Order of the Discalced Brothers was very popular with the inhabitants of Lima, who professed a great and legitimate veneration for these monks. Devoted to the point of complete self-denial, these monks went from door to door soliciting alms for the poor of the capital and every day distributed food to the hundreds of beggars who came to ring the bell of their monastery and were never sent away. They were veritable apostles who enjoyed immense popularity at Lima. When they passed, women knelt down before them, asking their blessing and kissing their hands devoutly. Men greeted them with respect.

Lastly, the Brothers of the Good Death had a costume which was more like that of the secular clergy. They wore a black cassock, on the front of which was sewn a large red woollen cross. They had a black cloak and on its left side appeared a second scarlet cross like the first one. Their hat was of black felt with silk tassels which fell down to their shoulders. As the name of their community indicates, their ministry consisted in assisting the dying. The services they performed for the community were many. So they were respected, popular, and deserved to be.

Such were the different types of clergymen who could be seen passing down the Alameda. Some—bishops on a visit, canons, seminarists—were going to the cathedral or some *tertulia*. Others —Brothers of the Good Death or discalced monks—were going to a sick man's bedside or asking for alms. The contrast between the silk cassock and the *mortaja* emphasized eloquently that sincere piety was increasingly rare, the senior secular clergy less and less evangelical, but that charity was still active and that when all was said and done it was really from the regular orders and not the administration that the poor, the unfortunate and the sick received bread, consolation and care.

THE UNIVERSITY AND COLLEGES

The viceroyalty was very proud of its educational system. 'By this means, religion asserts its dogmas and the civil and political government its best maxims,' noted Amat in his *Memoirs*,[13] thus emphasizing once again that religion was a State affair. But it did not seem that the practical achievements of the viceroys matched their ambitions.

The university—the only one—of Lima comprised chairs of philosophy, theology, law, medicine, mathematics and languages. The last-named chair was singled out for special preference by the viceroyalty. In fact, it was essential that the Indians should be instructed in the Spanish language. That was why a body of itinerant teachers had been sent to the most remote villages to teach the tribal Indians Spanish. On a higher level, there was at Cuzco a college for 'noble Indians' called St Borgia where the sons of the great native families received the education which gave them access to the highest posts in the viceroyalty. Spanish was the compulsory language for everybody and the use of Indian dialects had long been forbidden both in education and public administration. It was theoretically forbidden to 'speak Indian', which did not stop families in the rural communities remaining faithful to the language of their fathers.

So there was only one university in Peru, the University of San Marcos. It was the oldest in the Americas. Founded by an imperial *cédula* of Charles the Fifth, dated May 12, 1551, it enjoyed the same privileges and the same statutes as the University of Salamanca. At first installed in a building belonging to a Dominican church, San Marcelo, it was transferred to the Square of the Holy Office of the Inquisition under Viceroy Toledo, its protector, who laicized it.

It must be admitted that during the colonial period the university was the seat of pedantry and quibbling dialectic. But on the eve of the Revolution it became a centre of political agitation which the government did not succeed in pacifying. Three rectors were famous at that time. Baquijano y Carrillo fought against 'colonial servility' and the 'despotism of Madrid'. Rodriguez de Mendoza secretly spread the ideas of the encyclopaedists and fostered the

[13] *Memoirs of Viceroy Amat*, p. 123.

revolutionary spirit. Bartolomé Herrera tried to educate the new Republic and hold anarchy in check.

In the time of la Perricholi, although it had been secularized by the viceroy, the University of San Marcos remained 'confessional'. The Dominicans retained many privileges in it. All the religious orders were provided with special chairs. In addition, three royal colleges were attached to the university. The colleges of San Felipe, San Martin and San Toribio, which was under the direction of the diocesan seminary. The other colleges were considered to be on a lower level. They were the Augustinian college of San Ildefonso, the Jesuit college of San Pablo and the Franciscan college of San Buenaventura. Theology was naturally the principal faculty and the best endowed with chairs. Then came the faculty of canon law and Roman law, the worst endowed being those of mathematics and medicine.

Following the customs of all the great universities of Spain, the conferring of doctors' degrees was accompanied by a great deal of solemn show at the University of San Marcos. The scholar, who had successfully withstood the ordeal of the examination, began by placing his coat of arms topped by a canopy over the door of his house. Then, the day before the ceremony, he walked through the streets of the town, preceded by a band of kettledrums, trumpets and flutes. At the head of the procession floated the standard of the royal school, surrounded by lackeys and pages in livery. Then came the rector and all the masters and doctors, wearing their gowns and insignia and accompanied by a crowd of people on horseback. On the day fixed for handing over the diploma, the jury marched solemnly from the house of the future doctor to the cathedral. A dais was erected in the chapel of the Virgin of Antigua, decorated for the occasion with tapestries, hangings and silver vases. On it sat the president examining the thesis, who put a question in Latin to the candidate. The latter, standing in the midst of the assembly, answered, also in Latin. As a comical interlude, a student then read a humorous speech called a *vejamen*. Then the candidate knelt and made the profession of the Catholic faith in conformity with the Council of Trent and swore obedience and fealty to the king of Spain, his representative the viceroy, the rector and the university regulations. When that was done, the dean of the chapter, who was also the chancellor of the university, handed over his diploma, while his 'patron of the thesis' gave him the kiss of peace, put a ring on his finger, girded him with a sword and put gold spurs on his shoes, according to the rites of chivalry. The new doctor then bestowed the accolade on the rector and the members of the jury among whom he now took his seat. After a collection had been made among those present, the procession returned to the house of the new holder of the doctorate, who offered them a great banquet. The same evening, the procession returned to the Plaza Mayor to watch the bullfight which traditionally put an end to the rejoicings.[14]

There was another rather exceptional university manifestation: the reception of the viceroy shortly after his assumption of office and his solemn entry into the city. On that day, the university presented its homage to His Excellency in person, accompanied by all the official personages. He listened to the obligatory academic eulogy of his greatness and his virtues, then he distributed the prizes for the poetry competition that had been organized in his honour. The doctors laid at his feet a profusion of praises in which the respect due to the delegate of His Majesty assumed in turn the subtle forms of Gongorism and the pompous ostentation of the dithyramb. There is no doubt that more rhetorical affectation than self-seeking adulation entered into this laudatory concert. However, the panegyrical enthusiasts and versifying maniacs could not resist the temptation to overdo it, embroidering on the theme with the austere application of men performing a sacred duty and the fervour of the virtuoso executing brilliant arpeggios. Even strong personalities like Don Pedro Peralba lost all critical sense and could write sentences like this: 'The prince is a visible deity to whom our words can only be a hymn or a prayer . . .'

However, it should be emphasized that, within this frivolous town, in the heart of this university that was perhaps over-inclined to flatter authority, there reigned great application to study and a definite love of knowledge—knowledge that was still rudimentary, erudition that was heavy, but knowledge and erudition for all that.[15] Moreover, because of its receptions, its feasts and its theatrical performances, the university had become as it were the academy of the court of the viceroys. Lima was not the most important university town in the Spanish American Empire. It

---

[14] Raul PORRAS BARRANECHEA: *Pequeña antología de Lima* (according to José de la Riva Agüero), p. 170.

[15] *Ibidem*, p. 172.

came a long way behind Mexico and Cordoba—in the Rio de la Plata. But it had made itself a reputation as an intellectual capital, owing to the literary talents of its masters and their disciples. Among the teaching staff, from the loftiest professors and the wisest doctors to the starving *bachilleres de pupilos* (the ushers) and the multitude of 1,500 students who attended the courses, there were many who tried to attract the beneficent attention of the viceroy and the highly-placed authorities by their compliments. If one remembers the homilies written by men engaged in higher education or the obsequious tone of many administrative reports, one is pretty soon convinced that it was necessary to curry favour if one wanted to become a personage of high rank or simply obtain a *cátedra*.

Life in the colleges was freer and less subject to the caprices and wishes of the authorities. Many piquant anecdotes testify to this. Here is one about the College of San Carlos, related by Ricardo Palma.

During the rectorate of Don Torribio Rodriguez de Mendoza, a shoemaker called Halicarnaso had installed himself in a little shop built against the main door of the college. Halicarnaso was a friend of the students. In his back-shop, he kept the three-cornered hats and *comepavos*, vulgarly called dress-coats, which formed the college uniform in which on Sundays the pupils walked as far as the *portería* (the porter's lodge) and which they rapidly took off as soon as they were through the door to put on round hats and frock-coats, thanks to which they could pass unperceived and go on their escapades without being recognized.

During the recreation breaks, the shoemaker was entitled to enter the courtyards of the 'orange-trees', the 'jasmines' and the 'small boys'. Our man spent his leisure hours in the day-boys' courtyard, trying to learn a few Latin verses by heart or to solve two or three mathematical problems. Halicarnaso adored the students and was always willing to do their errands. The presence of Halicarnaso was indispensable at the processions and official feasts in which the pupils of the college took part with their rector and their teachers wearing the big blue ribbon, the supreme goal of their aspirations. The *tapadas* of the parishes of the Sagrario, San Sebastian and San Marcelo kept up a running fire of witticisms and compliments with the *carolinos*, while those of Santa Ana and San Lazaro militated under the banner of the *fernandinos*.

The collegians studied throughout the week. So it was quite natural that on Sunday they enjoyed themselves to the full. Purely as a witness, Halicarnaso took part in many of the jokes and tricks of the *carolinos*, but to hear him tell the neighbours about them, one would have thought that he was one of their principal authors. The only business in which he never got mixed up was the students' messages to their sweethearts. On this point his integrity was above reproach. But a quick-witted Lima woman managed to get from him in three minutes what the students had never been able to obtain. The students of canon law, i.e. those who were doing their first year of law, were the *consules*. They were entitled to go out on Thursdays from three or four o'clock until seven. One afternoon, a Thursday in fact, a *tapada* in a short skirt and high mantle and who, to judge by her uncovered eye, her plump arm, her curves, her swaying gait and short steps must have been one of those Lima women who make one's mouth water, appeared at the cobbler's.

'Master,' she said, 'may God give you a good end to the day.'

'The same to you, lady,' replied Halicarnaso, bowing double.

'Master,' went on the *tapada*, 'I must speak to a *consul* who is coming here soon. Here are four piastres for your cigars. Please let me go into your back-shop.'

Halicarnaso, who had not seen the colour of four piastres for a long time, rejected the money indignantly.

'Come! Come! What do you take me for? The cheek of it! For *entremises* of this kind, go to Margarita the Cat or Ignacia the Pest. That's the last straw!'

'Don't be angry, master. Good Heavens! What a cantankerous fellow you are,' the girl continued, without turning a hair. 'It was because I thought you were a friend of Don Antonio that I risked asking you a favour . . .'

'Quite right, Miss, I am a friend of Don Antonio, and a very good friend.'

'Well, you don't show it, since you refuse to let me see him in your back-shop.'

'With my awl and my person, I am a friend of this student and yours, miss. I am a cobbler and not Count of *Entre* and Marquis of *meter*. Ask me something that has to do with my trade and you will see whether I serve you on the dot and without having to be cajoled.'

'Very well. Mend this shoe for me, master.'

In a flash, the mischievous girl had broken some stitches on her white satin slipper with her nails. It was impossible for Halicarnaso to leave her bare foot on the ground, that is to say clad only in a stocking as fine as lace; he had to let her go into the back-shop. Of course, her gallant arrived on time. The cobbler set to work. He went very slowly, taking his time and winking at the *consul* and his girl. During this time, our lovers talked about the usual themes of lovers when they are together. The worthy Halicarnaso muttered to himself as he sewed: 'The moment it is a question of things to do with my trade, I have nothing to say. They chat and I sew; no reason or scruples there.' And, pushing his needle through, he sang:

> 'The flea and the louse
> wanted to marry
> it's the fault of the corn
> if they didn't do so.'[16]

[16] *Tradiciones peruanas* (French transl. by Mathilde Pomés), p. 784.

ECONOMIC LIFE: TRADE, INDUS-TRY, AGRICULTURE, TRANSPORT AND FINANCE

One of Viceroy Amat's great principles was that authority dominated the economy, in other words, there was no business without order. Forty years later Baron Louis said to Louis XVIII: 'Do you practise sound politics, and I will see that your finances are sound.' So Amat's policy was inspired by the economy, i.e. it tended to protect commerce, to the extent that the Treasury profited by it.

THE LAW, PROTECTOR OF COMMERCE

The thief was the regime's public enemy number one. So people were busy tracking them night and day. To this effect, squads of policemen made nocturnal rounds. It was during one of these rounds that a band of thieves was arrested and that eleven of them had their heads cut off without any kind of trial. At roughly the same time, a veritable round-up was organized in the mountains of the valley of Carabaillo, at three leagues from Lima, to catch a group of negroes who held travellers to ransom. Half of them were hanged and the others condemned to lifetime imprisonment.

It will be seen that the justice of the viceroyalty was expeditious. When it did not hang, it whipped. Corporal punishments were two a penny. A chronicler of the period, defending the whip as a legal punishment, said with cruel humour:

'Lashes with a whip are as salutary as a purge, for the bad blood spurts from the shoulders and is renewed. The Mayors need very little incentive for administering the whip and never give less than a hundred blows. It is only a question of round figures when they pronounce sentence. The whole secret lies in having enough strength of mind to bear the first blows until the shoulders swell up; once they have swollen, it is no longer difficult to withstand eighty or ninety blows. All those whipped as a measure of justice put on weight, for to make flesh, there is no better *medicina* than the whip, that is proved.'

The punishment of the whip was mainly reserved for thieves by the Inquisition and the *cabildo* of Lima. *'¡Alza la penca y dale!* Raise the whip and strike!' was the traditional phrase with which the punishment began.[1]

It will be understood that in these circumstances the thieves did their best to escape from the rigours of the law. They particularly sought out the 'holy places', where, as we have already seen, every fugitive had the 'right of asylum'. There were also in Lima so-called houses *de cadena*, which, by royal order, the servants of the law could not enter without the previous authorization of the master of the house—and what was more only in certain special cases and after having given weighty reasons. Heavy chains stretched in the vestibule and behind the entrance doors—hence the name of *cadenas* given to these houses—secret hiding-places, duplicate exits known only to the master of the house guaranteed fugitives an almost inviolable retreat.[2] Colonial history is full of quarrels between the civil and ecclesiastical authorities or between the *encapotados* and the owners of houses *de cadena* over the subject of this right of asylum. To tell the truth, it was not without some reason that the viceroyalty grew irritated with this custom, which, inaugurated originally with the laudable aim of giving aid to hunted persons, had gradually become an institution guaranteeing impunity to common law criminals. We can understand that the authorities did not tolerate it and that Viceroy Amat had imposed the restrictions mentioned in the preceding chapter on the 'right of asylum'.

THE TREASURY

Severe as it was with robbers, the viceroyalty was no less severe on swindlers and smugglers. The expenditure of the viceroyalty of Peru was considerable. The militarization of the territory and the costs of administration entailed considerable expenses which could only be covered by the collection of taxes. In order to increase the

---

[1] Quoted by Ricardo PALMA in *Tradiciones peruanas*, p. 566.
[2] *Ibidem*, p. 537.

resources of the Treasury, Amat had taken measures to encourage trade between the countries of the South American continent and had obtained the concession from the king of Spain that cotton, logwood, wood for dyeing, dried fish, wax and sugar should be exempt from tax on their arrival in Spanish ports. But they were taxed on their departure. The result was that the inhabitants of the viceroyalty were heavily taxed. Not that they did not do everything in their power to elude the revenue authorities. The clergy and the religious communities were past masters in the art of false declarations. It was one of Amat's preoccupations—and not the least of them—to set his *contadores* on the trail of defaulting taxpayers and make them pay up. In three years, from 1767 to 1770, the number of taxpayers had risen from 27,000 to 42,070.[3]

In the big agglomerations of Indians, contributions were levied not only on each person, but also on communities. In this connection, it is instructive to consult, *inter alia,* a list drawn up by the viceroy's accounting services, enumerating by provinces, districts and categories the number of Indians liable to tax and the sums brought in as a result. First of all, we note that in the seventy-seven provinces belonging to the eight 'departments' of Peru—Lima, Chuquisaca, Misque, La Paz, Cuzco, Arequipa, Guamanco and Trujillo—there were 2,298 tax collectors, that there were nearly twice as many Indians at Cuzco as in Lima and that fathers, mothers and children were taxed according to the same scale. This meant that the 181,869 Indian children in the viceroyalty, whatever their age, were inscribed on the tax register and contributed through the intermediary of their parents to the colonial revenue, each paying a full share. Thus, out of a population of 761,696 Indians, no one escaped taxation, not even the Indians called *reservados,* i.e. the most poverty-stricken of all. And the Treasury was enriched by the annual sum of 1,154,790 pesos, or more than 700,000 pounds sterling.

On occasions His Majesty himself worried about the collection of taxes in the territories coming under his authority. Then he used to send an important official, who was called the Visitor, to this or that capital of the New World. Some of these 'visits' went beyond the bounds of a simple administrative inspection and entailed serious consequences. By way of example, I may mention the mission of Don José de Areche in 1777—a bad year for Peru,

[3] *Memoirs of Viceroy Amat,* p. lvii.

which experienced simultaneously financial embarrassment, internal rebellions and war on its frontiers.

In this fatal year 'of the three sevens', the Crown sent to Peru Don José de Areche with the title of Superintendent and General Visitor of the Royal Hacienda, armed with the most extensive powers, so that those of the viceroy became ridiculous. The viceroy was Don Manuel Guirior, Amat's successor. His wisdom and his administrative qualities had earned him general sympathy. Areche's real mission was to increase taxes to the maximum. The natives' taxes were fixed at a million pesos. In the Assembly he created *diezmos* (tithes) and the tobacco shops, and the taxes on their sales brought in substantial amounts; he crushed the traders and miners with taxes and duties, and squeezed everybody so hard that a series of disturbances broke out at Huaraz, Lambayeque, Hyanuco, Pasco, Huancavelica, Moquegua and other places in the course of which the *corregidores, alcaldes* and officials were taken to task by the people. A vast conspiracy, at the head of which were Don Lorenzo Farfan and an Indian cacique, was opportunely discovered at Cuzco.

Guirior did his best to convince the Superintendent that he was on the wrong track, that discontent was general and that, in spite of the severity of his measures, he would not succeed in collecting the new taxes without putting the country in danger of armed revolt. But Areche, considering that the king had sent him to Peru to enrich the Royal Treasury at the expense of the viceroyalty, remained deaf to the counsels of prudence lavished on him by Guirior. Besides, the latter interfered with his plans to exhaust the country; he managed to get another viceroy appointed and after a reign of four years Don Manuel de Guirior was dismissed and recalled to Madrid where he died a few months after his return. But the affair ended in Guirior's favour. The viceroy emerged victorious from his judgment of residence and the secret council that followed it, and Areche was severely condemned. Devotion to the royal person was not always rewarded.[4]

THE TRADESMEN

Being a tradesman was not considered incompatible with nobility. From the beginning of the Conquest, the Crown had

[4] *Tradiciones peruanas*, p. 651.

206

decreed that 'the fact of being a merchant or shipper in the Indies would never be an obstacle to accession to the military orders of nobility'. This liberalism had not been in vain. 'One can truthfully say,' wrote Viceroy Montesclaros to his successor, long before Amat, 'that with the exception of those who are prevented by being ministers of the king, everyone here does business with their wealth without losing their prestige in the least.' But this restriction was pure courtesy. 'From the viceroy to the archbishop,' wrote a Portuguese Jew, alluding to the same period, 'all do business and are merchants, even working through foreign hands.'[5]

As the years went by, the number of tradesmen—most of them Creoles—increased, at the same time as their vanity flourished. They were rich and their wealth took the place of nobility for them. After all, it was they who made the country rich. But all these *'Bourgeois gentilshommes'* dreamt of some outward signs which would distinguish them from the common herd. The institution of the militias provided them with the means for satisfying their desire to be looked up to.

Instead of coats of arms and quarterings of nobility, they wore uniform.

The spectacle of these grocers in charge of manœuvres and drapers in full-dress uniform marching through the streets of Lima or some Andean pueblo made that serious-minded traveller Humboldt smile:

'It is not the military spirit of the nation, it is the vanity of a small number of families, whose heads aspire to the title of colonel or brigadier, which has encouraged the formation of militias in the Spanish colonies . . . Traversing the mountain range of the Andes, one is surprised to see on the mountain slopes, in small provincial towns, all the tradesmen transformed into colonels, captains and quartermaster-sergeants in the militia. As the rank of colonel confers the *tratamiento,* or title of nobility, which is incessantly repeated in family conversation, one can accept that it makes the greatest contribution to the happiness of domestic life and that the Creoles sacrifice an extraordinary amount of their

⁵ *Descripción anónima del Perú* (1620). MS. in the National Library, Paris, quoted by J. de la RIVA AGÜERO in his article on Don José Baquijano de Beascoa y Carrillo de Cordoba, in *Revista de archivos, bibliotecas y museos,* Madrid, vol. 76, p. 465.

wealth for it. Sometimes one sees these militia officers in full-dress uniform and decorated with the royal order of Charles III, seated gravely in their shops, going into the smallest details of the sale of their merchandise; a singular mixture of ostentation and simplicity of behaviour that astonishes the European traveller.'[6]

In reality, there was neither ostentation nor simplicity in the behaviour of these decorated shopkeepers, but a firm intention to show off their privileged situation by tangible signs. Their uniform, their gold braid and their insignia took the place of emblems which marked them as the whites of America in the eyes of the Indians, half-breeds and negroes.

TRADE AND SMUGGLING

Although Lima was the 'commercial market-place' where all business was handled, the port of Callao was the vital centre of the viceroyalty. The traffic that passed through it was immense. All kinds of merchandise and foodstuffs converged on Callao, the meeting place for Spanish ships arriving and departing. From Chile came ropes, leather, tallow, dried meat and corn. From the archipelago of Chiloé planks of Alerze, made of a very light wood, woollen goods and especially 'Turkish-style' carpets to put on daises. From Peru itself came the sugar of Andaguela, Guyaquil and other parts, the wines and spirits of Pisco. Guyaquil and its environs also supplied masts, ropes, rare woods, tobacco and honey. From Mexico and Guatemala came tar, wood for dyeing, sulphur and the balm which was called 'balm of Peru', although it actually came from Guatemala, as did Chinese silks (in this case smuggled). All these goods or raw materials were either used for local consumption or re-exported to the Metropolis.

It is possible to form an idea of the variety and importance of the traffic leaving Peru for Spain by studying the list of goods registered at the port of Callao with the port of Cadiz as their destination for the period 1761 to the end of 1775. We find, for example, 'on His Majesty's account': 2,600 loads and $23\frac{1}{2}$ lb. of cocoa at the rate of 78 per load, 10,918 cwt. 41 lb. of copper, 13 cwt. of vicuna wool, 885 cwt. of cascarilla (a variety of quinquina), 11,238 cwt.

5½ lb. of tin, 27 cwt. 3½ lb. of the plant 'known as Clahual', 185 lb. of crude mercury and 8 *arrobas* of powder in 4 barrels. We also find 8 small boxes of gold and silver coins 'returned by the royal house of the Mint', plus a 'bundle of special objects for the king'. The goods sent 'on behalf of private individuals' were also very varied. They consisted mainly of metals (55,381 cwt. of copper, 1,682 cwt. of tin, 1 cwt. of stones containing antimony, 4 bronze bells and 15 cwt. of bronze), textiles (1,880 cwt. of vicuna wool, 9 cwt. and 26 scarves of alpaca wool, 73 cwt. of 'ceiba' wool, 1,556 cwt. of cotton, 6 curtains, 12 pairs of gloves and a cotton tent, 2 woollen carpets) and exotic produce (chocolate, indigo wood, sarsaparilla, cascarilla, amber and coral).[7] But the most valuable cargoes were made up of the gold and silver extracted and worked in Peru which the viceroyalty sent to Spain. In fifteen years—from 1761 to the end of October 1775—the quantities of gold and silver sent from the port of Callao to the port of Cadiz, via Cape Horn, and destined either for 'His Majesty's Treasury' or businessmen and private individuals, reached a figure of 56,096,997 silver pesos and 14,770,529 gold pesos, a total of 71,677,526 pesos, equivalent to more than 50,500,000 pounds sterling.[8]

Ships flying foreign flags were forbidden to trade with the Spanish colonies. Those which anchored in Peruvian ports or were stopped and examined in territorial waters were confiscated if manufactured goods or Spanish money were found on board. This regulation was got round by both foreign smugglers and the Spanish authorities in two ways. The first consisted in landing at an isolated port or estuary. A shot fired from a cannon warned the inhabitants on the coast of the arrival of goods for sale. Unloading took place mainly at night. The captain took care only a few men were allowed aboard at the same time and had them searched on arrival and when they left to prevent theft. The second method was less dangerous, for it bore all the outward appearances of legality. Shunning desolate regions, the smugglers put themselves under the protection of the law the better to violate it. All they needed to do was to cause some accident on board their ship, such as breaking a mast or making a leak in the ship's side. The slightest damage was enough as long as it was compensated for by the 'present' that it was customary to give the governor and port

[7] *Memoirs of Viceroy Amat*, p. 230.
[8] *Ibidem*, p. 228.

authorities in such cases. The goods were put in a warehouse, the door of which was then locked up, but another door was left open by which the goods were removed during the night. To justify the presence of foreign goods on the market, the master of the ship asked the governor for permission to sell a part of the cargo to pay for the repairs. Once permission was given, these goods went to swell the number of those which had already entered illegally.

'In fact, the whole of Peru allowed smuggling to flourish quite freely and publicly, so much so that the government officials who tried to oppose it were powerless when faced with the general tendency . . . Lines of mules loaded with fraudulently imported merchandise went through Lima beneath the balcony of the viceroy himself. Nobody could put an end to this traffic.'[9]

This remark by Salvador de Madariaga confirms that smuggling in Peru was perfectly organized.

We must remember that the ban on foreign ships trading with Peruvian ports was alleviated by the decrees of the Bourbons of Spain licensing French ships to do business with the Indies, with certain reservations. It seems that long before these decrees the French managed very well, to judge by a document discovered in the National Archives by Régine Pernoud, referring to the beginning of the eighteenth century. The document in question is a letter written by La Rigaudière, commanding the French frigate *Aurore,* which was at Callao at the time. La Rigaudière was a daredevil. A specialist in raiding merchant shipping, he took part in an expedition against Rio de Janeiro three years later and it nearly succeeded. He had come from Bayonne to Peru 'solely with parcels from the King of Spain for the Viceroy who had just arrived and should be entering Lima at any moment'. His letter, dated June 30 ,1707, was addressed to du Casse, the famous pirate who 'took care of' the privileges granted by Spain to French ships in South America.

'A ship which is leaving for Panama gives me the occasion to have the honour to inform you of my arrival in this place on March 30th. The Viceroy was not yet here and only arrived on May 18th. I handed over to him a personal letter from his Catholic Majesty and the parcels . . . I can assure you, Sir, that it was high time that

[9] Salvador de MADARIAGA: *L'Essor de l'Empire espagnol*, pp. 172–173 and 174.

I arrived and it seems that God has brought us here as quickly as we have come, the crossing having taken only three and a half months. The bad news that has been rampant in this country had put everything in disorder, but my arrival has reassured people and things are going on in the normal way. I won't go into all the details of what is happening, for this letter might be seen, apart from the fact that I hope to be on my way back before it reaches you. I shall only say that the affairs for which I was sent here have so far borne little fruit. I do not know what will happen in the future, but I greatly fear that they will not have the result that was proposed . . . The Viceroy has promised to send me off at the end of August. I shall go to Chile to take on provisions and return as soon as I possibly can. He told me that he would give me what you had lent him and 30,000 piastres which the Company of the Assiente sent to him to remit to you . . . No enemy vessel has appeared in these seas; there are ten or twelve private ships which are doing very bad business here: the authorities have refused to receive them in this port or to permit them to carry on any business. The Viceroy has sent a message telling them to withdraw from these seas and that he does not want to see or hear about them.'

Reading between the lines, this missive reveals that the pirates served as intermediaries between the viceroy and the Company of the Assiente, i.e. the Spanish organization responsible for keeping the accounts of operations concerning the Assiente. The Assiente, or *Asiento*, was the name given to the monopoly of the sale of negroes in the Spanish colonies. It was ceded by Spain to England under the terms of the Treaty of Utrecht in 1713, which also gave it the right to establish offices in Rio de la Plata and at Buenos Aires and to send a vessel of three hundred tons there once a year at the time of the fair to trade. Needless to say, the English, strong in their right of *asiento* and abusing it, pushed their advantages and attempted commercial inroads on the coasts of Peru. On the whole, they were very badly received. In any case, it was quite natural for the Company of the Assiente to use pirates as messengers, or even as brokers. For the sum that La Rigaudière, in his polite letter addressed to du Casse, undertook to hand over to him on behalf of the viceroy probably represented his remuneration for the transport of a cargo of negroes.

So the ban on foreign ships trading with Spanish ports was

absolute in principle, but not so in fact, at least for English ships—as from the Treaty of Utrecht and in the interval in Hispano-British hostilities—and French ships. The welcome reserved for the latter by the authorities of Peruvian ports inevitably reflected the fluctuations in Franco-Spanish diplomacy which developed with the help of treaties between the two countries and in sympathy with the fortunes of arms on the European battlefields. So the system of *licencias* had its ups and downs, ranging from the utmost liberality to suppression pure and simple. The reception also varied according to the 'recommendations' which the captain could avail himself of, that of a pirate sometimes making up for the lack of a *licencia* or even being preferred to it. In that same year of 1707 when La Rigaudière's frigate anchored peacefully and under the protection of the viceroy in the port of Callao, the powerful company of the Indies found itself refused admission, if we refer to the evidence of the businessman Gauver:

'I found three ships of the Company of the Indies, loaded with a rather bad assortment of goods; they had written to the viceroy for permission to go to Callao, but he replied that that was against the orders of the king, his master. He refused them so courteously and politely that he seemed to be asking them not to approach Lima as a favour, and this letter was brought by a judge who had orders to prevent all trading by the French with Spaniards, with severe penalties against the latter, such as confiscation of property and exile to Valdivia for private individuals, confiscation of goods and exile outside Peru for monks and priests and exile to the Island of Callao for Indians and mulattos.'

The tone is much the same in Chapter Three of Part III of Amat's Memoirs, dealing with the arrival in the port of Callao of a French ship 'called *Saint-Jean-Baptiste*'. While solemnly declaring his friendship for the French, the viceroy, arguing from the fact that the Family Pact 'did not contain any clause excepting the subjects of the King of France and ships flying his flag from the general ban on trading with Spain', asked the *Saint-Jean-Baptiste* to put to sea again, not before he had most correctly seen to it that the ship was careened and the crew visited by the officer of health. Yet another ship that was not covered by a special *licencia* or the protection of a pirate! For, I should repeat, the tolerance of the Spanish Bourbons was not general. It was the subject of special regulations applying to certain ships and specific kinds of trade. The pirates saw to the rest.

A TALE OF SILK STOCKINGS

Round about 1788, the viceroy of Peru, Don Teodoro de Croix, received confidential messages from the Crown ordering him to put the country in a state of defence. It seemed probable that relations with England would be broken off. In spite of the mystery with which His Excellency surrounded himself, information leaked out and big business did not fail to take advantage of it. The following year and after a few months during which the holds of ships coming from Spain had not been inspected, a frigate from Cadiz, the *Santa Rufina,* arrived at Callao, loaded with a valuable cargo, which had miraculously escaped from the English cruisers.

Among the goods intended for Don Silvestre Amenabar, a Lima tradesman, there were two crates containing 240 pairs of ladies' stockings. But the customs officials declared that these goods were smuggled, because they had not come from a Spanish factory. The consignees protested, so two of the most eminent tradesmen were appointed as experts and they, after taking the oath and examining the thread, the weave, the marks and countermarks, begged to differ from the customs officials' opinion. Nevertheless, the viceroy decided that the two crates should be stored in the customs shed and samples and a copy of the file sent to Charles III in Spain, so that he could settle the matter. A similar measure was taken in the case of four more crates containing 576 pairs of stockings addressed to Don Manuel Zaldívar, shopkeeper in the Portal de Escribanos.

Ten months passed and the women of Lima, for whom the stockings held by the customs were intended, began to get impatient. They no longer went to balls, paid calls, walked in processions or went to the theatre, for they could not decently put in an appearance with stockings that were darned or in tatters. Both sides showed obstinacy and His Excellency grew more stubborn every day. The women of Lima declared open rebellion on the men, whom they accused *en masse,* since they were in revolt against a governor so unkind to the fair sex. As the viceroy was not married or under a woman's thumb, he understood nothing about feminine needs. In the end, the tradesmen, fearing that the women, tired of this verbal warfare, would resort to more effective means, decided to pay a deposit of 10,000 pesos to the royal coffers to make the viceroy go back on his decision and so put an end to a conflict which otherwise would not have finished until 1790, when the tradesmen received a reply in their favour from Spain. Each pair of stockings was sold for an ounce of gold and the whole cargo was sold out in eight days.[10]

WORKMEN, CRAFTSMEN, GUANO

In the time of la Perricholi, there already existed what we should call 'skilled workers' today. Most of them were mulattos.

Disdaining mechanical employment, which repelled them because of their pride and their indolence, the Spaniards and the Creoles left them to be taken up by their subjects of a darker colour who excelled in the trades of shoe-making, tailoring, haircutting, inn-keeping, carpentry and small shop-keeping.[11]

Not only did the mulattos practise these trades with enjoyment, but they also grew rich from them, if we are to believe Jorge Juan and Ulloa when they describe mulatto craftsmen parading through the streets of Lima 'wearing rich cloths of gold and silver, of such a quality that nobody of higher rank could have found better'.

The textile industry was very prosperous, owing to the raw silk imported from China, the cotton and the wool from vicunas, guanacos and llamas, which were woven on the spot and produced cloths which competed in quality with those which came from Spain and 'arrived in bad condition because the sea made them perish'. This was a survival of a native industry, a handicraft activity of local production.

On the other hand, it seems that certain crafts and manufactures were lost. We find an example of crafts being abandoned in the Secret Reports of Ulloa and Jorge Juan. Vicuna wool, finer than that of the two 'sheep of the Andes', the guanaco and the llama, was excellent for making hats. But nobody succeeded in making hats solid enough to compete with those which came from England and France and which were made of musquash. In 1737 an English hatter was established in Lima. His hats were so solid and so cheap

---

[10] *Tradiciones peruanas*, p. 717.

[11] *Gillepsie de Buenos Aires*, quoted by Salvador de MADARIAGA in *Le Déclin de l'Empire espagnol*, p. 146.

that he soon had more customers than he could cope with and made his fortune in five years. Then he went back to England

'but out of gratitude to the country which had made him rich and to one of the Creoles who had helped him to make his fortune in his early days, he wanted to reward him by revealing the secret which enabled him to give the hats their sheen, suppleness and good quality, so as to give these kingdoms a means of profiting by one of their natural resources'.

The Creole was either incapable of keeping the secret of this method or did not try to keep it, and in 1742 all the hatters of Lima made hats according to the English process. However, although they were all in possession of the secret, no one made them as well as the man who had received lessons directly from the Englishman. The technique had been lost.[12]

Although some trades disappeared because of their practitioners' lack of ability or because their product no longer met the requirements of the period, there were others which, practised from time immemorial, were still very much alive, for example the profession of the men who collected *guano*.

Guano is a manure composed of birds' excrement which is found in great abundance on the coasts of Peru. Its richness in phosphoric acid and nitrogen make it a marvellous fertilizer. Elisée Reclus, in her *Géographie universelle*, gives a poetic description of the guano islands:

'On the beaches, especially at Huacho, lobsters are caught by the million. They could be caught by the thousand million. Around the islets and rock which rise from the ocean near the coast, the fish teem in enormous shoals, so that the surface of the sea breaks on them as if on reefs and owing to this abundance of oceanic life, the birds of the air also whirl round in myriads: penguins, petrels, terns, skuas, and cormorants rise in mobile images above the islets and deposit masses of excrement which the miners extract.

This new type of mine ... was by no means ignored by the ancient Incas who used it successfully in their agriculture. Humboldt, visiting Peru in 1804, had the idea of sending a few samples to the

[12] Jorge JUAN and Antonio de ULLOA: *Noticias secretas*, quoted by Salvador de MADARIAGA in *L'Essor de l'Empire espagnol*, p. 371.

French chemists Fourcroy and Vauquelin for analysis. Little attention was paid to this discovery at the time.'

In any case, the collection of guano was one of the most flourishing industries in Peru, which aroused the rather naïve astonishment of Frézier, who described a visit to the island of Iquique as
follows:

'The island of Iquique is also inhabited by Indians and negroes,
who work there extracting guano, which is a yellowish soil believed
to be the droppings of birds, because in addition to stinking of
cormorants' excrement birds' feathers have been found deep in this
soil. Nevertheless, it is hard to understand how such a vast quantity
could have been amassed, because, for more than a hundred years,
they have loaded ten or twelve ships with it every year to manure
the land, and yet one scarcely notices that the island has decreased
in height . . . It is true that the sea birds are so numerous that one
can say without exaggeration that the air is sometimes darkened by
them. *And, after visiting Arica, Frézier observed:* The island of
Guano . . . is very unpleasant owing to the stench of birds' droppings with which it is covered . . . it is even believed that it makes
the port unhealthy in summer . . .
To transport the guano to the fields, the people of Arica generally
use the species of small camels that the Indians of Peru call *llamas*,
those of Chile *chillehueque* and the Spaniards *carnero de la sierra*.'

The extraordinary fertility of the valley of Arica owing to guano
fired Frézier with enthusiasm: 'This prodigy is achieved with the
help of these droppings or *guano* which fertilizes the soil so that it
yields four and 500 per unit of all sorts of cereals, corn, wheat,
etc. but especially of *agy*, when the farmers know how to use it
properly.'

MINES AND MINERS

The *Mercurio Peruano* tells us that there was, in 1791, in the
viceroyalty of Peru—without including the province of Quito, or
that of Buenos Aires, or even the famous region of Potosi which
will be mentioned further on—a large number of mines, either
being worked, or abandoned, undoubtedly because their owners
thought that they had got the maximum out of them. Or because

some natural catastrophe had made them unsuitable for working. In the department of Lima there were 4 gold mines, 181 silver mines, 1 mercury mine and 4 copper mines, all being worked. 70 silver mines had been abandoned. Up to that date nothing but silver mines had been discovered in the department of Cuzco. They numbered 19 and were all being successfully worked. In the provinces of Pasco and Huallanca, 227 silver mines were being worked and 22 were abandoned. In the department of Trujillo, 3 gold mines and 134 silver mines were being worked and 161 were abandoned. In the department of Huamanca, including the district of Lucanos, 60 gold mines, 102 silver mines and 1 mercury mine were being worked and 3 gold mines and 63 silver mines were abandoned. In the department of Arequipa, 1 gold mine and 71 silver mines were being worked and 4 gold mines and 28 silver mines were abandoned. In the department of Guantayaya, 1 gold mine and 20 silver mines were being worked and 19 gold mines and 31 silver mines were abandoned. Lastly, in the department of Huancavelica, 1 gold mine, 80 silver mines, 2 mercury mines and 10 lead mines were being worked, while 2 gold mines and 215 silver mines were abandoned. 'The majority of silver mines abandoned,' states the *Mercurio Peruano*, 'have been left because of floods against which they cannot be guaranteed.'

This list makes one think. Of course, these mines were not all equally important, ranging from the thin, quickly exhausted seam to the vast deposit with apparently endless reserves. But what a source of revenue! From the beginning of 1780 to the end of 1789, that is to say in an interval of ten years, these mines brought in a sum that can be evaluated, when turned into English money, at more than 50,500,000 pounds sterling. As for the silver mines of Potosi, not included in those which have just been enumerated, they produced, from 1547 to 1637, a sum equal to more than 72,000,000 pounds sterling. However, although it was very productive, the revenue from working the mines could have been multiplied tenfold. In fact, the Peruvians were far from having exhausted their possibilities. A statistician, Helm, notes in his *Journal d'un voyage de Buenos Aires à Potosi*, published at the end of the eighteenth century: 'Eighty years ago, part of a mountain not far from La Paz collapsed. People found there on the surface piles of solid gold weighing fifty lb. Even in 1787, the rains frequently uncovered pieces weighing two oz. and more.' This leads us to think that the reserves of precious metal in Peru were practically unlimited. There were two reasons why many mines were not worked, apart from those already mentioned. Firstly, the geographical situation of Peru's mines did not facilitate the extraction of metals. Humboldt was much struck by this fact, during his geological mission to Peru. He wrote on this topic:

'The biggest silver mines, those of Potosi and Pasco, are at great heights, very near the limits of the eternal snows. To work them, men, provisions and animals have to be brought from far afield. Towns situated on the plateaux where water freezes all the year round and trees cannot grow do not offer an attractive place of residence. Only the hope of getting rich can make a free man decide to abandon the delightful climate of the valleys to isolate himself on the back of the Peruvian Andes.'

Hope of making his fortune or simply of getting enough to eat. And Humboldt compares the situation in the mines of Peru with that of the Mexican mines.

'In Mexico, on the contrary, the richest veins of silver, those of Guanuajato, Zacatecas and Taxco, are at average heights of from 5,520 to 6,500 ft. The mines there are surrounded by cultivated fields, towns and villages; forests crown the neighbouring peaks; everything there facilitates the subterranean wealth.'

The second reason was that the mountain Indians showed no zeal in helping their masters to discover new deposits in which they would inevitably be sent to work. 'There are mines whose sites are carefully hidden by the Indians out of fear of being employed in work which they consider dangerous for their health and even their existence.'

Working conditions in the mines were very bad, even at Potosi, which kept up the appearance of an industrial capital. It had a population of more than 60,000 Indians and 10,000 Spaniards. Each of the surrounding villages was required to send to Potosi a certain contingent of Indians to work in the mines, which was called the *mita*. The *corregidores* sent the *mitayos* off on the day of Corpus Christi. The majority took their wives and children with them. Sometimes, after having completed their year of compulsory service, whole families of Indians did not return to their villages

218

and remained at Potosi, where they were at least sure of subsisting.

It was Carvajal, an officer of Francisco Pizarro's, who had discovered the mines of Potosi, to the south of La Paz, at a height of 13,600 ft. On the summit of this mountain of silver the Spaniards had built the highest town in the world. Beneath a colourless sky, houses in the Andalusian style flaunted their arabesques around gaping shafts. Prison and fortress at the same time, *la casa de la Moneda* (the House of the Mint) symbolized with its heavy portal and oppressive silence the power of the Lion of Castille. In it a whole group of wretches, shut up for a period or for life, minted the silver money of the king of Spain. Yet these coin-makers, working in workshops or in the open air, were considered favoured in comparison with the miners, who had to go underground to detach with pickaxes the pieces of silver mixed with sulphide of arsenic or antimony, or those mixed with sulphide of lead and copper pyrites. Brought up to the surface, these sulphides of silver were transformed into chlorides that were treated with mercury. The amalgam was heated and the result was silver.

It was said that Potosi was so cold that Spanish women could not give birth there. They were forced to go twenty and thirty leagues away so as not to run the risk of dying with their child. In this connection, Frézier notes:

'This effect of their delicate health was looked on as a punishment from Heaven, because the Indian women were not subject to this inconvenience . . .'

Describing the conditions of the *mitayos* in the mines, Frézier adds:

'However that may be, it is certain that strong fumes continually come from the mines. The Spaniards who live above them are forced to drink the herb of Paraguay or *maté* very frequently to moisten their chests, otherwise they suffer from a sort of suffocation . . . But these fumes are much worse down the mine, they produce such an effect on bodies which are not used to them that a man who encounters them for a moment emerges like a cripple, feeling such pain in all his limbs that he cannot move them; it often lasts more than a day and then the remedy is to take the sick man back to the mine. The Spaniards call this sickness *quebranta-huesos*, i.e. that which breaks the bones. The Indians themselves,

219

who are used to it, are forced to relieve each other alternately nearly every day . . .'

But even more than *maté*, it was *coca*, with its tonic effect on the anaemic constitutions of the Indians, that enabled them to keep going.

'To safeguard themselves against the bad air that they breathe in the mines, the Indians continually chew *coca*, a kind of betel, and they claim that they could not work there without it. [*And Frézier concludes:*] Only the Indians are fit for this work, on which it is impossible to employ negroes, because they all die. The latter are robust and infinitely harder workers than the Spaniards, who regard manual labour as something shameful for a white man. To be *hombre de cara blanca* is a dignity which exempts Europeans from manual labour; but they can be pedlars without blushing and carry their pack in the streets.'[13]

So nearly all the metals were found in the mines of Peru: gold, silver, copper, tin, lead and mercury. In addition there were salt, plaster-stone (gypsum), transparent alabaster, which was used as windows for houses, and a black volcanic stone, called the stone of the *gallinazo*, from the name of the urubu, whose colour it had. The viceroyalty also took a great interest in the mercury mines, of which Huancavelica was the most important. Working conditions in these mines were very arduous, because of 'the malignant fumes caused by the particles of mercury, which not only put out the lights with which the Indians work in the depths, but also cut these wretched workers' life-span short'. Thirteen provinces representing sixty-seven *repartimientos* supplied the mine of Huancavelica with the necessary manpower, more than 17,000 Indians.

These compulsory recruitments of personnel literally pumped the country dry, for the death rate was high and it was necessary to provide periodic replacements for the Indians intoxicated by the mercury fumes. Incidentally, the viceroy himself admitted this: 'Although the silver mines destroy many Indians, the mercury mines are incomparably harmful to human nature, which explains the depopulation of the villages in these provinces.'[14] It is fair to point out that the viceroyalty was worried about this state of

13 FRÉZIER, p. 379.
14 *Memoirs of Viceroy Amat*, pp. 240–250.

affairs and that it envisaged, in Amat's time, to stop working the mines of Huancavelica, a veritable tomb for the Indian 'live-stock'. Moreover, the condition of the *mitayos* had relatively and slightly improved since the Conquest. The *mineros* (mine owners) were forbidden to keep the *mitayos* beyond the legal duration of the *mita*. And Amat himself, though apparently far from sentimental, disapproved of certain inhuman practices and gave orders that they should be severely dealt with, for example, the practice of mine-owners selling to other mine-owners their Indian personnel, once the period of their *mita* was up. Amat vehemently denounced such trafficking, genuine slave markets 'contrary to divine and human rights', adding, as a practical man, that 'the health of the Indians was the sinews and principal foundation of the wealth of Peru'.

GOLD

The Indians of Peru had not waited for the arrival of the Spaniards to extract and work metals, which the Incas used in large quantities, especially gold. As for the Spaniards, they had been gold prospectors in all ages. In fact, from the most remote antiquity, gold mines had been worked in the Iberian peninsula. Strabo mentions them in his *Geography*. More specifically, Pliny describes the technique used at the time for treating gold: 'It is beaten, washed, ground into coarse powder and lastly triturated in a mortar.' That was still the method used in the sixteenth century. So the Spaniards knew that gold could be found either in the form of grains and nuggets mixed with sand, or mixed with sulphides, like quartz. Gold dust was extracted from rivers or river deposits. Gold incorporated with sulphides was found in mines. When the *conquistadores* arrived in Peru, the Indians, too, were familiar with gold and had been using it for a long time, but they preferred to look for it in the rivers. The procedure they generally used was washing. They let water flow down the sloping bottom of a wash-trough and gradually poured into it the powdery matter which contained the gold. The gold fell to the bottom, where it was retained by a mesh. Once it was washed free of the muddy particles, the gold thus collected was smelted with four times its weight of silver. This alloy was attacked with concentrated, boiling sulphuric acid which dissolved all the metals except gold. This was the refining. These two operations were known to the Spaniards,

221

although they also used, when refining gold, the ancient procedure also quoted by Pliny, consisting in substituting a mixture of copper sulphate, shale and saltpetre for the sulphuric acid.

Thus the Spaniards knew no more than the Indians about the extraction of gold. But they perfected the system and got the maximum yield from it. First of all, they discovered a new principle of purification called 'amalgamation in the *patio*'. The gold-bearing mineral was crushed with pounders by women and old men. It was then placed on a paved area called an *arrastro* which was surrounded by a channel full of water. Beasts trampled on this mineral turned mud. The whole was moistened with water, mercury was added and then a final bath completed the separation of the gold from the impure matter. The Spaniards were not content merely to improve the technique. As the method of prospecting in rivers seemed archaic to them and the results inadequate, they spread the extraction of gold in mines. Henceforth, thousands of natives were employed on this frightful work of hollowing out mountains, extracting sulphides with picks, crushing them by hand and pulverizing them in moulds. Washing and refining came next. So arduous was this work that the Indians preferred to live and die between the cyclopean walls of the *casa de Moneda* at Potosi rather than go down the mine where their conditions were not much different from those tradition atributes to Solomon's slaves in the mines of Manica dug for the Queen of Sheba. Some sections of Peruvian mines—with those black ghosts incessantly going up and down—recall Michelangelo's *Last Judgment* in which convulsed clusters of human beings seem to form a sinister chain.

However—to show how man cannot remain indifferent to his trade, amidst the worst misery—the *mitayo* had moments of exaltation in his dreary existence. What an event it was when the *catador* (the searcher) thought he had discovered a mine! All activity in the surrounding country was suspended. The shops were shut. The schoolmaster sent his pupils home. The parish priest had all the bells rung merrily. Indians and Spaniards ran towards the site of the miracle. People rejoiced and pushed each other about. If the discovery was confirmed, they feasted on the very spot where the vein had appeared. If there had been a mistake, everyone went home, not really disappointed. A curious thing was that Spaniards and Indians exhibited the same enthusiasm. Yet for the latter gold had no more value—even less, because of secondary utility—than copper and lead. Moreover, the discovery of a nugget or a gold-bearing area announced the martyrdom of the mine. Probably the Spaniards had communicated their gold fever to the Indians and they thought themselves generous in propagating the mirage of Eldorado among them in exchange for the actual metal.

MEANS OF TRANSPORT: MULES AND BAROUCHES

The main means of transporting goods between the coastal ports and the principal commercial towns of Peru—Lima, Cuzco, Puno and Arequipa—was the mule. Genuine beasts of burden, the mules literally died on the job. Consequently, they had to be renewed frequently. For this purpose 80,000 or 100,000 were brought from Tucuman and Chile every year. The herds or *recuas* were divided into several *piaras* of ten mules, each under the leadership of two men. They sometimes made daily marches of twenty-five miles in the high mountains without water or pasturage. It was necessary to have the herd followed by an equal number of spare mules so as not to have to abandon the goods carried by those which died on the road. The tracks of Peru were signposted by the skeletons of beasts that had died en route. Nevertheless, the people of the country and the merchants did not shrink from an expedition of 200 or 300 leagues to the coast to fetch goods from Europe. But the moment when the muleteers had to give proof of their skill and patience was when they had to make their beasts cross a bridge. For example, the bridge of Apurima, the most frequented in the whole of Peru, crossed a river the bed of which was carved out perpendicularly in a fault in the rock, with a depth and width of 120 spans, almost 600 ft. This bridge, made of ropes formed of the bark of trees six feet wide, interlaced with wooden cross-pieces, sagged slightly towards the middle. The mules, seized with giddiness, only advanced with difficulty. To pay for the bridge's upkeep, four *reales* had to be paid for each mule load. Everything in the way of foodstuffs and merchandise that circulated from Lima to Cuzco and in Upper Peru was forced to pass over this bridge, or else make a detour lasting six or seven days to pass elsewhere. This means of transport was also used by the travellers who ventured into the highest mountain regions. There were no others. Unless they resorted to the *cargueros*, of whom Humboldt, who had used them, said: 'They have a chair strapped on their back, on which the traveller is seated, and they average three or four hours' journey a day.' We can understand Humboldt when he adds: 'We preferred to go on foot.'

In town, the usual means of transport was the barouche, an open or simply covered vehicle, which must not be confused with the coach, a closed vehicle, fitted with windows and doors covered with gilding and lined with leather, which was reserved for the viceroy and a minority of nobles and highly-placed officials. These barouches aroused Frézier's admiration:

'As one counts the coaches in the towns of Europe to indicate their magnificence, in the same way, at Lima, one can count 4,000 barouches, the ordinary carriage of the country, drawn by mules. But to give an idea of the opulence of this town, it is enough to relate the amount of wealth the merchants exposed there towards 1682, on the entry of the Duke of la Plata, when he came to take possession of the town. They arranged that the Calles de la Merced and de los Mercaderes should be paved to the extent of two quarters with gold ingots which normally weigh about 200 marks, 12 to 15 inches long, 4 to 5 inches wide and 2 to 3 inches thick, which could make the sum of 80,000,000 écus and about 320,000,000 livres of our money, at the present rate. It is true that Lima is to some extent the depository of the Treasures of Peru of which it is the capital. It was estimated, a few years ago, that its expenditure was more than 6,000,000 écus. It is necessary to reduce this greatly today since the trade carried on by Frenchmen has brought goods from Europe cheaply and the trade they do at Arica, Ylo and Pisco diverts money which in the past came to Lima, hence the town is poor at present in comparison with what it was in the past.'

AGRICULTURE AND VEGETATION

The great variety of vegetation and the specific properties of the climate had made Peru a country well suited to agriculture, since the time of the Incas. In the past and until the earthquake of 1687, Peru was self-sufficient as regards wheat and barley; it was very rich in pastureland, sugar cane, olive trees, fruits and vegetables, and in vines which yielded excellent table wines. In spite of earthquakes and natural calamities, Peru had remained an agricultural country under the viceroys, owing to a wise policy.

San Miguel de Piura cultivated cotton which was shipped at Payta. Pisco was famous for its spirits, Iquique for its saltpetre. The quinquinas were one of the most lucrative branches of Peruvian trade; gathered in the Andes, their bark was carried to the coast on the backs of mules and alpacas by routes which could only be traversed by beasts of burden and Indians, as we have already seen.

The extreme temperature, on the coast at least, only varied, save in exceptional circumstance, between 53·6 and 59 degrees Fahrenheit, so that vines grew side by side with coffee, cotton and sugar cane. When the soil was properly irrigated, it could produce up to four crops a year. The technique of irrigation was very advanced, as proved by the numerous channels which meandered through the plains of the Rimac.

Almost all the European fruits grew in Peru: figs, apples, grapes, olives, etc. The West Indian fruits were also found there: pineapples, guavas, sweet potatoes, bananas, water-melons and melons. But there were species of fruits peculiar to Peru, of which the most esteemed were: *chirimoyas, paltas* (avocadoes), *granadillas* (a sort of pomegranate), *higos de tuna* (the fruit of a sort of prickly-pear or euphorbia), *lucumas, pacayos, pepinos* (cucumbers), *ciruela* (plums), etc.

Another plant very common in Peru was *coca*. This herb was used by the Indians, who appreciated its tonic virtues. In the order of medicinal plants I must also mention jalap, the root of which was much used in medicine, China root and *mechoacan* which the inhabitants called *jonqui*. Lastly, I must not forget *agy* or hot pepper. The Spaniards of Peru were so fond of *agy* that they put it into all their dishes, although it was so hot that it scorched the mouth. As it only grew on the high plateaux, caravans of merchants climbed up into the valleys of Arica, Sama, Tacuna and Locumba every year to make a clean sweep of the *agy* harvest, which they bought very cheaply and sold at ransom prices.

WEIGHTS AND MEASURES, COINS

Here are some details about the main measures in use in the viceroyalty of Peru.

The unit of length was the *vara* or three feet. For 'dry materials', including salt, the unit of capacity was the *cahis* (about ninety-six gallons) equivalent to twelve *fanegas,* the last named representing twelve *celemines.* The unit of weight was the pound, broken up as follows:

1 *libra*	=	2 *marcos*;
1 *marco*	=	8 *onzas*;
1 *onza*	=	64 *ochavos*;
1 *ochavo*	=	384 *tomines*;
1 *tomín*	= 4,608 *granos.*

For liquids, with the exception of oil, they used the *cántara* or *arroba* equal to eight *azumbres* (about 2½ gallons). It was divided into *media cántara, cuartilla, azumbre, medio azumbre, cuartillo* (very popular), *medio cuartillo* and *copa.* For oil, they used the *libra, media libra, cuarterones* or *panillas* and *mediaspanillas.* An *arroba* weighed twenty-five *libras* and a *quintal,* four *arrobas.*

Goods were designated by the place from which they came. Principally there was 'Asiatic' merchandise coming from Manila via Acapulco and 'European', also called 'Castilian', merchandise. The goods were packed in containers the dimensions and characteristics of which corresponded to the nature of the merchandise. These were the different types of packings:

fardos: bales
sacas: large sacks
costales: small sacks
botijas: jars
zurrones: shepherds' scrips or pouches (of leather)
cajones: cases
petacas: chests
canastas: baskets.

To conclude, let us come to the 'sinews of war', that is to say the coinage, which was either gold or silver.

The biggest gold coin was the *doblón,* also called *onza* and vulgarly *pelucona,* which was worth eight gold *escudos* or sixteen silver *pesos* or *duros.* The *doblón* had a gross weight of 27·064 grammes and as the Finance Act had fixed the title of the alloy at 916 thousandths, the net weight in gold of the *doblón* was 24·814 grammes. In addition to the *doblón,* the gold coins included the *medio doblón* or *media onza* and the *escudo.*

The highest silver coin was the *peso fuerte* or *duro* or *real de a ocho*, usually called *patacón*. It weighed 27·064 grammes. In addition to the *peso*, there were the *medio peso* or *real de a cuatro* and the *peseta* or *real de a dos*. The *real* properly so called was subdivided into the *medio real* and the *cuartos* or *cuartillos*. Lastly, there were coins in circulation made of an alloy containing a high proportion of copper and called *maravedis*.

MONETARY PROPORTIONS

As the bimetallic proportion, at the time of Amat's viceroyalty was 1 to 16, the gold *escudo* was worth 2 *pesos* or *patacones*; the *doblón* was equivalent to 8 *escudos* or 16 silver *pesos*. Lastly, the *doblón*, the *peso* and the *real* were worth 4,352, 272 and 34 *maravedis* respectively.

To form an idea of the relation between Peruvian money in the time of la Perricholi and money in 1960, the reader should note that the *patacón* was worth 50 times more than the *sol*, at the exchange rate of 28 *soles* to the USA dollar, 1960. Or it can be estimated that in Amat's day 1 pound sterling or 4 dollars was the equivalent of 5 *pesos*, in round figures and valued in gold.[15]

The financial policy of the crown tended to ship most of the gold to Spain, reserving silver for the local needs of Spanish America. This policy, added to the fact that America produced much more silver than gold, raised the relative value of gold (compared with silver) from 1 to 10·11 (1497), to 1 to 10·60 (1537), 1 to 13·29 (1609) and 1 to 16·55 (1686); from this maximum parity fell to 1 to 16 (1728), 1 to 15·07 (1737), to return to 1 to 16 in 1750. The royal *cédula* of December 23, 1642, still in force under Amat's government, instituted two different kinds of money: a 'heavy' coinage which remained in circulation in America and a 'light' coinage reserved exclusively for Spain. The firmness with which the Crown backed up the law and maintained the weight of its money in Peru made this Hispano-Indian money the international specie of the whole world for three centuries. The excellence—the health of this money was proverbial. It was used as standard on all the international markets, including those where the enemies

[15] I owe this rare and valuable information to the great kindness of Don Manuel Moreyra Paz-Soldan, one of the most eminent South American specialists in economic and monetary questions and whose works, especially *El Tráfico Marítimo en la época colonial* (Lima, 1944) are authoritative on the subject.

of Spain traded. An official of the State speaking of Dutch trade in the Pacific was in a position to say: 'The coin which the Dutch use is of "Castilian silver", for it is the most highly appreciated in the whole of the East.'[16]

Thus the money used in the overseas territories and especially Peru was 'good'. Without it, the Spanish Empire would certainly not have lasted three centuries.

[16] Quotations taken from *Relación del Procurador General de la Ciudad de Manila e Islas Filipinas a S.M.*, C.D.I.A.I., vol. VI, p. 391 *Carande*, pp. 139 et seq., quoted by Salvador de MADARIAGA in *L'Essor de l'Amérique espagnole*, p. 178.

CHAPTER THREE

INTELLECTUAL LIFE: LITERATURE AND THE FINE ARTS

If I have saved the pleasures of the mind till the end, it is not because they were negligible, but because they only appealed to a minority, what is conventionally called an 'intellectual élite'.

Mainly centred on Lima, the intellectual élite proclaimed, desired and asserted themselves to be Latin. This latinity was present everywhere. In the cloisters of the University of San Marcos where the pandects echoed. In the boudoirs of Lima, among the whistling birds, the heavy perfumes and the satin dresses. In the luxurious baroque colonial palaces where lords and great ladies did their utmost to ape European fashion down to the tiniest details. In the drawing-rooms of the court, where, for a century, the flashing jackets of the house of Bourbon had replaced the severe doublets of the house of Austria.

But Lima was particularly Latin owing to the sparkling gaiety of its women and the mordant wit of its men, clever at broadcasting epigrams and satires in the drawing-rooms and public places. The irony and sometimes the scurrility of society and popular gossip-writers filled the pages of the gazettes. From the earlier days of the viceroyalty, an Aretino of the drawing-room or crossroads responsible for keeping alight the torch of wit was always to be found. Used to a pleasant, unexacting way of life, frequenting the *corridas* and literary coteries, Lima society had one thing in common with Spanish society—it adored palace intrigues. Its vital preoccupation was to resemble as closely as possible the courtiers of Madrid whose manners it copied. So its eyes were turned, with a curious mixture of envy and mockery, in the direction of the metropolis, passionately attentive to everything that went on there and quite ready to adopt its customs and prejudices, though sometimes under pretence of criticizing them.

The advent of the Bourbon dynasty had helped to make the

manners of Lima society less strict. In fact, since Philip V, Madrid had become the relay station of French coquetry between Paris and Lima. But Lima was fond of more than the wig and the red heel. Another form of merchandize, subtle and invisible, passed under the customs officers' noses—ideas! It was a craze with the people of Lima not only to dress in the French manner, but also to think like the French. Who would have dared imagine that the solemn doctors of the University of San Marcos, tired of expounding Aristotle, would have welcomed the message of the Encyclopaedia with enthusiasm? But welcomed it was. Creole scholars revelled in Voltaire and Rousseau, though somewhat on the sly, because of the Inquisition. Even the bishop of Quito himself was not afraid to confess: 'Every day that passes makes me regret more the time lost to me by the barbarous education which the hair-splitters gave me up to the age of twenty-one.' Barbarous education? Strong words from the pen of a prelate. And the *Mercurio peruano,* organ of the new generation, proclaimed the sovereignty of free reason and the practice of the new science, while condemning scholastic philosophy 'which had infested the barbarous centuries of obscurity and darkness'.

LITERARY CIRCLES AND JOURNALS

Even more than the doctors and prelates, it was the youth who set the fashion. The time of la Perricholi, at least the last part of it, overlapped two generations: the old generation, traditionalist and faithful to Spain, and the young generation, which thought vigorously about emancipation and was already working for its coming. 'The students of 1800 were the insurrectionary leaders of 1820 and often the political leaders of 1830,' it has been said. For the time being, they were twenty, the age of great plans, if not of great achievements.

These young intellectuals were to be met in the *circulos*. I have already mentioned the *tertulias,* basically worldly meetings at which the main topics were cancans and frivolities. Quite different and much more serious were the circles (*circulos*), the meeting-places of students, journalists and young poets, all men of culture and 'advanced' outlook. The discussions held there often had a serious tone. Not only belles-lettres, but also the future of the country were talked about. Where did literature end and politics begin? It was very hard to say. In any case, these discussions caused quite a stir, especially because they were diffused by the press, which made itself the vehicle of current tendencies.

Peru seems to have acquired a taste for newspapers very early. The first news-sheet appeared there in 1594. It gave details of the capture of Richard Hawkins. The regular publication of news had begun in Lima in 1621. It is believed that, during most of the seventeenth century, the printing-house of Contreras regularly published a review of the news of each month up to 1711. In 1744, a new journal, *La Gaceta de Lima*, appeared every two months until 1777. In 1790, Viceroy Gil de Taboada founded *El Diario Erudito Económico y Comercial de Lima*, which in the following year became *El Mercurio peruano* and also *La Gaceta del Gobierno de Lima*. *El Mercurio peruano* was an interesting, well-produced paper, but it appeared irregularly. There were no daily papers; they usually came out weekly or fortnightly. But it can be said that, as from the middle of the eighteenth century, Peru was in touch with the public opinion, not only of Spain, but also of the world in general. The Madrid papers and especially *El Espíritu de los Mejores Diarios*, a sort of digest of world news, were received regularly, with the inevitable time lag owing to the hazards of the sea crossings.

TOWN AND COUNTRY LITERATURE: SATIRE AND
VIRGILIAN THEMES

The Peruvians read the papers. They also read books. Firstly those which came from Europe and whose entry into Peru was subject to censorship by the Inquisition, especially French books, which were judged subversive and capable of corrupting people's minds. But although the Holy Office retained the right to look at books, its look had become very indulgent. 'Forbidden' books circulated comparatively freely in Peru and often with the complicity of the clergy. A system of 'authorization to read' was practised and widely abused. In 1786, Fray Diego de Cisternas, monk of St Jerome, was denounced because he possessed books containing violent criticisms of the Holy Office. As the accused was on very good terms with the viceroy, one of the Inquisitors paid him a visit to make due apology and excuse himself for having deprived him of forbidden books. Don Ramón de Rozas, intimate adviser of the viceroy of Peru, owned, read and lent forbidden books and was none the worse for it. On several occasions, the Supreme Council of the Holy Office ordered books which had been confiscated by the local Inquisition to be returned to their owners. There were vast libraries at Lima belonging either to private individuals or to communities, which contained the best productions of European literature—Spanish, Italian and French. These books were exempt from all the duties and taxes that weighed so heavily on other goods; they did not have to pay *alcabala, diezmo* or *portaje,* which greatly facilitated their importation.

If the Inquisition closed its eyes to the traffic in French books, some viceroys, such as Teodoro de Croix, hunted them down pitilessly and prohibited the entry into Peru of the works of the Encyclopaedists under penalty of severe punishments. They entered all the same. How could people firmly determined to read certain books be prevented from doing so? Voltaire, Diderot and Rousseau entered in spite of the customs officers, concealed in mother of pearl cases, hat boxes and even in the false bottoms of casks of wine coming from France.

Apart from the books imported from Europe, there was also a literary production peculiar to Peru and its size and quality were by no means negligible. It had the following peculiarity: its style, or rather its manner, reflected the political characteristics of the viceroyalty. It was a literature inspired by environment, on the one hand, and topical, current events, on the other. Since the intellectual centre of Peru was not in the geographical centre of the country, but on the coast, the viceroyalty was divided into two parts: the coast, dominated by Lima, domain of the white man and the half-breed, residence of the ruling classes, was both the cultural and political capital, and the *sierra,* which was almost entirely Indian. It followed that the literature of Peru was incarnated by two completely distinct styles: the literature of Lima—urban, social and satirical—and the literature *serrana*—bucolic, elegiac and Virgilian. The satirical spirit showed itself at Lima in all its guises. Its origin was Spanish. 'It was a Spanish tradition that the people avenge their miseries and pay out their oppressors by making fun of them.' The Creole liked to poke fun at others, and himself even more, perhaps. This ability to laugh at oneself made Peru a first-class home for satire. The Peruvian *lisura,* genius of the coast, was well represented.

Already, fifty years earlier, Cuviedes, incisive and ferocious, had published a satire against doctors under the title *Diente del Parnaso.* Castillo, poet and writer of impromptu verses, depicted the life of Lima in the past and loosed off some malicious darts at his contemporaries. More caustic still, sometimes even violent and coarse, Esteban de Teralla, author of *Lima por dentro y fuera,* sent vollies of arrows at the people of Lima, gluttons, sensualists, liars and self-seekers. A book that appeared in 1773 had a great success. Its author, whose real name was hidden under the sonorous pseudonym of Concolorcorvo, had depicted for the first time in Spanish America the societies and human types encountered in the course of a journey to Argentina and Peru. This book, entitled *El Lazarillo del ciego caminante desde Buenos Aires hasta Lima,* The Journey of a Blind Traveller from Buenos Aires to Lima, gives a curious account of the manners of this period, although it must not be taken literally.

Satire was even accepted at the viceregal court, which showed apparent indulgence with regard to it. Teodoro de Croix, one of Amat's successors, was friends with intellectuals as different as the erudite Don Hipolito Unane, who published his articles in the *Mercurio peruano* under the pseudonym of Aristeo, Brother Cipriano Jeronimo Catalayud, of the Order of Mercy, who signed his articles in the same paper Sofronio, Doctor Davalos, 'highly praised' by the University of Montpellier, the priest Rodriguez de Mendoza, nicknamed the Bacon of Peru by his acquaintances, the Andalusian poet Terrala y Landa and many others. Apparent indulgence, indeed, for Teodoro de Croix, one day that a certain Brother Juan Alcedo, of the Augustinian Order, had handed him a satire on the behaviour of the Spaniards in America, sent that insolent rhymer back to Spain, guilty of irreverence with regard to the viceregal person and the Spanish fatherland.

It was fashionable to versify and even banter in the most elegant circles, including the viceroy's antechamber. Senior members of the clergy also followed the fashion. Distinguished prelates conformed to it, such as Don José María Perez y Armandáriz, twenty-fifth bishop of Cuzco, whose puns and epigrams were famous throughout Peru. This high dignitary of the Church was very charitable and gave away all his income as alms. Knowing that he was so indifferent to luxury and money, one of his friends, shocked to see that he kept a gold spittoon, remarked on it one day. The bishop immediately improvised this reply:

'I keep it, because it is
of gold, not another metal:
a good Christian should use
gold to spit upon.'[1]

The memory of this nonagenarian bishop and maker of puns was preserved for a long time at Cuzco. Here is an example. A certain Colonel Pedro had received a *papier* (letter) from a prelate in which he asked for mercy to be shown to a soldier. As the colonel had left the bishop's recommendation unanswered, the latter sent the following poem on the rounds of Cuzco. It is based on a pun on Pedro and *piedra* (Peter and stone in Spanish) and its realism is most unepiscopal:

'A Spaniard and a gentleman
is Pedro and it is his duty
to use paper
to wipe his behind.
This method does not surprise me
in such an animal;
but I who am only an Indian,
use stone for that purpose.'[2]

A contrived pun, for although it was true that the Indians used a stone for this purpose, the bishop of Cuzco was not an Indian.

'Virgilian' literature, i.e. literature that extolled the beauties of nature, also had its adepts. It was born on the *haciendas*. The Creole *hacendados*, living all their lives in the fabulous, limitless Andean landscape, were naturally led to sing its praises! The way had been prepared for them by foreign travellers, mainly French, such as La Condamine, Bompland, Jussieu, Mutis, Frézier and Humboldt, whose tales had excited their own curiosity.

[1] *Histoire de la littérature américaine de langue espagnole*, by R. Bazin, Hachette, Paris, 1953.
[2] Ricardo PALMA: *Tradiciones peruanas*, translated by Mathilde Pomès, pp. 205–206.

These travellers, at first absorbed by nature, whether they were engineers or geographers, soon took an interest in the people. Surprised and charmed by the exotic quality of Hispano-American societies, they tried to depict them, especially Frézier and Humboldt. Thus they taught the inhabitants of Peru not only to see their country, but also to see themselves.

This discovery of themselves and their country through the intermediary of foreign travellers had a stimulating effect on the Creoles. Stung by being taught about their own fatherland by foreigners, they saw it with a fresh eye and rediscovered it. At the same time, Peru was influenced by the physiocratic theories which proclaimed the principles that the earth alone created wealth, that the circulation of goods should be free and that taxes should only affect landed property. Formulated by Quesnay, defended by Mirabeau, Turgot and Malesherbes, physiocracy found an ideal soil in Spanish America, whose economy was essentially rural. Lyricism took hold of the economy. So that, under the combined signs of agriculture, geography and poetry, was born what can appropriately be called American Virginialism. It was a good deal more scientific than literary, to judge by the two following titles: *Observaciones sobre el clima de Lima* by Hipólito Unanue and *Memorias históricas, físicas, críticas, apologéticas de la América meridional* by José Eusebio de Llano Zepata.

PAINTING AND MUSIC

Classical colonial art was mainly Spanish. However, the Indian tradition had marked it deeply—hence those Madonnas with the impassive face of the half-breed and the stiff garments weighed down with gold, which recalled the hieratic quality of Inca art rather than Spanish Baroque. This alliance, this osmosis of past and present, was particularly visible in painting, especially in the painting emanating from the 'school of Cuzco'. In fact, the ancient capital of the Incas, the town with stone temples and palaces, had become an artistic centre. The viceroyalty had brought painters from Spain—Murillo's son, for example—who had taught the Indian and half-breed artists the secret of the Spanish technique. This had brought about the Cuzcan school of painting, which mainly dealt with religious subjects, but sometimes also with

235

episodes borrowed from contemporary history. Using themes which were inspired by the Italian Mannerism then in fashion and which the Spanish masters had imported into Peru—Francisco Albani and the influence of the Bolognese school—the Cuzcan painters also resorted to local representations. So that, drawing alike on Indian folklore and the Spanish repertoire, the artists of Cuzco did not hesitate to paint Spanish types, treated in the Italian manner, against a Flemish background. But the Cuzcan masters did not confine themselves to copying Spanish engravings, while adapting them to local taste. They had attempted the difficult art of portraiture. A difficult, but remunerative art. For the great ambition of 'donors' was to have themselves portrayed, generally in full dress, which gave the artist the chance to show off his technique, by paying great attention to the drawing of lace, ribbons and embroidery. The production of these painters was not all of the same standard. Sometimes they confined themselves to copying, more or less faithfully, pious lithographs: Stations of the Cross, Good Shepherds with or without sheep, Seated Madonnas, Madonnas with grapes, Madonnas with fish. Sometimes, on the other hand, owing to the originality of their inspiration and the freshness of their colouring, they surpassed their Spanish models and came close to the Italian primitives, for example, in the picture of St Antony preaching to the birds. On the left, the saint speaking to the birds and fish which shout 'Hallelujah!' At sea a caravel. In the woods a puma, a peccary, a tortoise and an ant-eater. In the first spurs of the Andes a town and in the foreground beggars drinking, smoking and playing dice.

There were not many painters who made their fortune. Painting was a risky profession in Peru, where fashion played a large part, where it only needed the whim of an important personage at the viceregal court to launch a painter. The dream of every Cuzcan painter was to have his material and colours sent from Spain. He installed himself in a vast, well-lit studio. He trained pupils who helped him to finish his commissions.

But the situation of the painters who did not manage to make a name was miserable. They painted with makeshift materials. In the absence of artists' colourmen at Cuzco, they looked for ochres and earth colours in the neighbouring ravines, and bought powdered colours from the apothecary, oil and turpentine from the grocer. They used powdered incense as a siccative and burnt bone and candle smoke to obtain bitumen and black. Their brushes were of dog's hair and they stretched their canvases not on a frame, but on a plank with nails. As for their palette, they used a broken plate.

Music had the advantage of being within everybody's reach, both cultivated and primitive. In the drawing-rooms of Lima high society, people played the harp, a favourite instrument of the Peruvians, and the guitar, and they sang. They also danced, either Spanish dances, or the minuet, which had come from France. But music was most appreciated among the people. The main instruments were the following: the *quena*, a bamboo flute with seven holes, five of them on the fore part, one on the back part and one smaller one, near the mouthpiece; the *charango*, a small guitar housea in the carapace of a *tatou*; the *bombo*, a bass drum; the *phucu*, a short flute; the *anthara*, another, long flute and the *tinya*, a tambourine, not forgetting the harp, very different from the European harp. The Indian melodies were melancholy, expressing sadness more often than joy, sometimes, such as the hymns sung at funeral ceremonies, frankly lugubrious, hymns of grief into which however slipped a note of hope, an echo of the popular soul. The music of the Church had its own instrumentation. Religious services were generally accompanied by the organ, which had been imported into Peru by the Jesuits. But organists were rare. So, in certain villages of the *sierra*, they resorted to trumpets made of shells which sounded during the elevation of the host, the honour of blowing them being reserved for mayors. And there was always some humble local artist to play the Peruvian harp, which was well suited for softening pious souls.

Though the people of the towns were not short of distractions —if only the spectacle in the streets—the Indian of the Cordillera had no other pastime but to modulate his *quena*, made with his own hands from a special wood which grew only in the Andean sierra. Seated on rocks almost inaccessible to anyone except himself and his flock, his legs dangling over some abyss, his eyes turned to the horizon, he played while his eyes filled with tears. He was sad and happy at the same time. Sometimes, accompanied by a comrade's *quena*, he sang sentimental chants, called *yaravis*, in a monochord tone. The words of these primitive airs were collected by professional musicians. They in turn made them into songs whose success was guaranteed by the young society girls who sang them in the drawing-rooms. Here are some passages from a *yaravi* so adapted:

'When a loving turtle-dove has lost her husband, anxious and shuddering, she leaves, turns and takes flight.

Pensive and restless, she wanders in the woods, seeking among plants and willows the object of her desires.

Her heart broken with despair, she weeps, not caring now about fountains, rivers, gulfs and seas.

Thus I live, alas, since the fatal moment when I lost you, a radiant enchantment, sweet charm of my days!

I weep and my tears are without consolation, for my sorrow is great, and I breathe nothing but grief, sadness and anguish.

My memories oppress me, when my heart, rediscovering your adored face, sees you always like icy marble, like a dead flower.

If I go to weep in the vast countryside, my sorrow increases: trees, mountains, valleys and meadows, all speak to me of you.

In my solitude, I perceive you bringing me sweet consolation, tender affection, gentle caresses.

In my dreams, you disturb my rest and you plunge me into perturbation and terror.

My memories torment me, but they please my heart, which constantly suffers, weeps and calls out.

My sorrow moves the universe and, seeing in me the most faithful lover, all mankind and the birds themselves associate themselves with my sadness.

As long as I live, I shall follow your wandering shade, without fearing fire or water. No, nothing will ever restrain the impetus of my eternal love!'

Thus atavistic Indian nostalgia found its best expression in pastoral themes.

THE THEATRE: THEATRES, PLAYS, ACTORS AND VARIETY SHOWS

Literature remained the achievement of an élite. At least one had to know how to read, which was not the case with all Peruvians! More than fifty per cent of the population was illiterate. As for painting and music, in spite or rather because of their frequently popular character, they did not interest everybody. Certain distinguished circles despised Indian folklore. The really universal 'pleasure of the mind', in which everyone, even among the humblest, shared, was the theatre.

Although originally the theatre was born in Peru, as in ancient Greece, as in modern Europe, in the form of a religious rite, it had become very secularized in the eighteenth century. But from the beginning, in the seventeenth century, the principal towns of Peru possessed their permanent theatre, their companies of actors and actresses, and the plays, written either in Peru or Spain, delighted everybody, nobles and plebeians. At Potosi, Salvador de Madariaga tells us,

'there were four companies of actors and actresses, and plays were performed every Sunday and holiday; the sale of tickets brought in three or four thousand dollars, without counting the price of the most comfortable seats which represented a fine income for the Royal Hospital, for a box for a family cost four or five dollars'.

But naturally the capital of the theatre was Lima.

The rise of theatre in Peru had been seriously compromised at the time of the earthquake of 1746, which had completely destroyed the big theatre of Lima, called the *Coliseo de Comedias*. Though this did not stop the festivities for the coronation of Ferdinand VI from being the occasion of a big theatrical performance. 'The people of Lima's love of the theatre must have been very great, for less than two years after the terrible earthquake of 1746, they were in a position to perform the works of Calderón and other local authors of less importance with such luxury and ceremony.'[3]

Therefore Lima decided to celebrate the proclamation of the new king in Spain by three theatrical performances, which were to take place in the palace of the viceroy, each preceded by fireworks set off the night before in the Plaza Mayor, with illuminations throughout the town. Everything was prepared for the month of February, 1748, in four months' time. Everyone took part in the preparations. Even the ladies of the nobility helped to make the actors' costumes. During the three nights preceding the 14th Feb-

[3] *El arte dramático en Lima durante el Virreinato* by Guillermo LOHMANN VILLENA, p. 399.

ruary, the date fixed for the beginning of the festivities, the viceroy presented concerts in the gallery of the palace which opened on to the illuminated Plaza Mayor. They included opera music, with a great number of players, some of whom were foreigners and were being heard for the first time or played unpublished works. The second patio of the palace had been chosen for the theatrical performance, because of its vast dimensions. It was arranged in a semi-circle so that nothing that was said or done on the stage should be missed by the spectators. A platform was provided for the ladies and, in the centre, opposite the stage, was the viceroy, surrounded by important officials. The play performed was one of Calderón's, *Not even love escapes from love*, a sort of mythological drama based on the legend of Cupid and Psyche. The work by Calderón had been chosen as the most appropriate in the circumstances, for it alluded to a town overwhelmed with benefactions by an absent sovereign and people saw in it an analogy with the town of Lima which was fêting a distant monarch. The spectacle began with a curtain-raiser composed by a Lima clergyman, Félix de Alarcón, and which was a panegyric of the sovereign. The performance went on for six hours and ended with a feast in the course of which the viceroy offered his guests lavish refreshments. The spectacle was given on three consecutive days.[4]

This custom of celebrating great events that had taken place in Spain by theatrical performances in Peru was to last until the Emancipation.

Thus, the accession of Charles IV was the occasion for bullfights, nocturnal illuminations, masked processions and operatic performances. Four floats traversed the streets of Lima on which allegorical scenes in praise of the king of Spain were played. The first represented Africa, the air and Music. The second: Asia, Fire and Autumn. The third: America, Water and Spring. In the last appeared Europe, Earth and Winter. All these scenes had been rehearsed the day before in the drawing-rooms of the palace before the viceroy himself. The actors were sumptuously dressed, but the text was mediocre.[5]

The viceroys were very responsive to these flattering perform-

[4] Reported by Abbé Courle de la Blanchardière in his *Nouveau Voyage fait au Pérou*, Paris, 1751.

[5] *El arte dramático en Lima durante el Virreinato* by Guillermo LOHMANN VILLENA.

ances, the more so because they sometimes made a profit from them, if we are to believe Ricardo Palma:

'In addition to the income which his Majesty granted his viceroys in Peru by royal decrees, the latter were always fêted when the requirements of the service made them go to the port of Callao; they were welcomed there by a salvo of cannon fire. But the viceroy was entitled to choose between the shots, which after all are only smoke and noise, and the value in money of what would have been spent on powder. It is said that the representatives of the Crown did not fail to opt for the second alternative, in which they acted sensibly.'

Another royal *cédula* provided that, when the viceroy attended a theatrical performance, the actors and their impresario were obliged to hand over to the major-domo or pastrycook of the palace a few *onzas* for the sorbets and pastries of His Excellency. I should add that many of these viceroys, including Manuel Guirior, Amat's successor, if they accepted these tithes immediately handed them over to charitable works.

We have seen that the most important theatre in Peru was the Coliseo de Comedias at Lima, so that is the one I shall describe. It was the Confraternity of the Hospital of San Andrés which undertook the reconstruction of the theatre, completely destroyed by the earthquake of 1746. Without neglecting anything that would guarantee its solidity, it brought off the remarkable feat of finishing it in one year. In April, 1749, the hall was open to the public, but more than 32,000 pesos (about 23,000 pounds) had been spent, and the Confraternity had had to make representations to the viceroy so that he would authorize it to incur this expense by decree. Neighbouring houses and courtyards had been bought in order to enlarge the new theatre. The interior decorations, the costumes and everything that was necessary for the actors had been extensively provided for. However, the building does not seem to have been a complete success and the place 'had the bad reputation of being harmful to the health, for an intake of air which was reflected back on a façade of the monastery of the Augustines swept into the entrance passage, causing a draught that was reputed to provoke pains and rheumatism'.

The new theatre opened its doors on Easter Day, 1749. 'There was one great cry of admiration for the success of the edifice, whose happy proportions reconciled the requirements of the stage with comfort.' The hall, the floor of which was of wood from Chile, was shaped like an amphitheatre and included 113 oak orchestra stalls. According to custom, this part of the theatre was exclusively reserved for men. As for soldiers, sailors and coloured people, they were not allowed there unless they were properly dressed. A corridor which opened to the right of the main entrance was reserved for the governors; it was lighted by gratings and lanterns, and gave direct access to the places reserved for the viceroy. These places comprised three boxes in the front row, draped with velvet and surmounted by arches set off with paintings. The three boxes opposite the viceroy were reserved for the *ayuntamiento* (the Town Hall). All the boxes, seventeen in number, were served by a wide corridor and each one could hold eight spectators, comfortably seated. There were also four stage-boxes situated on both sides and a little below that of the viceroy and the *ayuntamiento*, and also decorated. At the far end of the entrance corridor and next to the viceroy's box a small door led on to the floor of the stage and to the artistes' rooms. At the end of the hall was the part reserved for males 'of lower quality'. In the left-hand partition of the lower corridor was a staircase with wooden steps and banisters leading to the upper gallery on to which opened the second-storey boxes, twenty-three in number and separated by wooden partitions and heavy draperies. Two more staircases, starting from the right and left of the second gallery, led to the third storey, called the *cazuela* and always reserved for the ladies. The actors' dressing-room, although less luxurious, had an attractive appearance, especially when la Perricholi had marked it with her presence a few years later. There was also a shop inside the Coliseo that sold ices, sorbets, sweets and fruit.[6]

Closed for repairs in 1758, the Coliseo, embellished and renovated, celebrated its reopening in 1762 by putting on an opera, *Maquina Real de Muñecos*. In the interim, performances had taken place either in halls rented for the occasion or in official buildings, such as the festival given on June 19, 1760, in the palace of the viceroy, the Marquis de Rocafuerte, to celebrate the accession of Charles III. After the reopening of the Coliseo, music played

----

[6] Description taken from a series of articles by Don Luis Antonio Eguiguren which appeared in *La Prensa* of Lima under the title *The Streets of Lima*, in December, 1942.

a much larger part in the spectacles and the composer Bartolomé
Massa received the title of master of music in 1765 and became
stage-manager. But in 1770, as the result of quarrels that set him
at odds with Villaverde and Sacomano, he lost these posts for two
years. His contract was renewed on October 14, 1772, at the
request of Viceroy Amat, his protector. The general inventory of
the property of the Coliseo was then drawn up; it even enumerated
the actors' costumes. In 1777, Viceroy Guirior having succeeded
to Amat, Massa lost his protector and had to hand over the administration of the Coliseo to Villaverde. In 1789, it was decided to
re-cover the whole of the roof, which entailed closing down the
theatre again until December, when it reopened for the feasts in
honour of the accession of Charles IV.[7]

If I have dwelt at some length on the Coliseo and its vicissitudes,
it is because it was, after all, the national theatre of the viceroyalty
of Peru and, in that capacity, was much to the fore in the thoughts
of the people of Lima, who always showed great pride in it. Its
destruction, its reconstruction and its various rearrangements
inspired the most frequent remarks at nocturnal *tertulias*. '*¿Que
nuevo en el Coliseo?* What's new at the Coliseo?' The plays put on
there were also discussed. These were some of the plays advertised
by the Coliseo for the theatrical season of 1753: *The Creation of the
World* by Velez de Guevara, *The Power of Reason* by Añorbe,
God dispenses justice to everyone by Villegas, *Quality is better than
Quantity* by Bances Candamo and, most of all, many plays by
Calderón: *The Arms of Beauty, The Garden of Falerina, I am the
First, Enchantment without Enchantment*, etc. Theatrical performances were of varying degrees of length, but generally speaking,
programmes were heavily loaded. The programme for a certain
evening at the theatre of Callao comprised first of all the comedy by
Antonio de Zamora: '*Amar es saber vencer y el arte contra el poder,*
Loving is knowing how to conquer and art against power.' This
was the opener. Before the dramatic piece, an orchestra of violins
interpreted some music specially composed by an unknown author,
and other melodies accompanied the play by Pedro de Peralta, a
Spanish dramatist. Next came a sketch by the Aragonese Don
Geronima de Monforte y Vera, a fluid burlesque poet. Two
interludes composed by 'friends' of the viceroy and, to finish

[7] *El arte dramático en Lima durante el Virreinato* by Guillermo LOHMANN
VILLENA.

with, a ballet: *El Sarao de los Planetas*, The Dance of the Planets.

Now here are a few names of dramatic authors between 1714 and 1770. Father Francisco del Castillo y Tamayo, known as *El ciego de la Merced*, the Blind Man of Mercy, author of numerous sketches, interludes and plays, including *The Conquest of Peru* and *War is the Life of Man* (which is in the National Library at Madrid) and a historico-mythological piece, *Mithridates, King of Pontus*. The priest Felix de Morales, the Jesuit P. Miguel Carreño. In 1748, a comedy of Calderón's was staged, *Love frees itself from Love*, in which ladies from high Lima society condescended to act. Lastly, there were female playwrights, such as the Prioress of the Convent of Santa Catalina who put on in 1743 what is called a *zarzuela*, that is to say a vaudeville, generally in one act, the dialogue of which was mixed with couplets.

So dramatic production in Peru was reasonably varied, since edifying plays such as *The Life and Miracles of St Rose of Peru* by Calderón y Moreto alternated with popular sketches such as *La Clementina* by the Spaniard Ramón de la Cruz, accompanied by music by Boccherini. Gradually it became the habit to introduce dances into the spectacle. The performers danced dances that were *muy vistosas* (very showy), such as the *Fandango*, the *Don Mateo* and the *Matatoros*; others, of French origin, such as the minuet, and yet another called the *Mongol*, a sort of Chinese pantomime. An acrobat who danced on a tightrope, with his eyes blindfolded, drew the whole of Lima. Often, the 'pure' theatre was supplanted by 'amusements' that were highly prized by the public. That was how dancing academies were opened at Lima as from the second half of the eighteenth century. They organized competitions between themselves, in which their pupils took part. A certain Léandre Orléans, of French origin, had succeeded in attracting the whole of the Lima public to his academy to watch these competitions, which became as popular as the theatre. There was a danger in this for the theatre. People might begin to prefer variety spectacles of lower quality and increasingly lax morals. Conscious of this danger, which seemed to have escaped Amat's notice, Viceroy Teodoro de Croix, one of his successors, had to take measures in order to arrest, in his own words, 'the free-and-easiness dating from Amat's day'.

Censorship controlled the theatre, as it did the press and literature. But since Amat's arrival it had become more understanding, modelling its attitude on the viceroy's. The 'free-and-easiness' which was to shock Teodoro de Croix at the moment when he assumed office had indeed been the work of his predecessor, whose love of the theatre was so great that he no longer distinguished its moral frontiers very clearly. In such circumstances, how could the censorship have been stricter than the viceroy? However, although it was indulgent, the civil and religious police saw to it that morality and the royal authority were not handled too roughly. People still remembered an edict issued by the Inquisition on December 22, 1758, inflicting the penalty of excommunication and a fine of 500 pesos on those who, infringing its ban, 'retained' one of the manuscripts that circulated clandestinely under the name of *Titulos de comedias nuevas*. The latter, composed at Lima, were full of allusions and even specific details that could harm certainly highly placed personages of unimpeachable morality. The edict remained in force, but it was not applied; allusions to the viceregal court, the clergy and officials were tolerated, provided that they did not directly implicate the person of His Majesty.[8]

In the same spirit, theatrical criticism was not subject to restrictions. The paper *Diario Erudito Económico y Comercial de Lima* for the years 1790 to 1793 contains an account of the plays which were put on at the Coliseo during those years. The *Mercurio peruano* and the *Semanario Crítico* at the end of the eighteenth century gave an important place to theatrical criticism of both foreign and Lima productions.

The theatre was appreciated by everyone and in all parts of the country, even the small towns. Frézier tells us that he was present at the Feast of the Scapulary at Pisco, organized by the mulattos in honour of Our Lady of Carmel, under the aegis of the Fathers of Mercy. The rejoicings began with the performance of a Spanish play, *El Príncipe poderoso*, The Powerful Prince, which was a mixture of sacred and profane. The altar of the Virgin, at the back of the stage, was the main feature of the décor. The play began with the recitation, kneeling, of an edifying prologue. Nevertheless, throughout the play, obscenities and crude clowning succeeded each other. The next day there was a bullfight, then, at night, a mock race with torches, followed by people in carts or on horseback

[8] *El arte dramático en Lima durante el Virreinato* by Guillermo LOHMANN VILLENA.

who shouted, sang and danced, while calling upon Our Lady of Carmel. The following Sunday *The Life of St Alexis* was performed by talented mulatto actors, who passed with ingenuous facility from the sacred to the libertine manner. I should add that the mulattos of Pisco were not professionals, any more than a good number of the actors who performed in the colleges and church clubs for charity. On the other hand, those who shone on the stage of the Coliseo or went on tour to Callao, Arequipa and Cuzco, were professionals. Professional actors were comparatively numerous, but those who made a name in their career could be counted on the fingers of one hand. And even they were only billed for a few months. In Peru, as in Spain, theatrical glory was ephemeral and the people of Lima soon got tired of their idols. Among the male celebrities, we may mention the tragedian Roldan, a pupil of Isidoro Maiquez, the juvenile lead Rodriguez Cedaba, and Barbieto, who excelled in the part of a traitor. To remain a 'star' was even more difficult for women than for men. But when an actress was a box-office attraction, there was no hesitation in paying her lavish fees. In 1752, the major-domo of the Confraternity of San Andrés—responsible for 'theatrical affairs'—had included in the contract of Doña Maria Manuela de Iturriaga a lump sum of 1,000 pesos for her to buy costumes, about 720 pounds sterling. These high fees compensated for the salaries, which were uneven. Although in principle there was a scale fixing the earnings for each category of job, the directors did not always conform to it.

A little later, the most famous *comica* was to be she who was familiarly called Inés or Inesilla, whose celebrity, however, owed less to her talents on the stage than to her rivalry with la Perricholi.

AN ENCOUNTER WITH LA PERRICHOLI BY WAY OF FAREWELL

The reader will remember the melodrama by Alphonse Daudet and Bizet, *L'Arlésienne*, which tells the unhappy love story of a young Provençal lad. The heroine of the play—the Arlésienne—provokes, animates and concludes the drama. We hear the swish of her skirt against the scenery, we hear her laughter, we divine her presence, but she never appears. She is more provoking imagined than real. And yet la Perricholi was not a myth. She was a creature of flesh and blood—very much so! And then, not only did she incarnate the symbol of colonial life in Peru, but also the eccen-

246

15. a. Choir stalls, Cuzco Cathedral

b. Inner courtyard of La
Merced Convent, Cuzco

14. a. Henra's Balcony, Cuzco

b. House in Arequipa

tricities of her private life, the permanent scandal of her public life—her affair with the viceroy—were the periodic and even the daily topic of news in Lima. A new escapade by la Perricholi and the whole town gloated over it. For a better understanding of Peru in the time of the Spaniards, one would have to see la Perricholi acting on the stage of the Coliseo, walking down the Alameda, teasing the viceroy and during the latter part of her life going piously to church, as the people of Lima saw her or could have seen her every day for nearly half a century.

On September 28, 1748, on the eve of St Michael's Day, in an obscure suburb of Lima, and not, as certain authors claim, in the heart of the 'noble city' of Los Caballeros de Léon de Huanuco, a child was born to Don José Villegas, native of Arequipa, and Doña Teresa Hurtado de Mendoza y de la Cueva, a Lima woman. The child was Micaela de Villegas, known later by the name of Miquita. A few weeks later, the child was baptized in the Church of the Tabernacle, facing the Plaza Mayor of Lima, as attested by the certificate issued by Don José Patricio de la Barrameda, *Teniente de los Curas Rectores* of the parish. The fact that the baptism of Micaela figures in the Spanish registers testifies to the *limpieza de sangre* of the Villegas family. If a mulatto or half-breed child had been concerned, the inscription procedure would have been different. So Micaela was a Creole of good family. Of course, a few drops of Indian blood may have found their way into this Spanish blood in the past—no family in the New World was totally exempt from it—but very little.

At the time of her meeting with José Villegas, Teresa lived with brother Don Francisco, a magistrate by profession and heir to the name and fortune of the Mendozas, since the recent death of their mother, Doña Soledad. Both were lineally descended from the viceroys Don Andrés Hurtado de Mendoza, Marquis de Cañete, and Don José Antonio de Mendoza Caamaño Sotomayor, Marquis of Villagarcia. For two centuries the Mendozas had supplied the Crown with *corregidores, alcaldes* and royal treasurers, all of great ability and rectitude. When Teresa told her brother that she intended to marry José, the first thing he did was to ask what he was. 'A poet and musician,' confessed Teresa, blushing. A guitar strummer! But he had to yield to his sister's obstinacy. The marriage was celebrated on January 2, 1745, in the same Church of the Tabernacle in which Micaela was to be baptized four years later.

Francisco presided over the wedding, but vowed pitiless hatred against his brother-in-law.

The Villegas were to have six children, the last of whom was born in the same year in which Don Manuel de Amat y Juniel was appointed to the viceroyalty of Peru. Micaela was the eldest. At an early age she astonished her family and their friends by her natural aptitude for music and acting. She easily learnt whole scenes from Alarcón and Lope de Vega, which she recited immediately afterwards, without understanding a word of them. She played the harp. She was a good guitar player. She sang, she danced, she mimed. Friends and relations used to gather at night in the Villegas's humble dwelling to applaud Micaela's first attempts. She already showed that she had talent in several fields, for she passed easily from dramatic declaration to imitations of fashionable tunes, refrains that were whistled on the Alameda. A fine future awaited her. ¡Si Dios quiere! (God willing).

José Villegas did not see his daughter's first appearances on the stage. He died comparatively young, leaving his widow with the heavy responsibility of a family to bring up. Perhaps the Villegas's stay at Tomayquicua, in the environs of Huanuco, in the Andean sierra, dates from this time. The visitor is still shown the old house in which Micaela and her family lived for a time and the garden made fragrant with chirimoya flowers. Perhaps it is no longer the same house, nor the same garden, but the perfumes have not changed. Micaela's historiographers would like to explain certain traits of her character by the influence of the huanuqueño landscape. 'Our Perricholi is Andean like our Indian brother,' states Ventura Garcia Calderón. And he imagines her 'in the company of llamas and alpacas, watcher of the summits'. Inconsolable because Micaela was born, on her own admission, at Lima and not at Huanuco, they could not abandon the legend of a romantic Perricholi, steeping herself in the mournful Andean landscape and powdering her face with white ceruse to make herself look like a Creole, as the Indian mountain women did.

Teresa, undoubtedly thinking of Micaela's future career, returned to Lima. Meanwhile, Francisco had become an important figure in the Audience. There's a relation who could be very useful to the child, thought Teresa, who boldly went to face her brother. But he had not changed his attitude, in spite of his brother-in-law's death. He refused his niece help and protection.

Let her fend for herself! So Micaela did without her vindictive uncle.

Micaela probably made her first appearance on the stage very young. But for some years she confined herself to interpreting minor parts. The theatre where she really acted for the first time was the Coliseo, brand new in its renovated splendour.

Don Manuel de Amat assumed his high office on October 12, 1761. Micaela was thirteen years old at the time. Six or seven years passed before the viceroy noticed the young actress. But she did not wait that long to attract people and be loved. The beginning of her love life, like that of her theatrical career, remains obscure. On this point too, legend and history are intermingled. If we are to believe the *Drama de las Palanganas,* Micaela left her family to establish herself in a street of ill fame, the *calle de Huevo,* in which lived slaves and 'women of her rank', for 'a woman of the theatre is unworthy of mixing with ladies because of her profession'. But the *Drama de las Palanganas,* the Drama of the Wash-basins, is a pamphlet directed against Amat's administration. So it is advisable not to take its author's opinions literally; he was inclined to blacken anything remotely concerning Don Manuel. But it is not being disrespectful to Micaela's memory to recognize her great skill in matters of the heart. When still quite young, she knew how to cumulate the advantages of protector and genuine lover. Her first intrigue was with a certain Moteu—probably a Frenchman—who took her away from her mother's house. A man called Gamuzo succeeded him, then a juvenile lead who gave him his cue, José Estacio. She was said to be on very intimate terms with Maza, the administrator of the Coliseo, although it was not proved. This was all common behaviour in the theatrical world and no one, not even honest women, found anything to take exception to in it.

When Micaela conquered the viceroy, she was not quite twenty. Let us try to picture her. First of all, was she beautiful? Those who knew her agree in granting her incomparable charm, in the absence of extraordinary beauty. She was better than beautiful, she was charming. Small and on the plump side, she was pretty. Her complexion was a very pale brown, her eyes 'the colour of steel', at the same time ardent and languorous beneath thick eyelashes. She skilfully concealed traces of smallpox with make-up. A beauty spot above her upper lip made her rather thick mouth, with its small very white teeth, even livelier. Her hair was abundant and very black and her hands and feet tiny. Her white satin shoes could be held in the palm of the hand. With a round neck, a pretty nose, but of the type the Creoles called *nato* (flattened), her breasts bursting out of her corsage, Micaela passed for a lovely, sexually attractive, girl, *bien laminada* as the Peruvians put it.

That was Micaela on the day when she acted before the viceroy for the first time. He returned the next day, and the day after that. His eyes never left her, sometimes he winked at her and he applauded loudly. His enthusiasm increased until he could no longer moderate it. This serious man of sixty, who was considered the coldest magistrate in the Spanish Indies, became as crazy as a stripling in a few weeks. He stamped his feet, shouted and rapped the floor with his cane. The ladies of good Lima society watched the grimaces of the old gentleman with white hair with a very shocked air. Such a scandal had never been seen since Peru had been a viceroyalty. But that did not stop Don Manuel on the road to his conquest. Was it difficult? Did he use shock tactics or patient strategy? Undoubtedly the malicious child made the viceroy languish just long enough to attach himself to her for more than one night. Once she was sure that by losing her virtue—or its appearance— she would win much more than the coach of the legend, she yielded.

When a young lady of easy virtue met a protector or an actress had just been singled out by a minister, her first move was to change her lodgings. Micaela did so too, transporting her household goods to the middle-class parish of San Marcelo. At night, she visited the palace by an underground passage that led to the garden. From this moment, the viceroy's affair with the actress was considered official. Far from keeping it secret, it seems that Don Manuel experienced a mischievous satisfaction in broadcasting it publicly to his subordinates. It was his custom to spend his weekends at Miraflores, in the villa of his nephew, Colonel Antonio Amat y Rocaberti. He took his mistress with him, or rather behind him, because of the protocol forbidding anyone to sit side by side with the viceroy. From then on, every Saturday at the end of the afternoon, Don Manuel could be seen leaving the palace in his heavy gilded carriage, followed by Micaela mounted on a horse bedecked with pompons and little bells. She dressed like a man, or else wore a long sky-blue skirt embroidered with gold fringes and a toque of feathers.

Don Manuel was not the richest man in Peru—far from it. But

he held one of the most remunerative offices in the overseas administration. As we have already seen, his annual income was 60,000
pesos, to which was added the revenue from various tithes, some
12,000 pesos. Thus, during the fourteen years and nine months of
his government, Don Manuel received 1,080,000 pesos, apart from
the commissions he took on various livings, calculated at about
5,000,000 pesos for the same period. A smarter and more venal
girl than Micaela would have hastened to leave the stage, estimat-
ing that the love of the viceroy was well worth the sacrifice of a
theatrical career. Micaela did nothing of the sort. She loved her
profession and would have put it before Don Manuel, if he had
not insisted that she stick to it. He loved the actress as much as the
woman. And then this rich official was no spendthrift. The 150
pesos that Maza, administrator of the Coliseo, paid out annually
to Micaela had never seen the inside of the viceroy's purse. Lastly,
it should be added in praise of Micaela that she was not at all
greedy. Although she willingly received presents from Don Manuel
and sometimes asked for them, she never had the mentality of a
kept woman. Becoming the favourite of the representative of the
king of Spain did not make her lose her head. Her two loves were
freedom and the theatre.

Not only did Don Manuel do nothing to entice Micaela away
from the theatre, he even took an interest in her career. He went
to rehearsals and gave the actors advice. His familiarity with the
actors shocked the aristocracy of Lima, who were unused to seeing
the highest personage in the land frequenting people hitherto considered barely good enough to amuse them. The viceroy, disdainful
of what Peruvian class-consciousness might think of him, showed
an ever greater enthusiasm for the performances at the Coliseo.
Often he settled the conflicts that arose between Micaela and her
partners. They were numerous, for the actress was hot-tempered
But there was one which had serious consequences.

One summer day in 1773 when Micaela was acting in the play
by Calderón de la Barca, *Fuego de Dios en el querer bien,* her
partners. They were numerous, for the actress was hot-tempered.
'Come on! Put more life into it! Inés would do better than that.'
Inés, her worst enemy. In a paroxysm of rage, Micaela, raising a
cane that she held in her hand, lashed the impertinent actor's
cheek. The curtain fell and the public shouted: 'To prison with the
actress!' Without a word, but puce with anger, the viceroy with-

drew from his box on tiptoe and left the theatre. That night, he went to Micaela's house and said: 'After today's scandal, it's all over between us. You can be satisfied that I did not force you to beg the public's pardon on your knees. Goodbye, Perricholi!'

That was the launching of the word which was to make Micaela a historic figure. What exactly did it mean? Must we attribute to Don Manuel's Catalan accent or to the fact that he was gap-toothed the final deformation of Perra-chola? This last word may be translated as 'bitch of a half-breed' or 'precious little half-breed', the *perrita* being a small silver coin. In addition, the viceroy was accustomed to call his mistress, when he was caressing her, '*Mi joya, mi pretichol,*' from the Catalan word *pretixol*, precious little thing. Some scholars even claim that the word was never spoken by Don Manuel and that the nickname Perricholi attributed to Micaela was given her by a neighbour. In any case and as from that moment, Micaela was no longer Miquita, but la Perricholi.

The repeated and violent quarrels between the viceroy and la Perricholi did not last long. However, after the incident of the theatre, Don Manuel did not see the actress again for more than a year, at the same time that he strictly maintained the sentence debarring her from the theatre. She was replaced on the stage by her rival, Inéz de Mayorga, better known by the diminutive of Inesilla. Mischief-makers claimed that Inesilla was every bit as good as la Perricholi. But she was not la Perricholi.

The viceroy had broken with Micaela, but he continued to frequent the actors of the Coliseo. Undoubtedly he sought in the theatre's marble halls the shadow of his beloved, who consoled herself, it is said, with a Colonel from Navarre, Don Martín de Armandáriz. Each as spiteful as the other, neither la Perricholi nor the viceroy made the first move. The reconciliation of the two lovers on September 17, 1775, was the work of the actor José Eustacio and la Perricholi's triumphal evening that of November 4, 1775, when the actress made her return to the stage of her first appearance after a year and a half's absence. Wilder than ever, with burning eyes and a smile of triumph on her lips, she reconquered her public, who acclaimed her like a long-lost queen. She sang and her voice had never been more beautiful. Maza had begged her pardon—by order! Inesilla fled to Lurin whence she was brought back by force and thrown into prison, for breaking her contract without notice! The viceroy, standing in the first row of the dress-circle, beat time. The story is even told that to encourage la Perricholi—intimidated, it seems, although not showing it—Amat called to her: 'Come on! There's nothing to have stage-fright about. Courage and sing well!'

That was the beginning of a triumphal period for la Perricholi. The viceroy insisted that she be paid the honours reserved for personages of high rank. A child was born to them in the meantime, the fruit of their reconciliation. He was called Manuelito like his father. A group of sycophants crowded round the child, dressed with incredible luxury and wearing round its neck a broad red ribbon like that of the Knights of the Royal Order of St Januarius. As in the past, they resumed their departures by carriage from the palace of Pizarro for the countryside at Miraflores. A gay company escorted the viceregal couple. People acclaimed her en route. Micaela organized pantomimes and sketches in the open air. She danced the pavan on the lawns. Then, with everyone sitting in a circle in the shade of the service-trees, they ate sorbets and jam; Micaela took a sweetmeat at random and, with a shout of laughter, put it on the tongue of the viceroy, who ate it with half-closed eyes. Or else the two lovers went alone to Cerrito de la Arena, where Micaela sang, accompanying herself on the guitar.

Don Manuel, seated at her feet, contemplated her as if she were an idol. She smiled as she hummed:

> 'Yo no sé qué demonios
> los dos tenemes;
> mientras más regañamos,
> más nos queremos.'

> I don't know what devil
> has got hold of both of us,
> the more we quarrel,
> the more we love each other.'

And when la Perricholi asked the viceroy what the news from town was, he answered casually: 'La Pila, el Puente y el Pan, como se estaban se están, The Stoup, the Bridge and Bread are all just as they used to be.' Which boiled down to saying: 'There's nothing to write home about.'

But la Perricholi was vindictive. She had not forgotten that for a long time she had been an object of scorn to Lima society, whereas her rival held the stage at the Coliseo. She was not fooled by the respect that was paid to her. She would never be considered a great lady, or even a lady pure and simple, she was well aware of that. She knew that to everybody she remained a schemer and a *cómica*, in the pejorative sense that the smart world used it. How could she humiliate them in their turn? She had an idea. More tenderly than ever, she put her request. Don Manuel protested and refused point blank. Micaela insisted and became even tenderer. He had given her everything until then. Was he going to refuse her permission to drive through the streets of Lima in a coach? Don Manuel did his best to persuade la Perricholi that only the *grandezas*—and then only those of Castile—could travel in such a vehicle and that if he authorized her to go out in a coach, the whole town would be up in arms. The viceroy's arguments made no impression on his mistress's will. Finally, Don Manuel agreed to la Perricholi's request. He ordered a coach to be built specially for Micaela, for there could be no question of her sitting with him in his own coach. They agreed that the viceroy should go ahead in his coach and that Michael should follow in hers. As an additional safeguard, Don Manuel had a small window put in the rear of his carriage so as not to lose sight of his lady.

For her arrogant demonstration, Micaela chose August 2nd, the day of the great Franciscan feast of the Portiuncula, celebrated by the Discalced Fathers. The afternoon was drawing to a close when the blue and gold coach of la Perricholi turned into the Alameda. The whole of the aristocracy had arranged to meet around the trees enveloped in the winter mist—the *garúa*—and the orange-trees bowed down with fruit. Behind could be seen the bell-towers of the Patronicio, of San Francisco de Paulo Nuevo—built with the collection made in the Plaza de Toros—and Santa Liberata. Further away the arches of the Bridge of Montesclaros loomed up vaguely in the approaching night.

But suddenly the *tertulias* were interrupted. Smiles froze. People recognized the first carriage and the second, too, which moved slowly, pulled by four white mules, driven by postilions wearing silver braid. *¡Es un escándolo!* An old priest was crossing the Via San Lazaro. Two choirboys accompanied him, candles in hand. He was taking the viaticum to a dying man. Remorse seized la Perricholi. She had her coach stopped, invited the priest to get into it and followed the carriage on foot. Later, she made a present to the parish of San Lazaro of this coach which, from an instrument of vengeance, became the most luxurious of alms.

That was how on this foggy day of the Portiuncula, the aristocracy of Lima were able to admire one of the last performances by the most famous actress in the New World. Dressed in a ball dress with a long silk train, entangled in her furbelows, stumbling on the jagged paving-stones, running breathlessly behind the carriage travelling at full gallop, spattered with mud . . . Tears ran down her face. She seemed sincere, perhaps she was.

Although all the chroniclers are in agreement about the authenticity of the episode of the coach, they argue about the kind of turn-out. Barouche or coach? The inventory of the Parish of San Lazaro mentions several coaches, not to mention several *coches* and *calesas* (carriages and barouches). Was it the state-coach attributed to the wife of the Viceroy Joaquim de la Pezuela or simply the carriage *de última moda*? Ricardo Palma swears that he saw it with his own eyes, as does Manuel Moncloa. But it was not the same one! 'With a coarse, heavy shape,' says the former, whereas the second says 'inlaid with mother of pearl and pink seats'. As for the inventory of la Perricholi's property, it specifies: 'a barouche with used accessories'. What else, then, can retrospective admirers of la Perricholi do but dream in front of the blue and gold coach, attributed to the Torre Tagle family, which is at the top of the great staircase of the Quinta de la Presa? And supposing it was the right one?

The incident of the coach, even if it established the 'viceroyalty' of la Perricholi, had irritated Lima society, which looked on it as a challenge. It inspired the gesture of another rival of la Perricholi, Mariquita Castellanos. She was a very beautiful woman, 'a dish for an archbishop, bait for an auditor', Ricardo Palma assures us. She owed her situation to a certain fabulously rich count who guaranteed her a more than viceregal income. She was known in Lima by the nickname of Marujita. La Perricholi's exhibition had irritated Marujita. 'So she wants to show that she's better than la Castellanos? We'll see about that!' And people did see. It was fashionable at the time for every woman in the public eye to have a little lapdog, which she took out on every possible occasion. Marujita's was an adorable doggie, combed and pomaded like a fop. She called it Cupidon. One day, on the feast of the Rosary, people saw la Castellanos arrive at mass, quite modestly dressed, followed by a maid carrying her mistress's little dog in her arms. There was nothing scandalous so far. But what was the spectators' surprise when they saw, at the time of the procession, that the dog wore a gold collar studded with diamonds round its neck! Their surprise was even greater when they learnt, a few hours later, that dog and collar had been given to the most needy hospital in the town by its mistress. Everyone in Lima understood the allusion perfectly and the enemies of la Perricholi applauded loudly this performance by la Castellanos, who could say from then on: 'No one can show that she's better than la Castellanos!'

La Perricholi's career did not end with the episode of the coach. Contrary to legend, she had not yet been touched by grace. Her repentance had only been momentary. On the contrary, as if she had a presentiment of the impending end of her fame, a sort of anguished frenzy caught hold of her. The viceroy, for his part, was approaching the end of his term of office. So he had no scruples —if he had ever had any—about being seen everywhere with his mistress. Sometimes his eyebrows wrinkled. He was thinking of the 'judgment of residence' which no viceroy could avoid and which he would soon have to undergo. Bah! He would see. Don Manuel was less and less at the palace, more and more at the Quinta del Rincón, which he had had his major-domo, Jaime Palmer, buy. It was situated behind the monastery of the Prado. It was there, in the most voluptuous of settings, that the two lovers spent the last months of their love affair. It was a sort of Trianon adapted to the colonial style, with many salons with red and gold hangings, oblong mirrors and rosettes. The Rococo manner was married to Spanish Baroque.

The wrought iron grilles and the miradors, together with the stucco cornices and the slender statues, made up the strangest whole. Snake motifs painted on the walls suggested sorcery. There was a navigable pool, a vast hen-house, a coach-house and stables. The garden, enclosed with walls like a Moorish seraglio and bathed in sirupy perfumes, was like the gardens of the Alhambra, if the dead-straight alleys and the rectilinear lawns did not recall French inspiration. In the centre was a miniature theatre. All round were little arbours of greenery, concealed behind tunnels of vine shoots and pink marble swimming pools where the brown skin of la

Perricholi reddened under the jets from the fountains. For water flowed everywhere. The viceroy had had the course of the Rimac diverted and it flowed to this temple dedicated to la Perricholi through silver channels.

That was the scene where the ageing Amat's last courts of love were held. Only the privileged—and the discreet—were invited to these dinners by lanternlight paid for by the viceroyalty. Exquisite nights when the oval mirrors reflected the flame of the candles and the ironical smile of la Perricholi. Like an Emir of Granada, Don Manuel enjoyed the last days he still had to spend in Peru. Outside, dragoons and halberdiers awaited his signal to escort him back to his palace. Might that moment come as late as possible! One night there was no water. What had happened? La Perricholi begged the viceroy to go and fetch some from the Rimac. It was dark, but not dark enough for Don Manuel to pass unnoticed, in his shirtsleeves and with the Grand Cross of the Order of St Januarius hanging round his neck. What did it matter! That was the rig-out in which he went to the Plaza Mayor 'to draw from the fountain a glass of water, of the only water that could quench his beloved's thirst at that moment'. Eccentricities and scandals followed each other. The devout crossed themselves when they passed *la casa del pecado*, the house of sin.

At the end of the month of May, 1776, a vessel from Spain dropped anchor in the little port of Paita. It had on board the successor to Don Manuel de Amat y Juniet, the very excellent Don Guirior. The arrival of the new viceroy was received with satisfaction by the population of Lima, tired of Don Manuel's indiscretions. There were many grievances against him, including that of having commissioned public works solely to please his mistress, such as the Paseo de Aguas. He was also blamed for having made his fortune. But the main reason why people were in a hurry to see him go was to be able to watch la Perricholi's downfall. The ladies of Lima got ready to savour their revenge. They spied maliciously on the departing viceroy and the fallen favourite. But the two lovers did not show themselves much in town. Micaela was no longer on the stage. Don Manuel had handed over his office to Guirior in July, 1776. He did not leave Lima until December. They spent these five months' grace at the Quinta del Rincón. The night fell on their love. They had stopped quarrelling. They ended by telling each other what they had not had time to say before. Micaela was nearly thirty, Don Manuel seventy-two. Nevertheless, when he left the house of his follies for ever, he left Micaela pregnant. A daughter was born.

Don Manuel returned to his native Catalonia. At the age of eighty, he married his niece. As for la Perricholi, she knew how to dominate her destiny. This affair—which could have been no more than a passing fancy—had lasted more than ten years, from October, 1766, to December, 1776. Micaela knew that it would come to an end one day. So she had long since made her arrangements and put some savings by. She was rich. Three years after Don Manuel's departure, she put the administration of her property into the hands of a manager. Then she acquired a villa on the corner of the Alameda and the Copocabana. She lived there for some time, after she had decorated it tastefully. In the meantime, she went back to the theatre, not as an actress, but as an impresario. She trained pupils and earned money. Her wealth and the respectability it gave her enabled her patiently to support the campaign of calumnies which broke over her as soon as her powerful protector had left. Pamphlets circulated, including the *Drama de las Palanganas*.

One day in 1795, Micaela heard of the death of Don Manuel. He was in his nineties. Until then, she had considered herself tied to him, in spite of his departure. Now there was nothing to stop her doing what she wanted. She married, in the parish church of San Lazaro, Don Firmin Vicente de Echarri, her co-director in a theatrical enterprise. Having become solidly middle-class, she wound up her joint enterprise with Echarri, sold or rented her houses and bought others. Micaela was approaching fifty. She was a rather heavy and very worthy lady. She led a quiet, respectable life, which was only disturbed by the periodical escapades of her son, Don Manuel de Amat y Villegas, who, fifteen years later, was to sign his name at the bottom of Peru's Act of Independence. No one was a bit surprised that he took a long time to learn common sense and that his youth was stormy—this viceregal bastard to whom his grandfather used to say when he was playing in the patio of his mother's residence: 'Keep out of the sun, child, for you are not just anybody, but *hijo de cabeza grande*.' (Literally, son of big head.)

We know little about the existence of la Perricholi between her marriage and her death on May 15, 1819, when she was over seventy years old. It appears that her last years, devoted in equal parts to business and worship, were exemplary. The poor blessed her name. The Church praised her piety. Did she wear the habit of the Carmelites? There is nothing to prove it and nothing to refute it. But a nun rooted in prayer would be an admirable conclusion to the theatrical figure la Perricholi had been.[9]

Out of this humble daughter of a Lima suburb, who became a star at the Coliseo, then favourite of a viceroy, to end as a doer of good works, as some say, nun, as others say, and as if such a career was not enough in itself, people have also tried to make her a revolutionary and to add to the list of her adventures of the heart the quite platonic one she is supposed to have had with Pablo Olavide. Pablo Olavide was the magistrate of the audience of Lima, who, with the money raised by the sale of property seized from the Jesuits, had established in 1767 'Population Centres' where agriculture and industry flourished. But he attracted the attention of the Inquisition, which denounced him for having obscene paintings in his house, but really because it suspected that he professed heresy. Although a search of his house revealed nothing but edifying books and religious objects, he was imprisoned and then condemned in 1778 to have his property confiscated and to eight years' retirement to a monastery. He fled to France where he made friends with the Encyclopaedists, including Voltaire, and took part in the Revolution. Returning to Spain in 1798, he died in 1803. It was tempting to associate this curious figure, a progressive with advanced ideas, with the bantering actress; tempting, too, to oppose, to right and left of la Perricholi, Viceroy Amat, the incarnation of old Spain, traditional and conservative—and Olavide, precursor of the Revolution. Admitting that this encounter took place, it would be quite wrong to draw too far-reaching conclusions from it. Non-conformist by temperament and living on the edge of society both because of her profession and her affair, la Perricholi had never cut a figure as an agitator. While

---

[9] There is an extensive bibliography about la Perricholi, ranging from the purely romantic to the scholarly thesis, from the *novela realista* by Jesús Víctor FAJARDO, *Desenfrenos de Miquita Villegas*, to the remarkable and quite recent works of Raul Porras Barranechea. The author, for his part, has mainly drawn on the works of the last-named, as well as those of Ricardo Palma, Guillermo Lohmann Villena, José M. Valega, Lavalle, Radiguet and the *Memoirs* of Viceroy Amat, all works quoted in the bibliography, not forgetting, of course, the very fine play by García Ventura Calderón.

disapproving of the regime perhaps in her heart of hearts, she had done very well out of it. And if her heart went out to the people, the worthy lower classes from which she came, her interests drew her to the side of the proprietary class into which she was finally incorporated. Nevertheless, the fact that la Perricholi's love affair with the viceroy took place in the pre-emancipation period is worth remembering. The scandal they caused may possibly have precipitated the fall of a regime which had outlived its time and was obviously worn out. Such was la Perricholi's contribution to the Peruvian revolution, without her knowing it.

In the play he devoted to la Perricholi, Ventura Garcia Calderón makes one of his characters, Martaniera, secretary and confidant of Viceroy Amat, say:

'The other day I read a book by one of those French unbelievers who send them to us hidden in the false bottom of casks of wine. Abominable books about liberty and atheism which are beginning to circulate in our town. Well, one sentence surprised me. It is when the author admits that if God did not exist, we should have to invent him. With all due respect, one could say that if la Perricholi did not exist, we should have to invent her.'

Let us simply say that she has been 're-invented' many times, so much so that in the eyes of the Peruvians of our own day she has become as topical as she was in the time of the viceroys.

Lima, Spring, 1958
Paris, Spring, 1961

BIBLIOGRAPHICAL SUMMARY

GENERAL BIBLIOGRAPHY

MANDIBURU (General Manuel de): *Apuntes históricos del Perú,* Lima, 1902.

CAPPA (Father): *Estudios críticos acerca de la dominación española en América,* (20 volumes).

BARRANECHEA (Raul Porras): *Fuentes históricas peruanas,* Lima, 1955; *Pequeña antologia de Lima,* Madrid, 1935.

MADARIAGA (Salvador de): *L'Essor de l'Empire espagnol d'Amérique,* A. Michel, Paris, 1953. *Le Déclin de l'Empire espagnol d'Amérique,* A. Michel, Paris, 1958. (Both translated from the Spanish.)

TORIBIO MEDINA (José): La Biblioteca Hispano-Americana *(1493–1810)* Santiago, 1898 and 1907, 7 vols. *La Imprenta en Lima* (1584–1824), Santiago, 1904 and 1907, 2 vols.

VARGAS URGATE (Father Rubé): *Manuscritos peruanos en las bibliotecas del extranjero* (mainly the *Bibliothèque nationale* at Paris).

FUENTES (Manuel A.): Lima, *Esquisses historiques, statistiques, administratives, commerciales et morales,* Firmin-Didot, Paris, 1866.

MIRÓ QUESADA (Aurelio): *Lima, Ciudad de los Reyes,* Buenos Aires, 1946.

PARRA-PÉREZ (C.): *El Regimen español en Venezuela,* Madrid, 1932.

ARANZ Y VELA (Nicolás Martínez): *Historio de la villa Imperial de Potosí (1705 1735),* Buenos Aires, 1943.

VELARDE (Héctor): *Arquitectura peruana,* Mexico, 1946.

THE COLONIAL PERIOD

LAVALLE (José Antonio de): *Galería de retratos de los Gobernadores y Virreyes del Perú (1533–1824),* Lima, 1891.

PALMA (Ricardo): *Tradiciones peruanas completas,* Madrid,

1952. Partial translation into French by Mathailde Pomès, Institut international de coopération intellectuelle, Paris, 1938.

ALFONSO (Luis Hernandez): *Virreinato del Perú,* Madrid, 1930.

VALEGA (José M.): *El Virreinato del Perú, Histórica Crítica de la época colonial en todos sus aspectos,* Lima, 1939.

AMAT Y JUNIET (Manuel de): *Virrey del Perú 1761–1776, Memoria de Gobierno.* (Preliminary study by Vicente Rodriguez, Seville, 1947.)

DURRET: *Volage de Marseille à Lima et dans les autres lieux des Indes occidentales,* Paris, 1720.

COREAL (François): *Relations de ses Voyages aux Indes Occidentales,* J. Frederic Bernard, Amsterdam, 1738.

BOURGER and LA CONDAMINE, de l'Académie royale des sciences envoyés par ordre du Roy pour observer aux environs de l'Equateur. Avec une relation abrégée de ce voyage, qui contient la description de ce pays dans lequel les opérations ont été faites. La figure de la terre déterminée par leurs observations, Paris, 1749.

PRADIER-FODÉRÉ (Camille): *Lima et ses Environs,* Paris, 1897.

PERNOUD (Régine): *L'Amérique du Sud au XVIIIᵉ siècle, Mélanges anecdotiques et bibliographiques,* 1942. Cahier No. 3. Mantes, Press of the 'Petit Mantais'.

LACROIX (M.): *Pérou,* L'Univers pittoresque, Firmin Didot, 1843.

LOHMANN VILLENA (Guillermo): *El Arte dramático en Lima durante el Virreinato,* Madrid, 1945.

SANCHEZ (Luís Alberto): *La Perricholi,* Santiago, 1940.

ACCOUNTS BY TRAVELLERS

FRÉZIER (Amédée François): *Relation du Voyage de la mer du Sud aux côtes du Chili et du Pérou,* Paris, 1716.

LABAT (R. P.): *Voyages aux Isles d'Amérique,* Club des Libraires de France, Paris, 1956.

JUAN and ULLOA (Jorge): *Relación histórica del Viaje a la Américameridional hecho de Orden de S.M., para medir algunos grados de Meridiano terrestre,* etc. Printed by order of the King at Madrid, 1748 (4 vols.).

HUMBOLDT (Alexander von) and BOMPLAND (A.): *Voyage aux régions équinoxiales du Nouveau Continent (1799–1800–1804),* Paris, 1814.

RADIGUET (Max), Secretary to Admiral Dupetit-Thouars on the frigate *Le Reine Blanche* (1841–1845):
Lima et la Société péruvienne, articles published in *La Revue des Deux-Mondes*, April–June, 1852.
Souvenirs de l'Amérique espagnole, Paris, 1856.

LAVANDAIS (Eugène de) and BOTMILAU (Adolphe de): *Voyages dans les Républiques de l'Amérique du Sud*. Articles published in *La Revue des Deux-Mondes*, April–June, 1850, and January, 1851.

MARCOY (Paul) (Laurent de Saint-Cricq): *Voyage à travers l'Amérique du Sud*, Paris, 1869.

TRISTAN (Flora): *Pérégrinations d'une Paria*, Arthus-Bertrand, Paris.

ANGRAND (Léon): French Consul at Lima in 1836. In 1887 donated to the Bibliothèque nationale at Paris a very rich collection of original drawings of Peru.

JOURNALS AND REVIEWS

La Revue de Deux-Mondes, for the years 1850–1851–1852.
Revista de Archivos, Bibliotecas y Museos, Madrid.
El Mercurio peruano de Historia, Literatura y Noticias públicas. Collection for May, June, July and August, 1792. Library of Rivas-Agüero, Lima.

1700–1705 Count de la Moncloa, twenty-third viceroy.

1705–1707 The Royal Audience.

1707–1710 Don Manuel Oms de Senmenat, Marquis de Castel Dos Rius, twenty-fourth viceroy.

1710–1716 Don Diego Ladrón de Guevara, Bishop of Quito, twenty-fifth viceroy.

1716 Don Diego Morcillo Rubio de Auñón, Archbishop Charcas, temporary viceroy.

1716–1720 Don Cármine Nicolás Caracciolo, Prince of Santo Buono, twenty-sixth viceroy.

1720–1724 Don F. Diego Morcillo Rubio de Auñón, Archbishop of Lima, twenty-seventh viceroy.

1724–1736 Don José de Armendáriz, Marquis of Castelfuerte, twenty-eighth viceroy.

1736–1745 Don José Antonio de Mendoza Caamaño y Sotomayor, Marquis of Villagarcía, twenty-ninth viceroy.

1745–1761 Don José Manso de Velasco, Count of Superunda, thirtieth viceroy.

1761–1776 Don Manuel Amat y Juniet, thirty-first viceroy.

1776–1780 Don Manuel Guirior, Marquis, thirty-second viceroy.

1780–1790 Don Agustín de Jaurégui, thirty-third viceroy.

1790 Don Teodoro de Croix, Knight of Croix, thirty-fourth viceroy.

1790–1796 Don Francisco de Taboada y Lemos, thirty-fifth viceroy.

1796–1801 Don Ambrosio de O'Higgins, Marquis of Osorno, thirty-sixth viceroy.

1801 The Royal Audience.

1801–1806 Don Gabriel de Avilés, Marquis of Avilés, thirty-seventh viceroy.

1806–1816 Don Fernando de Abascal, thirty-eighth viceroy.

1816–1821 Don Joaquín de la Pezuela, thirty-ninth viceroy.

1821–1824 Don José de la Serna e Hinojosa, fortieth viceroy (on the southern coast and in the southern and central mountains).

INDEX